MY GREATEST SAVE

MY GREATEST SAVE

BRIANA SCURRY

THE BRAVE, BARRIER-BREAKING JOURNEY
OF A WORLD-CHAMPION GOALKEEPER

WITH WAYNE COFFEY

ABRAMS PRESS, NEW YORK

ABRAMS
The Art of Books

For my parents, Ernest and Robbie Scurry

CONTENTS

FOREWORD

BY ROBIN ROBERTS

I can see the spectacle even now, more than two decades later, three thousand miles away in the *Good Morning America* studio in Manhattan. It's a steamy July day in Pasadena, California. I am with my ABC colleagues, getting ready to broadcast the final game of the 1999 Women's World Cup between the U.S. and China. I am not even supposed to be there, but over the previous six weeks the U.S. Women's National Soccer Team has become one of the biggest stories in the country. Over ninety thousand fans have packed into the Rose Bowl. Millions more are watching on television.

I've always believed the most iconic sports events transcend the actual competition and become something much more, a sociocultural marker of sorts. That's exactly how it feels in the Rose Bowl for the World Cup championship. I see mothers and fathers and their daughters tailgating in the parking lot. I see tens of thousands of young girls and boys—many of them wearing their Mia Hamm or Kristine Lilly jerseys—in the stands with their families or teams. I look up to the upper reaches of a stadium made famous by football, now filled to the top row because of futbol.

Women's futbol.

What is going on here? I say to myself.

As I watched the drama unfold that day, through ninety minutes of regulation and two extra-time periods and then the penalty-kick shootout, I found myself captivated by one player more than anyone else: Briana Scurry, the U.S. goalkeeper. I'd met Bri in the runup to the 1996 Olympic Games in Atlanta and was impressed with her competitive intensity and strength of character. She is the kind of person you sit down next to and feel determination and power all but pour out of her. Not because she is loud or defiant or swaggering. Bri's determination is the best kind. It is quiet. Unyielding. Deep.

And when she got between the goalposts, it doubled.

It's not easy being the "only". . . no matter what club or company or team you are part of. Bri was the only starter of color on the U.S. team. To my knowledge, she was the only player on the team who openly acknowledged that she was gay. She was the only girl on her first soccer team, the only Black kid on every one of her youth teams, the only Black female in her high-school class. It is not an easy way to grow up. I know, and maybe that's one of the reasons we connected so effortlessly. I was a military kid who moved around a lot. I was the only player of color on a lot of my sports teams. I was the only girl who was as tall as, or taller than, a lot of the boys. I was forever the new kid. You know that you are constantly being watched, evaluated—that you are Different, capital D intended.

Being a goalkeeper, of course, also makes you different. Ten other players are running around, and they are your teammates and you love them, but you are the only one between the posts, the only person with a singular mission: Keep the ball out of your net.

Bri was better at that than anybody in the world. That's not me talking. That's what her coach—the late, great Tony DiCicco—said. She was never better than she was in the shootout against China, making a breathtaking stop of a PK by China's Liu Ying. Moments later, Brandi Chastain drilled the World Cup winner into the upper right corner and then whipped off her No. 6 Team USA jersey, falling to the turf and clenching her fists in what instantly became one of the most recognizable images in the annals of sports.

It was a moment for the ages, legitimately so, but as the ensuing exultation rocked the Rose Bowl, I found myself wondering, *What about Bri's save?* This is not meant in any way to diminish Brandi and her clutch kick. The point isn't to parcel out who deserves the most credit. Briana Scurry made a phenomenal save, under massive pressure. Brandi Chastain made a phenomenal kick, under equal pressure. All I am saying is that it seemed to me that Bri's heroics were a little bit underplayed. She would never say that. She probably doesn't even want me to write it here. That's just who she is. Briana Scurry has never been about glory. She has always been about substance, and humanity.

In a Hall of Fame career, Briana Scurry won two Olympic gold medals and that World Cup title, but to me, she is more of a champion now than she has ever been. Bri's competitive career ended in 2010 because of a serious brain injury she sustained while playing for the Washington Freedom in Women's Professional Soccer—the forerunner of today's National Women's Soccer League. She took a hard knee to the head as she came out to play a ball, colliding with an onrushing forward. Under ten minutes remained in the first half. Bri made the save. It took her awhile to get up, but she did. She stayed in the rest of the half, then wobbled off for the locker room. She was never the same. And she never played soccer again.

The years after her concussion were the darkest of Bri's life. She suffered through memory loss and pounding headaches and crushing depression, all of it made much worse by bureaucratic obstacles and medical professionals, retained by an insurance company, who told her it wasn't that bad. Though she was close to giving up, she not only powered through and prevailed in the greatest battle of her life, she became a vocal and passionate advocate to raise awareness of the horrors and perils of traumatic brain injury. As great as Bri's World Cup title performance was in 1999, I believe this advocacy will be her most enduring legacy.

To me, the measure of a person's accomplishments isn't the number of championships you win or awards you earn. It's what you must overcome to get there. It's the character you show when you've been knocked down and the way you carry yourself, and the way you treat people when nobody is watching. There are more famous athletes in the world than Briana Scurry. There are few who can match her humanity. She is an extraordinary woman. She's an extraordinary advocate for those of us in the LGBTQ+ community. She is a person who lives her life, and her truth, with uncommon grace. She has a powerful and uplifting story to tell. I hope you enjoy it as much as I did.

Robin Roberts
New York, New York

PROLOGUE

I am fifty years old and have spent almost half of those years guarding soccer goals, all over the world. It is a job that brought me a measure of fame, if not fortune, along with some of the greatest thrills of my life, and the greatest pain, too. What can I say? I have a thing for extremes. The thrills—watched and celebrated by millions—included a World Cup title in the most historic soccer match ever played on U.S. soil, and two Olympic gold medals. The pain—experienced only by me, as private as the thrills were public—left me broke, broken, brain-damaged, and so psychologically battered that when I was living in a studio apartment in Little Falls, New Jersey, a little over ten years ago, I would sometimes stand at the edge of a nearby waterfall and think about jumping.

I came close a few times, but I always chickened out because it seemed too slow and violent, taking a plunge and getting tossed around the cold churning water like a rag doll. Plus, I can't swim, which probably would've triggered an anxiety attack on my way to the water. So I'd go back inside and lie on my bed and have this recurring vision of myself with a gun in a dumpster, ending my life in a pile of garbage, nice and quick.

The demons came at me hard, and loud.

Once you were the best goalkeeper in the world, they said. *Now look at you. You are a pathetic shell of what you used to be. Go ahead. Do it.* The only reason I didn't was that I couldn't bear the thought of what it would do to my mother. She was over a thousand miles away and had Alzheimer's disease, but she had devoted her whole life to her nine children and had always told me I could do anything and be anything, and that I should go after every single dream I had. I never would've gotten close to a World Cup or an Olympics without my mom or my dad, who had already passed.

Could I imagine the heartbreak it would bring on my mom, even in her impaired state, to find out her baby girl was gone?

No, I could not.

The thrills I've experienced, naturally, are much more pleasant to talk about. But I always said that if I ever told my story, it was going to be real, not some sanitized, tissue-thin tale that could pass for a Disney movie. When I was a kid, one of my favorite things to do was to ride my all-terrain vehicle. I'd get up to fifty or sixty miles per hour on dirt trails in the woods near my house, a little Minnesota motocross mama. I don't scare easily and don't do anything half-assed. If I am in, I am all in. I promise you are going to get all the details—about the good, the gory, and the in-between.

About what it was like to be a person of color on a team—and in a sport—that was historically as white as a bedsheet. About the traumatic brain injury I suffered in the last game of soccer I would ever play, charging out of the net to pounce on a ball the way I'd done a million times, and about the hell that ensued. For almost three years I kept my plight a secret from almost everybody in my life, even the teammates I stood alongside at the top of the medal stand, too stubborn and proud to let them see me in such a state. I prided myself on being strong and self-reliant, and now I was as far from that as you can get, desperate and vulnerable. I said nothing and suffered in silence, mostly gutting through it, sometimes self-medicating with Vicodin and alcohol, trying to get my brain back and taking the edge off the jackhammer headaches that pounded on me all day long.

It didn't work.

I will tell you about the shame I felt about pawning my Olympic gold medals so I could buy food and pay rent, and the whole truth about what went down at the 2007 Women's World Cup. It was not just the low point of my pro career, but probably the low point in the illustrious history of the U.S. Women's National Team—a fracture brought on by the toxic, self-centered agenda of a single player who put herself above the team and stomped on the culture that has made the USWNT one of the most dominant forces in global sport for going on four decades.

It hurt like hell, but you do your best to get closure and move on, and not carry around regrets and resentments like steamer trunks on your back. My life is better than it has ever been. I have the most amazing wife in the world, two great stepchildren, a lovely home, a backyard oasis, and a flourishing career as a motivational speaker. I feel so much gratitude for all those gifts I can't find the words to express it. A therapist friend once told me, "You are what you pay attention to." What good would it do me to let an ugly old wound fester, when I wake up every day next to a woman who I am madly in love with, and have joy and abundance everywhere I look?

• • •

Brad Friedel, the Hall of Famer who spent thirteen years in goal for the U.S. Men's National Team and seventeen years in the English Premier League, once said, "For a goalkeeper, there is no hiding place." All I can say is: *Amen*. A soccer goal measures eight feet high by eight yards wide. That makes it a 192-square-foot rectangle—the biggest goal in any sport. It can feel like the size of a small state when you are the one standing inside it, all alone. It's eight times the size of a hockey goal, and more than five times the size of a lacrosse goal.

Hiding? I don't think so.

There are ten teammates in front of you, and nobody behind you. You are literally the last line of defense. In most games your performance will have more impact on the outcome than any of those other ten. It's a daunting responsibility, but it's what you sign up for when you are a goalkeeper, and I loved it. I loved wearing a different colored shirt than everybody else and being able to use my hands and reflexes and jumping ability and, well, whatever it took to keep the ball out of the net. I couldn't guarantee we'd win the game if I did my job well, but I could guarantee we wouldn't lose if I didn't allow any goals. I have always been a logical person, a gift from my dad. This logic was most appealing to me.

I didn't mind being different. In fact, I kind of embraced it.

By the time I was in the net for the National Team, I'd had a lot of practice at it.

In all my years in grade school and middle school, I never had a classmate of color. There was a Black guy in my high school and that was it, and all my youth soccer teams were similarly homogeneous. For most of my seventeen years and 173 matches with the U.S. Women's National Team, it was the same thing—at least among the core players. My former coach, April Heinrichs, once described me to a reporter as "the fly in the milk," and while I didn't much appreciate the comment, she wasn't wrong. I am the only African American woman in the U.S. Soccer Hall of Fame, and I'm pretty sure I'm the only Black lesbian goalkeeper who has been on the cover of a Wheaties box. (Do I get a prize for that?) I didn't set out to be a pioneer or trailblazer, or some sort of Uber Underdog, but let's be real here: If people were made on an assembly line and were free to select their preferred options, do you think there would be a crush of folks signing up to be female, Black, and gay?

Me neither.

But I wouldn't change a thing. I love who I am. I love the path I've walked.

• • •

I didn't set out to be a soccer player, either. My favorite sport as a little kid was football, which makes sense, I suppose, since both sides of my family come from Texas, Land of Friday Night Lights. The Scurrys and the Gordons (my mother's side) go back generations in and around Galveston and Brazoria counties, on the Gulf Coast. They arrived there from West Africa, via New Orleans, in the same manner that almost all people of color arrived in America: on a slave ship, shackled together in the dingy darkness of the ship's hold, sitting in their own waste, getting just enough food to keep them alive. I know this only because of my wife's sister, Nicole Zizos Gulledge, who is a world-class genealogist. Nicole goes into Ancestry.com and you might not see her for days. She did a deep dive into the Scurry/Gordon family tree when I started this book and traced my ancestry back to Cameroon and Nigeria; she even unearthed a manifest for a slave ship called *The Union*. It left the Port of Baltimore for New Orleans, arriving on October 9, 1848, under Captain P. G. Hooper. *The Union* had fifty-seven enslaved people aboard. They are listed on the manifest as if they were the roster of a sports team, including age, sex, height, and skin color (black/brown). One of the people on the roster was a five-foot, nine-inch man. His age was twenty-two, his skin black. His name was Henry Gordon. He was my great-great-great-great-grandfather.

Like his fellow passengers, Henry Gordon was sold at the New Orleans slave market and was bought by a plantation owner in East

Texas. As far as I can tell, he spent the rest of his life toiling in the cotton or sugarcane fields in Brazoria County or Galveston County. I'm sure there are many other enslaved people in my family history, which makes me no different from millions of other African Americans, but somehow when you come across a document that has the name of your own flesh and blood on it, that shows them for how they were treated—as a piece of human cargo—it drills down deep. Every time I look at Henry Gordon's name on that manifest my insides go cold. I think about how his parents or grandparents must have felt to be ripped away from their family and kidnapped and herded onto a slave ship for the trip across the Atlantic, and how they must've suffered on that passage, and how Henry suffered on his own passage on the way to New Orleans. I think about how his grim existence would only get worse when he started his new life, if you can call it that, working all day in the searing Texas sun.

For no pay.

With no options.

With no hope.

One hundred and fifty years later, Henry Gordon's great (x four) granddaughter wore the crest of the U.S. Women's National Team and won a World Cup in front of a jam-packed Rose Bowl. One day maybe I'll be able to wrap my head around that.

• • •

Almost a century after the Civil War abolished slavery, my parents had their fill of life in Jim Crow Texas. Lynchings weren't as common as they had been earlier in the century, but you still heard about them. One of my father's good friends, Otis Turner, was married to a white woman from Sweden. The Turners traveled to see his family in Mississippi and only his wife returned; Otis Turner was strung up at a gas station for having the temerity to wed a white woman. I never heard about someone in my own family being lynched, but the indignities of daily life—segregated schools, buses, water fountains, lunch counters, movie theaters—wore on my parents, nonetheless. "The reminders that you were an inferior human being were everywhere, and they were constant," said Dr. Randolph Campbell, an eminent historian and expert on the history of slavery in Texas.

So my parents packed up and headed north. They had relatives who had recently moved to Minneapolis and decided to give it a try. Soon after I came along, they moved to Dayton, a small town wedged between two rivers, one famous (Mississippi) and one not (Crow), dotted with some of Minnesota's Ten Thousand Lakes, about a forty-minute ride from Minneapolis. The lakes were pretty to look at, but didn't do much for a non-swimmer. I was an active kid and my dad, Texan that he was, signed me up for a youth football league. It was a hundred or so boys and me. I played both ways, but my favorite was defense. I loved to put on all the gear, including the neck roll. I could run as fast as most of the boys, and faster than a bunch of them. I lived to make big hits. My mother could barely stand to watch because she was afraid I would get hurt. I slept with a football and would watch NFL games with my dad in the family room on Sundays, reenacting the plays and rooting not for the hometown Vikings but the Washington Football Team, because that was my dad's favorite. I was the happiest eleven-year-old kid in Dayton when John Riggins and his teammates ran over the Miami Dolphins to win Super Bowl XVII.

My football career lasted only a couple of years, unfortunately. The problem wasn't an injury or my ability to compete; it was a deal I'd made with my mother. She never wanted me to play in the first place, so she made me promise to stop once I hit ninety-five pounds, which required me to move into a different division. As a new season approached, I stepped on a scale and it delivered terrible news:

One hundred and two pounds.

Like a wrestler trying to make weight, I spent a few frenetic days exercising in a rubber suit, running around like a nut, limiting my food intake. It didn't work. It *couldn't* work. I was growing and I was always hungry. I gave up and had a big bowl of Lucky Charms. I would never see ninety-five pounds, or a neck roll, again.

• • •

I became a goalkeeper by accident. The truth is, a lot of things in my life happened by accident, starting with my birth. I arrived nine years after my nearest sibling and was not what you would call planned. But there I came on September 7, 1971, in a Minneapolis hospital, and faster than they could say, "Oops," my parents found themselves

A rare stationary moment at age 4.

reimmersed in the diaper-changing, midnight-feeding world they thought they'd left behind.

They also found themselves with the most active, thrill-seeking kid they had ever had. I'd tear around the house and dive-bomb off the couch and treat my bed like a trampoline. They knew I needed an outlet for my energy, so sports were a must. Once football was out, we scouted around for other athletic options. One day in school they handed out a flyer announcing tryouts for an all-boys soccer team in the area. There was no girls team. My knowledge of the sport was skimpy. I knew the ball was round, and that the equipment didn't include a neck roll and you couldn't knock other people down. It involved a lot of running. I was good at running, so why not give it a try? The coach had other ideas when I showed up on Day 1.

Daddy's little girl.

"Why don't you go over there and get in goal?" he said.

It wasn't quite an order, but it was close. I could tell my input wasn't all that welcome. I found out later that the coach was concerned I might get hurt mixing it up with the boys. I'm glad I didn't know that because it would've ticked me off. I would've told him I was a hard-hitting defensive back who would do just fine going for fifty-fifty balls against boys. Except for cameo appearances on the field here and there—always to take advantage of my speed—I stayed in goal for the rest of my career.

• • •

Nobody saw me play more soccer games than my parents, Ernest and Robbie Scurry. I called them Pops and Meresie (*mere* is the French word for mother; I tacked on the *sie* for added affection), and their loyalty was as unwavering as the tides. You hear all the time in youth sports about overbearing parents who make asses of themselves, getting into it with coaches and fans and referees, who want the whole world to know their kid is more gifted than everyone else, and why can't you see that? That was not my parents, thank God. Near the end of one game when I was on my club team, the Brooklyn Park Kickers, we had a breakaway on the other keeper when suddenly a chubby parent from the opposing team came running across the field, belly bouncing as he went, until he caught up to the ball and kicked it away. That's one way to support your kid's team, I guess. All hell broke loose and the guy was escorted from the premises. My parents were just the opposite. They supported me and my team, cheered when appropriate, and never caused any ruckus. I always appreciated their steadfastness, and their restraint. They would set up their folding chairs along the end line, about ten yards from the corner flag, so they could get a good view of their goalkeeper daughter. At halftime, they'd fold up their chairs and walk down to the other end line and set up camp in the same place. My mom didn't get overly technical in her exhortations.

"Get the ball out of there!" she'd say when the opponents got inside the eighteen. "Kick it!" Knowing they were there, over by the flag, just filled me up, bolstered me. When I stole a look and saw them in their chairs, it was as if the ground under my feet was a little bit firmer.

"You play the goal like you're a panther," Pops said during one of our traditional postgame trips to Arthur Treacher's Fish & Chips. The panther comparison became a theme for my parents. I liked it.

"You pounce on the ball. You go after it like you're stalking your prey," Meresie said.

During a break in U.S. Women's National Team training early in 1996, I went to Mardi Gras with my then-girlfriend, Lori. I'd been thinking of getting a tattoo for a couple of years . . . a tattoo of a panther. A tattoo that would always make me think of my parents. We were making our way down Bourbon Street one night in crowds so thick you didn't even have to walk; you'd just kind of get lifted and moved along with the human tide. I don't know whether it was the masks or the beads or all-around debauchery, but I decided then and there it was time to get the tat. Lori and I walked into this little shop and were greeted by the owner/artist, who had a shaved head and two extremely inky arms. I told him I wanted a tattoo of a panther.

"I've got a good selection," he said.

I was briefly deflated—I wanted to be original—but got over it. I leafed through several books he showed me and found an image I liked, the outline of a panther, muscled and menacing, baring its teeth.

"That's it—that's the one," I said. I told him I wanted it on my upper back, behind my left shoulder, facing off my body, as if it were ready to stalk, or make a save. The artist led me into a back room and closed the curtain, where he does his work when more privacy is required. He prepared his stuff and I took off my shirt and bra and lay down on a table. An hour later he was all done. When he showed me my tattoo—still my one and only—in the mirror, I was thrilled. It was even better than I'd hoped for. I got dressed, paid him $150, and rejoined the hordes on Bourbon Street.

For more than a quarter century, my inky panther has had my back. Five months after I packed up from New Orleans, she and I headed to Athens, Georgia, and the 1996 Olympics, where women's soccer made its Games debut. It went well. So well, in fact, that I made good on a bet and didn't just take off my shirt and bra. I took off everything. You will get the details, don't worry.

My panther and I never had a more electrifying experience, though, than in the final two rounds of the 1999 Women's World Cup. The semifinals were in Stanford Stadium in Palo Alto, California, the finals in the Rose Bowl in Pasadena, about 350 miles to the south. More than seventy-three thousand fans showed up for the semis, and way more than that in the Rose Bowl for the final, still the biggest crowd to watch a women's sporting event in history.

My first World Cup, four years earlier in Sweden, did not end the way I wanted. When I ran out to protect my goal in the Rose Bowl, I had one thought in mind:

We have one chance to change the ending from the last time, and this is it. One chance, dammit. No excuses. No mulligans. Let's go.

Having this World Cup contested on U.S. soil was a massive help, of course, but we goalkeepers are self-reliant sorts. I loved the crowd, but I wasn't counting on the crowd. We finished third in Sweden, and that sucked. There was one way to ensure a different outcome: to pitch a shutout. I was twenty-seven years old, still with no place to hide, and still not wanting one. The tournament had grown from twelve countries to thirty-two countries in just four years, morphing into a three-week crucible that was going to challenge our hearts, minds, and bodies to the max. The massive crowds, and the excitement over the U.S. hosting the Women's World Cup for the first time, jacked the stakes up even higher. The journey began in a sold-out Giants Stadium in East Rutherford, New Jersey, against Denmark. Mia Hamm was already a cult hero, the world-class face of the sport, and now other players—Michelle Akers, Kristine Lilly, Joy Fawcett, Carla Overbeck, and their soccer sisters—were getting justly celebrated, too.

When the introductions and national anthems in Giants Stadium were complete, I did what I always did, sprinting toward my goal and jumping up and grabbing the crossbar, swinging on it for a few moments before dropping to a knee on the Meadowlands grass, and said a prayer:

"Lord, please give me strength and agility and a clear mind. Help me to be decisive and committed. Keep me safe and fortify me with what I need to perform my best. Amen."

I said this prayer, or some variation of it, before almost every game of my career. I never prayed for victory. God isn't my personal genie, ready to automatically grant my wishes, if only I pray hard enough or earnestly enough. I don't see faith working that way. I am a spiritual person, but not a religious person. I believe in a Supreme Being, a Higher Power, whatever you want to call it. I do not believe in randomness. I believe things happen for a reason, even if we mortals can't comprehend what it might be. We're not supposed to comprehend it; that's why we're mortals.

My prayer left me feeling centered, energized, my body and mind steeled for the challenges ahead. I belong to the glass-half-full club, and always have, and in that moment my innate optimism was as robust as it had ever been. The whistle blew, and the World Cup was on. It would take us from one coast to another. Over six games my ritual never wavered: the sprint to the goal, the swing on the bar, the drop to the knee, the prayer for clarity, strength, decisiveness, belief. When you can summon these qualities and hold tight to them, who knows where you might wind up and what adversity you can get through?

I never expected to spend my life guarding soccer goals, or to even be a soccer player, or a person who would write a book, for that matter. I've learned a whole lot along the way. This is my story.

CHAPTER ONE

MY PEOPLE

I am shaky on my own family history. I like history and love my family, so this is not something I am proud of, on either count, but it's the truth. There are Scurry people on one side, and Gordon people on the other, and after that it gets a bit murky for me. Mostly it's because I came along so late in the game, nine years after my nearest sibling, that my own family was practically a rumor. It's also because we are spread out all over the country, from Texas to California to Minnesota, and other locales. I have nieces and nephews, and grandnieces and grandnephews, that I've never even met. Sometimes it feels as though I need a scorecard to keep track of everybody. Robbie Gordon, my mom, and Ernest Scurry, my dad, had nine kids between them. My mom delivered five babies over a twenty-year span. (That is some serious childbearing work.) A generation or two down the line, this family tree is going to look like a forest. We were a blended family at times, less blended at other times, as siblings went off to build independent lives. One thing that I do know is this:

If it weren't for the Busy Bee Taxi Company of Galveston, Texas, I wouldn't be here and you would be reading somebody else's book.

My dad was a hustler, in the best sense of the word. Before he got established in his ultimate career—a machinist—he would do whatever he had to do to earn a buck, whether it was working maintenance in a nursing home or doing custodial work wherever. He also was accomplished in other activities, such as running numbers games and poker games. I never witnessed this part of his life, of course, but I do know that now and again he had a wad of bills in his pocket. I didn't ask where the money came from, and he never told me. If something good happened with one of his after-hour pursuits, well, power to him, and good for us, I guess. But my father never counted on that to support the family. He kept hustling. One of his gigs before he moved to Minnesota was as a driver for Busy Bee, a Black-owned enterprise that is still going in greater Galveston today. Busy Bee taxis are bright blue and easy to spot, either in town or going back and forth on the causeway that connects Galveston with the Texas mainland. I wasn't around yet, but my brother, Ronnie, told me that one of Ernest Scurry's best Busy Bee customers was Robbie Gordon, who worked as a nurse's aide at John Sealy Hospital. My mom already had two kids by then—she had Ronnie when she was sixteen years old—and left them with her mother at her home on Avenue L in Galveston when she had to go to work. After my mom's shift, she'd call Busy Bee to get a ride to her mother's, and my father became her regular driver. Fares ultimately turned into something more. I have few details about how the courtship unfolded, but it moved fast. About a year after they met, Ernest Scurry and Robbie Gordon got married at the Galveston County Courthouse. That same year—1961—they decided to get out of East Texas and move twelve hundred miles due north to Minneapolis. The marriage lasted for the rest of their lives.

It was ten years after the move north that I came along. By then my parents were ready to make another move, this one only thirty miles, to the little town of Dayton. They wanted more space and better schools for Daphne, my older sister, and I. It wasn't my parents' intent to be integration trailblazers in Dayton, but apparently that is exactly what they were. My parents weren't color blind. How could they be? Black people have never had that luxury. They had spent their whole lives in Texas being looked on as inferior and being discriminated against, the same as every other person of color. At one point my brother Ronnie and his wife wanted to buy a house in a nice—that is, white—neighborhood in Galveston. Ronnie was a Galveston police officer who put in thirty-seven years of service by the time he retired. He and his wife could've easily afforded the house, but oddly enough, as soon as they made an offer it was taken off the market. Soon it came back on the market and was sold to people with a more agreeable skin color. My parents knew that Dayton was as white as snow and understood what that could entail. But it didn't stop them. Why waste energy shouting at the rain, when you know you are still going to get wet? If they were ever threatened or arrived home to see a cross burning on the lawn, they never shared it with me. If they were bitter about not being welcome at Galveston's lunch counters or having to sit in the back of the bus, they never shared that with me, either. They knew there would be barriers they would have to face, and they faced them. That's the way they rolled, the way they taught me to roll. My parents carried themselves with uncommon grace, and I'm sure it had a lot to do with their Christian faith. They weren't Bible-thumpers, but they went to church every Sunday (as did I, for awhile), and their faith was their bedrock. They knew the Lord had their back. They didn't make a big deal out of anything.

Once a month, always on a Saturday, I'd go with my mom to this big, blocky building that was surrounded by a bunch of other big, blocky buildings. I loved those outings. My mom never seemed bothered or burdened by it. It wasn't a tedious trip to a gargantuan, gray warehouse. She turned it into an adventure, in a town called Osseo.

"You ready, Bri? Time to go get us some Government Cheese!"

We'd park the car and walk in and get on a long line that snaked around a room that was the size of an airplane hangar. The line moved slowly. Some people had four or five coats on and rolling metal carts with them. The carts were packed with stuff. I thought it was a little odd that they would have so much clothing on, even when it wasn't five below zero in January. I had no idea what Government Cheese was, or that all these people were in line because they needed food for their families. When we got to the table at the front of the line, my mother showed the people a card and they handed her a bright orange (think the color of Velveeta) brick of cheese that was five inches high, five inches wide, and probably eighteen inches long. It looked like a mini railroad tie and if it had an expiration date, it would've been the end of the decade. They'd pack up two grocery bags full of canned yams and vegetables, pasta, instant mashed potatoes, and other non-perishables and we'd be on our way. When we got home, my mother would make me grilled Government Cheese on Wonder bread. Other than her Southern fried chicken (cooked to crispy perfection in a vat of Crisco), my mom's orange, gooey grilled cheese was my favorite. We had some form of Government Cheese almost every day and it would still last almost the whole month. That's what it was supposed to do.

I didn't feel embarrassed or stigmatized because we got food assistance. It was just what we did, and who we were. I never felt poor. We had a split-level, stucco house in a modest neighborhood. I'm sure I wasn't the only kid in school who didn't get a back-to-school wardrobe every August. I wore my clothes until they didn't fit any more. Our idea of a special meal out was Red Lobster. Otherwise, it would be White Castle or Arthur Treacher's, after my games. Mostly my parents worked hard and stayed home. My dad became a foreman at a manufacturing plant. My mom was a nurse's aide, and on Friday nights would work as a bartender at the Nacirema Club, a favorite destination for African Americans in South Minneapolis. The club (its name is American spelled backwards) started when the city was largely segregated and Blacks had few social, or even residential, options. It hosted parties and fashion shows and other community events but was probably best known for becoming a go-to venue for top Black artists, who for years weren't allowed to play in the white clubs. Prince played at Nacirema a few times. So did a popular soul singer named Wee Willie Walker, and his band, Solid On Down. Weekend nights featured jazz musicians. After my mom worked her late shift behind the bar, my dad would go there the next morning and clean up. I'd go with him to help. The place smelled gross to my adolescent nostrils, reeking of stale beer and cigarette smoke. The floor was as sticky as duct tape, strewn with empties and cigarette butts and other detritus

Don't you love school photos? Me, circa sixth grade.

from a long night of partying. While he swabbed the floors, my dad collected bottles and cans and put them in a garbage bag, and later we'd go get the deposit money. The Nacirema had little round tables all over the club. My job was to collect the glasses on them, put them on a tray, and bring them over to the bar. Our deal was that if I found any money on the floor or the bar I could keep it. I could count on finding a fistful of coins and the occasional bill every week. It wasn't anything that changed my life, until one Saturday morning. I was near the bar with an overloaded tray of glasses when I happened to look down to see a crumpled-up bill next to a swizzle stick on the floor. I put the tray on the bar and bent down. I uncrumpled the bill and saw the face of Benjamin Franklin, and the number "100" in all four corners.

I ran to show my father.

"Pops, look what I found!"

"You never know what you are going to find, do you?" he said. He smiled. He honored our agreement and let me keep it. I bought a bicycle.

$$\bullet \ \bullet \ \bullet$$

My mother was a songbird. She sang when she cooked. She sang when she did dishes, and made beds, and at Christmas time she sang so much we didn't even have to put a record on. She could hit the high notes and she could belt it out, too. Every year at my elementary school we had this show called "The Dayton Follies." My mother's singing was always the highlight. I remember being upstairs in my room doing homework and hearing the notes of Kenny Rogers's "Lady" filling the whole house. Her rendition of "Hallelujah" was right there with Leonard Cohen's, though in a different octave. My mother probably would've loved to go through life singing, and once she had a chance. She was singing in a club called Gus Allen's Lounge in Galveston one night, a few hundred feet from the seawall and the Gulf Coast.

Galveston was a musical mecca then, and everyone in the business knew it. A producer for Bobby Bland, a well-known R&B artist, happened to be in the house. When my mother's performance was over, he approached her and introduced himself.

"You have a beautiful voice," the man said. "Would you be interested in touring with Bobby Bland?"

My mother thanked him and said she would have to get back to him. When she got home, she told her mother—my grandmother—about the offer. Meresie was twenty-one years old and had two kids under the age of six. It wasn't a long conversation.

"You ain't runnin' around the country singin' while I'm here takin' care of your babies," my grandmother said.

• • •

Minnesotans like to call their home the State of Hockey. So I was in the right place. It was February 22, 1980. I was downstairs in the family room, watching the Winter Olympics, which were being held in Lake Placid, a village in the Adirondack Mountains in upstate New York. I was eight years old and had never heard of Lake Placid. All I knew was that the U.S. was playing the U.S.S.R. in an Olympic semifinal, and I was transfixed. The arena throbbed with "USA, USA" chants. The Soviets swarmed the U.S. goal, killer bees in red sweaters, but Jim Craig, the U.S. goaltender, kept fending them off. He was diving, kicking, sprawling, stabbing. His limbs were moving in all directions, as if he were a marionette. I could not take my eyes off him. He was a one-man David, using his glove and stick and pads to stone Goliath. There were other U.S. heroes, for sure. Mark Johnson, the Americans' best player, scored two goals. Mike Eruzione, the captain, scored the game-winning goal. Up and down the roster, so many guys played the game of their lives. But the greatest performance of all was from Jim Craig. Not even two weeks before the Olympics the same teams met in Madison Square Garden and the Soviets won, 10–3. Nobody gave the U.S. a chance in the rematch, but late in the third period, the U.S. had a 4–3 lead. As the clock ticked down, the tension mounted and my stomach was doing somersaults. It was under two minutes, then one minute. Why was the clock moving so slowly? The U.S. tried to play keep-away and waste time in the corners. The throbbing got louder. I felt as though I was right there in the goal with Jim Craig, No. 30.

Finally it was down to ten seconds, and on the ABC telecast, Al Michaels began his countdown. With a second or two left, Michaels shouted, "Do you believe in miracles? . . . YES!"

"Yes!" I shouted, just as loud as Michaels.

I believed in miracles. I believed in Jim Craig. I believed that anything was possible if you had the courage to go after it. I danced around the room, and as the U.S. players dogpiled on Craig, I told myself, "One day I am going to be an Olympian, too."

I know this is straight out of Hokey Central. A few million other American kids wanted to grow up to be an Olympian that night. I don't know about those other kids, but I truly meant it—at least as much as an eight-year-old can. To me it didn't feel like an idle thought from a starry-eyed grade-school kid. It felt as if I'd found my calling. I told my teacher, Mrs. Swanson. I told my parents and my friends. I knew my future wasn't in hockey because ice skating wasn't my thing, and swimming sure wasn't. But I was going to make it in something. I was going to be someone who makes a difference . . . someone whose teammates can count on her . . . a female David who isn't afraid to stand up to Goliath.

A few years went by, and my sports career began. First it was football, then soccer, and before long I started playing basketball and softball and running track, too. I loved to compete and loved the way I was able to pick up sports easily. And every four years (now it's every two years) I loved watching the Olympics, Winter or Summer.

I loved all sports as a kid, especially football,
and the gear that came with it. I'm with my
niece, Tenecia.

The hold that Jim Craig and February 22, 1980, had on me never went
away. Of course it wasn't as supercharged as it was that Friday night
in our family room, but the core commitment to myself . . . "I am going
to do that one day". . . was undiminished.

When I was fourteen, I formalized the commitment. I got out a
pencil and a white poster board, and wrote:

OLYMPICS
1996
I HAVE
A DREAM

Eleven years later, the Summer Games came to Atlanta, Georgia.
It marked the Olympic debut of women's soccer. I was in goal for the

United States of America. I had a crazy Friday night in Lake Placid, and Jim Craig, to thank.

• • •

Early in my seventh-grade year at Jackson Junior High School, we had a parent–teacher conference with Mr. Repiesch, my teacher. The conference went well because I did my work and didn't cause trouble, though I did get called out for having a messy desk. (I plead guilty.) Mr. Repiesch discussed my grades (in the B/B+ neighborhood) and the coursework for the year and made a few suggestions that would help me as a student (clean up your desk) and praised me for my analytical mind.

"I think Briana could be a great lawyer," he said. My mom liked hearing that. She liked it a lot.

"I think she could be a great lawyer, too," she said. "In fact, I think she can be whatever she wants to be if she puts her mind to it."

If there is a single sentence that captures the essence of my mother, that is it. She saw no limits for me and wasn't shy about sharing the opinion. My dad was the same way. I'm not sure why they had so much belief in me. I was smart and athletic, got along well with most everybody, and did what I needed to do. But it's not as if I came out of a completely different gene pool. I have a number of smart, talented siblings. I think that when "Oops" happened and I came along so many years later, my parents were in a different stage of life. I was eight brothers and sisters away from being an only child, but it sometimes felt like that, because my closest sister in age, Daphne, was out of the house when I was in junior high school. Without an entire platoon of kids to care for, my parents had more time and attention to spare, and they devoted it to me in heaping amounts, though not in a suffocating way. I never felt harassed or pressured; I just felt empowered. I remember one morning in the kitchen when my mother and I talked as

I wolfed down a bowl of Frosted Flakes (it was impossible for a cereal to have too much sugar in my book). In the corner, a twelve-inch black and white TV, complete with rabbit ears, was tuned to *The Flintstones*. I don't recall the exact context, but most likely I was telling my mother about what I was going to do in the Olympics, and how I was going to make a difference.

"Shoot for the moon," my mother said. "If you don't, you'll never know."

The message got through, no doubt about it. It powered me in ways I didn't know at the time, and touched me so much more later, when I learned about Bobby Bland's producer asking Robbie Gordon if she wanted to go on the road with a big-time band.

People who heard my mother's voice when she was young said she could sing like Diana Ross or Whitney Houston. I can barely imagine how thrilled she must've been to get that invitation to become a professional singer, and how hard it must've been to have her mother nix it. My mom never had a chance to shoot for the moon. The moon was far away; her babies were right at her side, crying to be fed. It was her choice to be sexually active and become a teenage mother, and if she were with us now, she would not dispute that. My mother had her babies and nurtured them and raised them. That is what dutiful and moral people do. They take ownership of their lives and responsibility for their decisions. Not one time did I ever hear my mother sound as if she were a victim. Not once did I hear her say, or even intimate, that she could've been a famous singer if she hadn't been a mother so young. Quite the contrary. She loved those babies, and she gave them everything she had. And by the time I came along, she gave everything she had again. Instead of being resentful of the opportunities that started coming my way that she didn't have, her attitude was *You go for it. You can do it. I know you can do it.*

Pops and Meresie were a perfect team of parents, their greatest assets fitting together like a hand in a glove. My dad was a tinkerer, a fixer, a builder—a supremely methodical man who could take apart anything and put it back together better than ever. He rebuilt the front end and engine of a red Oldsmobile and we drove it all the way to Texas, twice. He wired an industrial-size cable dish, the kind you'd see outside a television station, in our backyard, the better to feed their TV habit. (My parents were television junkies. We had one in just about every room in the house, and one of our regular activities was watching *The Dukes of Hazzard* together. Why an African American couple from Texas would get hooked on a good-ol'-boy program that featured the Confederate flag and a car named for General Robert E. Lee is not something I was ever able to figure out.) My dad was good in math, especially geometry, intuitively understanding angles and spatial relationships. My mom was all heart, full of empathy and kindness and loyalty, and a passion for life you could hear every time she sang. I will never rebuild an engine, but my mind is wired similarly to my dad's. My singing voice will never be compared to my mother's, but I think my heart beats the same way hers did. Meresie and Pops gave me everything a kid could ask for. I thanked them often, but there's no way I ever thanked them enough.

CHAPTER TWO

SEARCHING

My life in mischief was short and hot. Playing alone on the floor of my room one day, I found a pack of matches. I don't remember how, but I got my six-year-old mitts on them, struck one up, lighting it on my first try. I moved the flame close to the dust ruffle because I wanted to see what would happen. What happened was that the dust ruffle caught fire and I burned my fingers because I held on to the match too long.

The flame grew to about eight inches. I started to scream and cry. My sister Daphne came running, arriving to find the bottom of my bed on fire. She doused it with a couple of glasses of water and no 9-1-1 call was required. This was the beginning and end of my pyromania phase, but not the last time Daphne came to my rescue. A few years later, I was at the bus stop in the morning, waiting to go to school. We had just arrived in Dayton. A kid called me "Darkie." His name was Robert, and he had a smirk on his face. He was a couple of years younger than me, but that didn't stop him from being a bully.

"Darkie! Darkie! Darkie!"

The look on this kid's face scared me. It was mean and full of hate. I started to cry. When the bus came, I sat as far away from him as I could. Daphne wasn't there that day, but she made a point to hunt down Robert a few days later. She grabbed him by the arm and dug her nails into him.

"Ow! Ow! You're hurting me!" he said.

"Don't you ever call my sister names again, you hear?" Daphne said.

Robert didn't immediately respond. Daphne tightened her grip.

"I said, 'Do you hear me?'"

"Yes, yes. I hear you."

Daphne let him go and put her arm around me. I can't tell you how many times she did that. In our sprawling Scurry/Gordon family, Daphne was closest to my age and the only other child of Ernest and Robbie, the one sibling who really grew up with me. Daphne wasn't just a big sister. She was a superhero. I felt protected when I was with her, always knew she would never let anything bad happen to me. You know how some big sisters want their little sisters to just go away and stop bugging them? That was never Daphne. Even if she ever felt that way, she never showed it to me. She made me feel loved and cared for. She did my hair and drove me to taekwondo lessons and taught me about music. She was like my dad, loved cars and the mechanical workings of things. Daphne had posters of Firebirds and Grand Ams in her room, so that's what I wanted, too. She listened to groups like Chicago and Journey and Boston, so that's what I listened to, too. When I heard Daphne singing "More Than a Feeling," I turned it into a duet. My dream in life was to grow up to be like Daphne Scurry.

The only thing I regretted was that Daphne wasn't closer to my age. It wasn't her fault, of course. But when she graduated from high school and left home and got married, I had trouble understanding why she wasn't still in the downstairs bedroom. I had a really hard time with that. As much as I loved Meresie and Pops, I felt as though my sister had ditched me. I held it against her for a long time, and that was totally unfair.

Daphne did not ditch me. She moved on with her life, as she should've done. The most important thing was that she was always there when I needed her. I have never forgotten that.

• • •

Teddy De Luca was my best friend. He lived close by us in Dayton and we did everything together. Teddy was olive-skinned and good-looking, a lanky, athletic kid who was a fast runner. It made for an instant bond. In gym class or recess we'd rule in dodgeball or red rover, and especially when we'd play "Smear the Queer." (How awful and homophobic that name was, and how little we understood that.) Basically, all "Smear the Queer" amounted to was a brutal game of keep-away. We'd roll up a T-shirt or grab an old football or Nerf ball, and it would be Teddy and I against everybody. The one and only goal of the game was to get the person with the ball—aka The Queer. Tripping, tackling, horse-collaring—you could employ any tactic you wanted to get The Queer down, before you ripped the ball away from him.

"Smear the Queer," everyone would yell as they ran. Teddy and I were faster than the others, and we'd toss the ball back and forth when the herd got close to one of us. We were very often The Queers and almost never got smeared.

Away from school, Teddy and I tore up the trails of Dayton on our three-wheelers. I'd motor out of my driveway, turn right, meet him on a dirt path, and off we'd go on our fire-engine-red Hondas. We had a whole network of trails to choose from. We liked to ride on a trail along a ridge and eventually make our way down into a quarry-like pit, where we'd spin around in circles, Three-sixties 'R Us, laughing as we went. I was a maniac on that three-wheeler. I'd put the helmet on and turn into Evel Knievel, always looking for a near-wreck experience without actually wrecking. Teddy wasn't one to play it safe, either. For all the hours we spent riding, we never crashed or got hurt. Teddy and I were good drivers. We were also lucky as hell.

Often we'd ride to the local convenience store, where we'd get custard or candy and play *Donkey Kong* until we were out of quarters. Teddy and I grew closer and closer. It was so much fun to be with him, so effortless. He totally got me, and I got him in the same way. I was at his house one day when I was thirteen years old. We were sitting on his bed. He was playing with his pet ferret. I looked at my best friend Teddy and just came out with it.

"I like you more than as a friend," I said.

Teddy did not see this coming. Honestly, I didn't either. I just said what was in my heart. Teddy smiled awkwardly and looked away. He was quiet for a moment.

"I really like you, Bri, but not in that way," he said.

It hurt to hear that, but it didn't surprise me. Teddy had never given me any indication that he wanted to be my boyfriend. I did my best to hide my disappointment, but it wasn't easy, given how awkward it was.

"That's OK. We're cool. We'll hang out and ride," I said. And I was good to my word. We continued to ride the trails and do our daredevil thing. I was confused for a long time whether I truly wanted Teddy to be my boyfriend, but honestly it was all part of an adolescent's search for her sexual identity. The labels gay and straight, heterosexual and homosexual, meant nothing to me. My body was changing. My life was changing, as I went from little girl to young woman. I had dreams about Teddy. I had dreams about one of my female soccer teammates, too.

What's going on? I have feelings for Teddy, and I was just dreaming about making out with a girl. What is that all about? I thought when I woke up.

I was in exploration mode, and all over the place—the trails, the soccer field, and soon, the basketball court. It's not as though I felt alarmed or panic-stricken about the dream with the girl or felt a pressing need to change the sexual channel back to Teddy as soon as possible (as if that could've been an option). I was just a kid living my life day by day, trying to find my authentic self. I felt attracted to my soccer teammate when I was awake, too. I never told her, the way I told Teddy. A lot of young gay kids do that, whether it's out of confusion or shame or a hope that the feelings will just go away. Mine did not go away. Nor were they going to. Even when I felt attracted to Teddy, I already knew on some level that I was gay. After I met Kelly (not her real name), any lingering doubts were erased.

Kelly was a ninth-grade classmate. She was into music and I was into sports, but our different orbits proved no impediment at all. She was nice and cute and we hit it off from the outset. We started writing notes to each other and exchanging them between classes. In no time we became inseparable. One day in school I visited her in the band area. Kelly played the flute. There was a soundproof room where the band members would go to practice. Kelly and I found ourselves alone in the room. I can't tell you who initiated it—I am guessing it was mutual—but we kissed. And we kissed again, and again. It was a fun and exciting five minutes, and the acoustics were sublime. I have no clue why we picked such a high-risk location—somebody could've barged in on us at any time—but it was probably part of the thrill.

And so began my first romantic relationship. Kelly was my new best friend and my girlfriend, all in one. Even though I was only fifteen, there was a depth and a substance to our connection that I'd never felt before. It was exhilarating, and my first insight into what would become my *iceberg theory of human relationships*, which asserts that what you see above the surface is vastly smaller and less significant than what there is below the surface. I was physically attracted to Kelly, for sure, but the emotional connection was what really drew me to her.

Kelly and I never made out again in the Anoka-Hennepin High School band sound room. We found other locations. One of them was my bedroom. Kelly's house wasn't far away from mine, so it was an easy commute. We were in my room one time, surrounded by my trophies and my homemade Olympic dream poster. The lights were off and the TV was on. We kissed and cuddled and talked softly to each other and it was all lovely until my father opened the door. We weren't kissing at that moment and I don't know what he saw in the darkened room, but he closed the door and said nothing.

I knew we were busted.

Not even five minutes later, my mother called upstairs and said it was time for Kelly to go home. She kissed me goodbye and left. Moments later, I was at the dining room table with both of my parents. My mom did the talking. She was completely calm, even gentle.

"Honey, I know it's probably fun and exciting to be close to your friends," she said. "When I was your age I did the same thing. It's good to have those friendships, but in time I got past it. It was just a phase for me. I'm not upset at all about whatever you and Kelly were doing, but don't make a habit of it."

That was the end of the discussion. I never spoke to my parents again about my sexuality.

It wasn't about hiding or keeping secrets. Between dreams I had and my relationship with Kelly, I was awakening to the reality that I was a lesbian and was totally at peace with it. There was no reason for me to issue some sort of declaration and have it notarized and countersigned. I embraced who I was, loved who I was. And because my parents loved me unconditionally, I knew that my sexuality would have no impact on their devotion to me. They never said a word about finding a nice young man, never pressured me to be different from the person I was. All my parents ever gave me was encouragement and endless amounts of love.

My relationship with Kelly deepened. I celebrated my fifteenth birthday on September 7, 1986. Kelly and I made plans for her to come over that night to dinner and birthday cake. Five o'clock turned to six o'clock, then seven o'clock.

What was going on? I kept waiting. And waiting.

Kelly never showed.

Was she sick? Was there a family emergency? Something terrible must've happened. Kelly was the person I cared more about than anyone outside of my family. It was my birthday. She would never do this to me.

I was sad and worried and went to bed but couldn't sleep. All I could think about was Kelly. A little after midnight, I couldn't take it anymore. I got out of bed, threw on some clothes, went downstairs, and grabbed the keys to my father's yellow Cadillac. (My father always drove Cadillacs. That was his thing.)

In the driveway, I slipped the Caddy into neutral so it could roll onto the street without a sound, and without waking up my parents. Then I turned the ignition and put on the lights and went for a two-minute drive.

To Kelly's house.

The house was dark. The whole block was dark. I parked on the street, turned off the ignition, and tiptoed toward the house. I had spent many hours in Kelly's room, so my destination was clear. My heart was pounding, hard. I knew what I was about to do was stupid and reckless, and maybe illegal. I didn't care. I clambered onto the woodpile to hoist myself up to a lower section of roof, then scrambled up to the second story, and Kelly's window. I tapped on it once, then again, then a third time. Finally, a light snapped on. Kelly came to the window, rubbing sleep out of her eyes.

"Bri, what are you doing?" she whispered. "Are you out of your mind?"

I choked up immediately. I fought tears and lost. I whispered, too.

"Kelly, you were supposed to come over for my birthday. How could you do this? I thought you were my best friend."

Kelly was quiet for a second. Her eyes were welling up, too.

"I'm sorry, Bri. I am really sorry, but I can't do this anymore. You have to leave now."

She left the window and turned out the light. I sat on the roof for a few moments, trying to take this in, crying even harder now. I shimmied back down the roof, to the woodpile, to the ground. I drove home and went back to bed. I tried not to think about all the times I'd spent getting close to Kelly on this very same bed. It was no use. I hugged my pillow and for the first time in my life I cried myself to sleep. It was my first broken heart. It made for a crappy birthday.

• • •

Time healed my hurt, and sports accelerated the healing. The rhythms of my life were defined by the sports season: soccer in the fall, basketball in the winter, track and softball in the spring, and then club soccer with the Brooklyn Park Kickers in the spring and summer. Whatever sport I was playing in the moment was my favorite. I loved soccer, but when that was done and I moved inside to the gym and went from goalkeeper to slashing, ball-hawking forward for the Anoka High School Tornadoes, basketball was all I thought about, and it was the same in the spring, when I turned into a sprinter and long jumper for the track team, and a shortstop in softball. All I can say is, thank God I didn't grow up in an era where you had all this pressure to play one sport and stick with it exclusively, lest you fall behind your peers. I knew one thing, and my parents knew the same thing: I had a passion for sports and I was blessed with athletic gifts that made me good at them. Nobody ever told me, "You have talent. If you don't specialize right now you are going to miss out on a chance to get a scholarship." Playing sports wasn't an obligation or a means to an end, ever. I felt happiness that approached complete rapture when I was competing and, truth be told, felt it more when I played basketball than anything else. The pace of the game, the explosiveness and quickness it required, was squarely in my genetic wheelhouse. I fantasized much more about being the next Sheryl Swoopes or Dawn Staley than I did the next Michelle Akers or Mia Hamm. Whatever sport I was engaged in, though, I played it for the purest of reasons: It brought me joy. I see so many kids these days who stop playing because that joy is drubbed out of them, whether by pressure to get a college scholarship or overinvolved, overzealous parents hell-bent on getting a return on the thousands of dollars they've spent along the way. It's so sad. Why play if it's not fun?

A local high-school sports historian once told me I am the only female athlete in the history of Anoka High School to make all-state in three sports. Who knew? As I went from Anoka High to UMass to the USWNT, the stakes got higher, but the enjoyment that powered my journey didn't change. It was never about ego fulfillment or individual acclaim or a pressing need to be the GOAT. I just wanted to be happy and be the best Me I could be. That was the sum total of my agenda.

• • •

When I was fourteen years old, girls club soccer finally made it to my corner of the world. I became a member of the Brooklyn Park Kickers and started playing for a man named Pete Swenson, who was a traveling textile salesman by day and a coach the rest of the time. Like most good salesmen, Pete could talk, and he could persuade. He grew up on Long Island and had the New York accent to prove it. When Pete said, "Get the ball out of there," it sounded like "Get da bawl outta dare." When he complained to the referee about a hard foul against a Kicker, he'd say, "Dat's a yellow cawd! She almost moidered my playah!" Pete called me Kermit—he still does—because I did a good Kermit the Frog impersonation. He wasn't looking to compete with Alex Ferguson as a soccer strategist, but he was smart and knew about sports and competitive makeup, and he sure knew how to motivate. Players who needed a little coddling, he coddled. Players who needed to be challenged, he challenged. I was in the latter category. One time we were playing a team called the Burnsville Blaze. The Blaze were a major power in our part of the state. All you had to do was ask them. They had a paid coaching staff and snazzy warmups, matching backpacks and top-of-the-line uniforms. They looked as if they'd stepped out of a high-end soccer catalog. We Kickers were much more of a blue-collar crew. Pete not only didn't get paid, but I am positive that he lost money coaching us. When we had to travel for out-of-state tournaments, the costs climbed, money that my parents didn't have. Pete never said anything, never made a fuss. But I played in every tournament and that didn't happen by magic. He would routinely take care of entry fees and other expenses, not just for me, but for other kids whose families didn't have the means to cover it. It's just who he was . . . a kind and generous man.

I never cared for the Blaze. I thought they had an attitude about them, though maybe I was just ticked off because we could never beat them. We were warming before the game and Pete was in the center of the field, exhorting us in his usual way.

"No letup today. Not for one second. We can beat this team if we never let up," he said.

That was Pete's constant refrain. When it's his time, 'Don't let up' should be on his tombstone. As he strolled around the field that day, Pete heard one of the Blaze kids say, "Hey look at their goalie." Some

Portrait of a Teenage Keeper

tittering followed. I never heard a word. Pete casually walked over to the girl who said it and asked her what she meant.

"It's just that we don't have any Black people around here," she said.

I was in the goal, getting loose, when I saw Pete approaching me. He told me about the "look at their goalie" comment. It wasn't a slur. It's not like she said the N word. But clearly I qualified as something out of a freak show.

"What do you think, Bri? Maybe it's time to show them what a Black goalie can do?" Pete said.

"I think so, Pete."

Maybe it was just a coincidence, but I played one of my best games of the year and we beat the Burnsville Blaze for the first time ever, 4–0. The Black goalie enjoyed the match immensely.

• • •

The Kickers did a lot of winning. We punched way over our weight class and we were proud of it. In Pete's mind, we were forever "da undadawg." We won tournaments against teams that were more skilled and more athletic than we were. We did it by not letting up.

In the summer of 1989, we surprised people by winning the Minnesota state title in the U.S. Youth Soccer Association U-19 tournament, advancing to Omaha, Nebraska, to compete in the Midwest Regional Championships. It was the biggest tournament I'd ever played in. I was a neophyte compared with the other goalkeepers at this level, but I had no doubts that I belonged, thanks to my parents, who nurtured me with affirmation and positivity the same way people water their gardens. It wasn't that I thought I was better than anybody else—just that I had a strong belief that I would be up to the challenge. There were two brackets with four teams apiece in Omaha, the top two in each moving into the semifinals. We won our first game against a formidable North Dakota team and then had to play a club from Kansas, who were even better. The air was as thick as porridge and so hot the tar was melting in the parking lot. It was my favorite kind of weather to play in; having sweat dripping off me fueled my intensity. (Field players tend to disagree.) Kansas was a favorite to make the finals—which put the match right up Pete's motivational alley.

"You can beat this team if you play together and never let up," Pete said.

• • •

The whistle blew and Kansas was all over us, playing a beautiful, slick-passing style, from one side of the field to the other. They dominated the first fifteen minutes and a kid ripped a low, hard shot toward the right post. I dove but couldn't stop it.

I bounced to my feet and I was pissed.

"No more," I shouted to my team.

And that was what I believed. I was beginning to learn the most important skill a goalkeeper, or any athlete, can have: a short memory. The shot that I didn't save was history. Why dwell on it? The present moment was all that mattered, the only thing I could change. Lamenting the past and worrying about the future were a waste of energy. Carpe diem.

The game went on and the Kickers, indeed, did not let up. Denise Swenson, Pete's daughter, a lethal striker, tied the game and then scored again to give us a 2–1 lead. The game moved into the final ten minutes. Kansas pushed its midfielders and defenders forward. My heart ratcheted up a few hundred beats.

If I don't allow another goal, we advance to the semifinals.

Of course it was not just me; everybody had a job to do. But that's how a goalkeeper's psyche is wired. We can be the heroes. We can be the GOATs. It's not all on us, but a whole lot is on us.

All I kept saying in my head is: *Keep the score 2–1.*

Fewer than five minutes remained. It felt as if Kansas had twenty-two players on the field, and all of them were on the attack. A Kansas defender looped a dangerous ball into the box. A forward got on the end of it and knocked it toward the right post. I punched it away and scrambled to my feet. The rebound went to a Kansas midfielder, who one-timed it, her shot heading to the upper left corner. I sprinted across the goal and made a fingertip save, the ball bouncing a few meters away. Another Kansas player was on it, and pounded the rebound, hard. A rocket. I got in the path of the ball and caught it in front of my face. This time there was no rebound.

Man, those were a crazy fifteen seconds, I thought. I clutched the ball and let the clock tick.

"C'mon, Keep, don't waste time," the ref said sharply.

I punted the ball downfield. My teammates were battling their asses off and I loved it. They were doing everything possible to disrupt Kansas's last-ditch attack.

It's got to be close now. C'mon, ref. Blow the damn whistle already and let's get out of here.

A Kansas midfielder was about to launch a long ball across the field when the three whistles mercifully sounded. I sprinted out of the goal and my teammates sprinted to meet me, a delirious group hug by the top of the eighteen.

"I've never seen anything like what Bri did in those close minutes, making three saves—bang, bang, bang," Denise Swenson told her father. It was nice of her to say, but in my mind, Denise Swenson was the hero of this game, hands down. Not only had she scored both goals, she did so after getting her ankle stepped on by a Kansas player and playing in terrific pain.

The best part of the victory was that every single Kicker left it all out on the field. Nobody let up for a second. Pete Swenson was a happy coach. I was a happy keeper.

CHAPTER THREE

SWIMMING WITH THE MINNOWS

I told you Pete Swenson could talk, and sell. I wasn't kidding. In the summer of 1989, before my senior year at Anoka High, Pete made it his mission to help me get a college scholarship. It wasn't so easy. I had started to make a name for myself locally, but Minnesota is not exactly known as a soccer mecca. A hockey and ice-fishing mecca, yes. But for most college soccer coaches, Minnesota is strictly flyover country. I had drawn interest from the University of Wisconsin and Florida International University. Northern Iowa also recruited me, but for basketball. As much as I loved basketball, I sensed that a five-foot, eight-inch swing player with physical skills but not much of a perimeter game was not going to light it up at the Division I level. I visited Wisconsin and really liked it. It was tantalizing to think about attending Big Ten games at Camp Randall, the Badgers' historic football stadium, and when Greg Ryan, the Wisconsin women's soccer coach, offered a partial scholarship, I thought I'd be going to Madison. (Yes, this is the same Greg Ryan who will come back to the story later.)

Pete, though, was convinced I could do better. He knew I had zero interest in the local Big Ten school, the University of Minnesota, or in any other Minnesota schools, so he didn't even bother. The U, as Minnesotans call it, had a whole lot going for it, but from a young age I vowed to myself I would go away to college. Minneapolis was a bit more than a goal kick from Dayton and did not qualify as "away." I wanted to be on my own, to start my own journey. That was non-negotiable. It seems odd to me even now that a kid who was so close to her parents would feel that way, but I had an almost primal longing to bust out and challenge myself by going to a different part of the country. My parents were fine with it. Pete explored several long-distance options and reached out to a man named Jim Rudy. I had never heard of him. He was the women's soccer coach at the University of Massachusetts, one of the top programs in the country, and a renowned goalkeeping expert. Jim and Pete had become friendly when Jim was recruiting Denise Swenson for the University of Central Florida, where he coached before moving on to UMass. (Denise wound up going to the University of Connecticut.) Pete told Jim he needed to make a trip to Minnesota.

"I have a goalkeeper you have to see," Pete said.

"I don't need a goalkeeper," Jim said.

"You need this goalkeeper," Pete said.

A bit annoyed at Pete's insistence, Jim explained that he had a topflight keeper who had three years of eligibility left. He couldn't see spending precious scholarship dollars on a position where he was all set.

Pete was undeterred.

"When you see her play, she is going to change your mind," he said. "Trust me on this, Jim. She's the only goalkeeper I've ever seen in my life who jumps so high she hits her head on the crossbar."

Jim Rudy came out to Minnesota. He stayed at Pete's house and watched the Kickers play in a tournament near the Twin Cities. All the top teams in the area were there. Pete told me beforehand that coach Rudy would be in attendance.

"That's cool," I said.

Of course I knew something very good could come of his visit if I performed well, but I wasn't nervous in the least. I didn't feel as though I had to play the tournament of my life. I didn't feel as though I had to do anything different whatsoever, except channel my parents' message: Do your best. Do everything in your ability to be first, but if you put all you have into it—whether it's a geometry test or a hundred-meter dash—you can hold your head high. It's Parenting 101, and borderline trite. OK, more than borderline. But it sunk in. My parents were smart people but didn't overcomplicate things. They were comfortable with themselves and passed that on to me.

As the first game of the of the day was set to begin, I saw Jim Rudy on the sideline with a notebook and my parents on the end line with their folding chairs.

Be your best, I told myself. *Keep the ball out of the net. Play your game.*

• • •

We won our first three games by an aggregate score of 16–1. We were just crushing people, smothering them with our high pressure, forcing turnovers. I didn't have much to do in goal, but when called upon I was on it. It's one of the biggest challenges of being a goalkeeper. You don't have the luxury of playing your way into the game, settling into a rhythm. You might be a mannequin for an hour and then in an instant have to make a stop that could decide the game. For a keeper, the mental challenges are as intense as the physical challenges. You can't afford to spend a second looking at how pretty the clouds are. You must be hypervigilant all the time, in a similar way that airline pilots or soldiers have to. No, the outcome of a soccer game is hardly a life-and-death situation, but you get the point. You can't turn concentration on and off as if it were a water faucet. I hadn't been a goalkeeper for all that long. In many ways I was raw and unrefined, getting by much more with athletic ability than technique and constant alertness. Mostly what I prided myself on was stopping shots other goalies wouldn't get to.

I talked to Jim Rudy in between games, about soccer, school, family, everything. He visited with my parents, too. He made this trip not just to see me in goal, but to get insight into my makeup as well.

How does she treat her teammates?

How hard a worker is she?

How does she respond after a goal or after she makes a mistake?

How is her body language?

Is she a leader?

Before he was going to commit to a pile of scholarship money, Jim Rudy wanted to know more about the person who he might be spending the next four years with. I didn't have a good read on what he was thinking, but the Kickers were having a good day and so was I, though we were about to face the toughest test of the day.

Our opponent in the championship match was the Bangu Football Club. Bangu isn't a town in Minnesota. It's a neighborhood in Rio de Janeiro, and the club adopted its name, and the trademark Brazilian playing style, which is characterized by ball skill most American players can only dream about.

Bangu was a talented side. They seemed to have the ball on a string. The match was tight from the start and my eyes were on high beam, watching them knock the ball around. I made a couple of difficult saves early on, but they also beat me twice and the score was tied and they were coming for more. A quick counterattack sprung a Bangu forward free. I came out to cut down her angle. She deked left and tried to beat me on the right but I made a sliding tackle that got all ball and no Bangu, even though she took a spill and threw up her arms, a stunt that all forwards learn in Scoring School. The threat defused, Denise Swenson buried her third goal of the game with a defender hanging all over her. Sometimes coach's daughters get their playing time because of who is making out the lineup. Not Denise. She was a big-time finisher, with speed, skill, and toughness.

"Way to go, D," I yelled from the goal.

Bangu pushed numbers forward to get the equalizer. One of their players ripped a shot from twenty yards out, high and rocketing right at me. I leaped and punched it over the bar. I grabbed the ensuing corner in traffic and then waited and waved for everybody to get out of the box, and then waited a little more, a stunt that all keepers learn in Goalie School. I punted the ball as far as I could, toward the sideline. Not a minute later the game ended, and the Brooklyn Park Kickers were champions. Jim Rudy came over to congratulate me, my four-game showcase complete. I wondered what he was thinking.

• • •

Coach Rudy came over to our house for a post-tournament barbecue, and Ernest Scurry served his world-famous ribs, which, per usual, he started slow cooking early in the day. (My dad was a professional-quality chef, and if there were a Grilling Hall of Fame, he would be in it. Everybody told him he should open a restaurant. It was a lifelong dream of his to do just that, and he was close to making it happen. It was going to be called Bri's Family Barbecue. He even had the sign made up for it. And then the local zoning board torpedoed it at the last second. I don't think I ever saw my father angrier, or more disappointed.) After lots of ribs and fun, Jim Rudy said goodbye and told me he'd be in touch. He called shortly after he returned to Massachusetts and said he wanted me to come in for an official visit. I flew in, met the other players, toured the campus, and had a meeting with an academic advisor and told her I was interested in pre-law. By now I was ninety-nine percent sold on UMass. Ninety-nine turned into a hundred when Coach Rudy offered me a scholarship package that covered almost everything. In the fall of 1990 I would be a University of Massachusetts Minutewoman. It never would've happened without the huge heart and superb sales skills of Pete Swenson.

• • •

A few months later I was back in goal for the Anoka Tornadoes. It was my senior season, and I had one mission in mind: Go out with a state title with my people: Colleen Carey, Laurie Menke, and Shannon Jaakola. We were part of a core group that changed the DNA of Anoka girls soccer from losers to winners, and all of us had the same mindset: we were seriously competitive people on the field and had a whole lot of fun off of it. We weren't into partying—I never had a sip of alcohol until I was in college—but we knew how to have a good, wholesome time in Anoka, a metropolis of seventeen thousand people with a Main Street that was made to cruise. And cruise we did, from Burger King on one end to the movie theater on the other end. Usually we'd be in Laurie's car, driving super-slow, singing along with the radio as it blasted out the old standby from Queen, "Another One Bites the Dust," or a much newer hit, "Baby, I Love Your Way," by Will to Power.

Our bond was forged as freshmen, after we were "welcomed" to high school by the upperclassmen on the soccer team, via the usual means—a rite of initiation. Here's how it went down: The older team members conspired with our parents to leave our houses open so they could enter in the middle of the night. I can't speak for the others, but my abduction involved getting roused from my sleep by a gaggle of upperclassmen, who forced me to wear clown-type clothes and a goofy polka-dot hat and wouldn't even let me brush my teeth, wash my face, or comb my hair. Then I was marched downstairs, whisked into a car, and taken to the bridge over the Rum River at the end of Main Street, where I was Saran-wrapped to a light pole at four thirty in the morning. Colleen and Laurie were wrapped to nearby poles. (Shannon had to wait a year to get wrapped, because she was on the JV that season.) I don't know how long I was wrapped to the pole, but it felt like a whole soccer game could've been played. The upperclassmen clearly had done this before, because their wrap job was fast and tight. By the time they came back to get us, I'd managed to half-wriggle my way free, but they weren't done with us. They made us walk around in public and go into a few of the open stores, and then we had to sit down and eat breakfast in Perkins Pancake House in our ridiculous outfits. They showed mercy on us after that, allowing us to go home and change into our regular school clothes.

Our team was tight from the beginning; our new coach, a local legend named Dave Tank, made sure of it. Coach Tank was an outstanding all-around athlete in his day and became a top basketball coach later in his career. He was one of those rare people who was so gifted as a coach that his specific knowledge of a sport hardly mattered. If he'd never been to a volleyball game, he would've still found a way to coach the volleyball team to unprecedented heights. That was pretty much how it was with soccer. Anoka girls soccer had been, to put it mildly, a laughingstock for its entire history. After the team finished 3–17 in 1986, the athletic director asked Coach Tank to take the job, no matter that he may not have known a midfielder from an outfielder. Coach Tank said he'd do it for three years. He found out that he had a lot of talent coming in, and a lot of work to do, because the talented players were from different club teams and geographic areas and had little use for one another. So his first team-building challenge was to blast through the regional divide and make it clear to anyone who resisted him that she was welcome to turn in her uniform.

"We're going to be a team, and we're going to back each other up, and every single player is going to abide by the same set of rules.

If you break those rules, you are going to sit, and I don't care who you are," he said.

Early in the year, he scheduled a practice on the same day as the state fair. The fair was a big end-of-summer event that most of us wanted to go to. One of coach's rules was that if you don't go to practice, you don't play in the next game. Three of our best players decided to go to the fair.

They sat. We lost our first game—our first two games, actually—and Coach Tank didn't care. Rules were rules. Everybody got the memo. Coach Tank also made a point to intermix the different groups in drills and scrimmages. There was no chance you were going to be playing with your best friends. Coach Tank called us "the Minnows," and his main message was that if the Minnows stick together and play hard and have each other's back, they can swim with the biggest fish in Minnesota. Not unlike Coach Pete, he taught me that a coach with passion, commitment, and the ability to motivate can work wonders. There were better teams in Minnesota, by far—teams with rich history and deep talent. The genius of Coach Tank was that he convinced us that none of that mattered. When that sort of belief begins to take root, watch out. The Tornadoes went 9-4-1 in Coach Tank's first year and made it to the regional semis—by far the greatest year the program had ever had. A year later, we finished 11-3-2 and again advanced to the regional semis. In our senior year, we were 15-3-2, losing only one game after an 0-2 start.

Our belief—and our closeness—never wavered. Coach Tank's emphasis on togetherness and discipline never did either, though he did cut me a little slack on a late-season road trip. One of his ironclad rules was that the bus leaves at three o'clock and you had to be in your uniform and on the bus by that time, or you weren't going to play. The bus waited for nobody. I never missed the bus, but this one time I *did* forget my uniform. I had left it at home and in the pre–cell phone era, I couldn't text my mother to let her know. I got no answer on the home line, so I got on the bus and hoped for the best. My mother came home from work and saw my equipment bag—which included my uniform—by the front door. It was a little before three o'clock. My mother and my sister Daphne got in the car and hurried over to school. They arrived a few minutes after three and saw the bus pulling out of the school parking lot. Before the bus got on a major road, my mother pulled alongside it and Daphne held up the bag out the passenger window.

"Bri, look!" one of my teammates said. "Your mother is here with your uniform!"

Talk about a big-time save.

In the back of the bus, my teammates held my feet while I leaned out of the window—way out of the window—reaching out as if I were trying to stop a PK heading for the corner. I grabbed the bag from Daphne, who was doing her own reaching. The transfer was consummated. I got changed on the bus, and we won the game. After Coach Tank found out what happened, someone asked him if he had relaxed the rules.

"There are no rules about whether a player is permitted to get her uniform while we are in transit," he said.

That was how the year went. We swept the first three postseason matches without letting up a goal, becoming sectional champions for the first time. The Minnows were on to the states.

We were seeded fifth and not expected to last long. It was fine with us if people believed that. It dovetailed perfectly with Coach Tank's message that whatever chatter was going on outside was irrelevant; when players are truly a team, they can do anything. We opened the state tournament against Stillwater, a traditional downstate power. The game was at Carl Tonn Field in Osseo, not far from where we got our Government Cheese. We'd played Stillwater twice this season, losing and tying, and not managing a single goal. The game was intense and fiercely contested, and was still scoreless well into the third quarter, when a Stillwater player came in alone on me. She dribbled inside the eighteen and then I bolted right at her. She put a move on and tried to catch me off guard, shooting early. I made a sprawling stop. Minutes later, still in the third quarter, a Stillwater forward, unmarked in front, took a shot from four yards out. Had she kicked it with any authority or direction it would've been a goal. She side-footed it and didn't hit the ball cleanly. I dropped down and smothered it without much difficulty. I breathed a sigh of relief, and then another, when an ensuing Stillwater shot smacked into the crossbar and bounced away.

The fourth quarter was more of the same, Stillwater taking up residence in our half, taking three or four shots for every one we have. We mounted a counterattack here and there but didn't seriously threaten. The game went into sudden death overtime. I believed we would have the edge if it went into a shootout, but I much preferred to see us find a way to score and win it on the field.

We kicked off, and OT began with our star forward, Laurie Menke, who had more than fifty goals over the past two seasons, carrying the ball down the left flank. Laurie crossed to Colleen Carey, our center midfielder and her Saran Wrap pal (and my fellow Brooklyn Park Kicker), who lofted the ball artfully back to Laurie, another BP Kicker. About twenty-five yards out, Laurie drove a left-footed shot to the upper right corner. The Stillwater keeper jumped but couldn't get it. The ball was in the back of the net and the Minnows were into in the semifinals, against St. Paul Academy.

• • •

Star athletes are usually friend magnets in high school, but that wasn't my experience at Anoka. I was never one of the popular kids and didn't try to be. I wouldn't call myself an outsider, but between my Black skin and my intense eyes, I often felt that people found me unapproachable—a person they needed to be wary of. My sports teammates would tell you just the opposite, so it was hard for me to figure out any of this. A good friend once told me, "Being different in Anoka was a ticket to isolation," and there was no doubt I was different. Still, I didn't feel isolated or shunned. I had no interest in going to the big post-football game parties, or hanging with the "in" crowd because they were typically big drinkers, and I didn't drink. I just did my own thing, with the people I cared for. In my senior year, I invited a bunch of kids over to our house for a get-together. We were downstairs in the family room, where my parents had a bar. Only later did I find out that a few hard-partying types sneaked behind the bar and wiped out most of my parents' liquor supply. That was all the confirmation I needed to know these weren't my type of people.

• • •

The semifinals and finals were both scheduled to be played in the Metrodome in downtown Minneapolis. Coach Tank wanted to be sure we weren't going to be awestruck about playing in the biggest and most famous stadium in the state, home of the Twins and Vikings and such stars as Kirby Puckett and Cris Carter. The man thought of everything. The day of the semifinal, he pulled us out of school early so we would have extra time to get acclimated. After a forty-minute bus trip, we were inside the Metrodome. We walked through the vast concrete underbelly and peeked in the locker rooms, and then he took us out on the field. I felt like a little kid in an amusement park. He instructed us to lie down on the turf, close our eyes, and visualize what was going to unfold when we played St. Paul Academy in a few hours. He wanted us each to see ourselves doing our jobs, laying it all out there, committing to dig deep for that extra effort that just might make the difference. It was my first visualization experience. I thought it was damn cool.

• • •

Half the school and the marching band showed up for the game, and that made us feel at home, even in the cavernous dome. Laurie scored early and then buried another one. In the third quarter, Shannon Jaakola curled a world-class free kick from thirty yards out into the corner. Before the fourth quarter began, I was so happy that I thrust my arms overhead in a "V" shape and jumped over our bench. Our defense was superb throughout, and nobody was more of a bull-dog than a ninety-pound sophomore, Kirsten Romness, who was recovering from mononucleosis and hadn't practiced in weeks. Here was this little twig of a girl—we called her Squirt—stopping every threat that came anywhere near her. St. Paul scored in the final ninety seconds—the first goal we had conceded in seven games, but it didn't dampen our spirits even a little.

Our opponent in the finals was Park Cottage Grove, which had made a surprising run of its own. Coach gave us some last-minute instructions about playing hard and playing for each other. Both teams were cautious at the outset, content to stay compact defensively, the ball pinging back and forth in the middle for a good part of the game. Park smothered Laurie wherever she went; we had a hard time finding openings. The game was scoreless at the half, scoreless through three quarters. Regulation ended the same way, and twenty minutes of overtime did not change the script, either.

As we ran out for the penalty-kick shootout—the first in state championship history—I visualized nothing but good things. We'd lost in a shootout in the sectionals the year before, and Coach Tank had us work on our penalty kicks at the end of every practice. "Pick a corner you are comfortable with and stick with it," he said. "Don't

Your 1990 Minnesota State High School Champions—the Anoka High Tornadoes.

overthink it or get cute." Our forwards told me all year that having to go against me during our shootout practices made them better. I hoped that was true.

Both teams were tight and missed their first two PK attempts. Shannon got us a lead, and then I made a lunging stop to turn away Park's third attempt. Now Coach Tank called on me to go from goal-stopper to goal-scorer. I picked my spot—lower right—and put us up 2–0.

Park broke through to make it 2–1, but now we were just one PK away from a state championship, and it rested on the foot of Melissa Lindquist, a junior. Melissa's spot was the lower left corner. She took a short runup and pounded it . . . into the lower left corner.

We poured onto the field as fast as any Twin or Viking ever ran on that turf. We hugged and cried and Dave Tank, the coach who created a culture that celebrated the whole and not the parts, reveled in it as much as anyone. Two days earlier, the Minnows had

It was a rollicking bus ride back to Anoka after the championship. Check out the braces.

visualized themselves as state champions. Now no visualization was necessary. We had a raucous bus ride back to Anoka, a convoy of cars following us, a procession that culminated with a big celebration back at school, where we got our state-champion medals. I liked this champion concept a lot.

CHAPTER FOUR

COLLEGE GIRL

I arrived in Amherst, Massachusetts, in early August of 1990 with two suitcases and no fear. It was farther from home than I'd ever been. Some of my siblings made a wager about how long I would last. I don't know who won the bet, but I do know it wasn't the person who took the under. It was the start of my new life as a UMass student-athlete. They called us the Minutewomen, which was a dumb name, but not nearly as bad as the Lady Minutemen. I looked at it as a great new adventure, and even my roommate couldn't change my thinking. She was OK in the beginning, but she seemed chronically unhappy and I think part of the problem was that she didn't like sharing a room with a Black girl. She never expressed that to me, but she talked about it to enough other people that I had no reason to doubt it. She left after one semester and went to live in a sorority. I wasn't too broken up about it.

It took no time at all for me to get comfortable with my team-mates and Coach Jim Rudy and his staff. We had a lot of talent and I couldn't wait to get going. There was only one teammate I had a hard time figuring out. Her name was Skye Eddy. Skye was a sophomore and the incumbent goalkeeper, and a very good one at that. She won five games as a freshman and tied two others, with a goals-against average of just 0.77. I understood that I would probably be Skye's backup, at least at the start. Coach never said it in so many words, but it made sense since Skye already had a year in the program and had done well. I wasn't worried about it. My focus was on bringing my best to each training session and to get better every day. Where it got awkward for me was that Skye was the first teammate I'd ever had who didn't seem happy I was there. Colleen, Laurie, Shannon—they were my soccer sisters in high school. It was the same way with my Kicker teammates. It wasn't as though Skye was overtly hostile to me when I arrived, but she didn't roll out the welcome wagon, either. Just about every player on the team introduced themselves to me and made me feel part of the family. Skye did not. I felt as if she was watching my every move. If I made a good save in training, I could almost feel her body tense up, as if she had to do better. I thought the competition would be good for both of us. She, clearly, did not.

"Why did you come here when you knew I was here?" she asked me one day.

I didn't know what to say, so I told her truth.

"I didn't have any idea who was here," I said. "Coach offered me a spot and I said yes."

The whole thing seemed odd. I tried to put myself in her cleats. Maybe coach didn't tell her he was recruiting another keeper, I don't know. Either way, I didn't let it rock my world, or impact anything I did. There were two of us and one goal, so we might as well get at it. It wasn't anything I could change, so why worry about it? To me, worry is a negative emotion that can do a lot of harm, an emotional sump pump that sucks positive energy out of you.

So the competition began, and it was intense. I studied Skye and she studied me, and I came to appreciate how good she was. We were completely different keepers. She was far superior technically when I was a freshman. She knew how to position herself and cut down angles and was excellent with her feet. She was a good athlete and sound in all the fundamentals. She always seemed to be in the right place. I was more kinetic, less technical, relying on pure athleticism to jump, dive . . . do whatever I had to do to keep the ball out of the net. I wasn't good at all with my feet; Coach Rudy made that a priority and let me know it.

"You are some ball stopper, but you can't punt worth a damn," he said, smiling.

Skye and I got to the point where we'd even keep track of goals in practice to see who let up the fewest. In a rapid-fire drill one day in which players were going one-on-one with me, a teammate decided to get cute and chip the ball over me as I charged out of the net. The ball went in and I went off. We were supposed to be working on breakaways.

I was ticked off. I guess the competition was getting to me.

"That's weak shit—chipping me," I said.

We opened the season on the road against Rutgers in Piscataway, New Jersey. Coach named Skye the starter and she would've been in goal except that she got food poisoning the day before. (It wasn't me, I promise.) I stepped in and we won 3–0. I'm sure that didn't make Skye's stomach feel any better. As the season went on, we pretty much alternated starts. I had no problem with it, but Skye wasn't thrilled and at one point went into Coach Rudy's office and said she wanted to be named the starter for the rest of the year.

"I can't do that," he replied.

We had a good season, but not a great one, by UMass standards, finishing 10–5–2. I started eight games in goal, with three shutouts, and got into a few extra games because coach used me as a field player on the front line. I was the fastest player on the team; I guess he figured, why not try to steal a goal with my legs? The keeper rotation would've remained the same my sophomore season, but Skye missed the entire year with an injury. I started all nineteen games and had twelve shutouts and, thanks to the tutoring of Coach Rudy, was getting better all the time. I liked the way this was going.

• • •

I wasn't on a full athletic scholarship at UMass; there was a work-study component to it as well. The job I liked best was working as a referee for intramural sports, including soccer. For twelve dollars per game, I got to be outside and run and play sheriff, too, upholding the law of the pitch. It wasn't always easy, especially games involving fraternities. Some of them had intense rivalries, and frat boys being frat boys, it wasn't uncommon for things to get out of hand. During one lopsided contest, an international student completely dominated the game. He was little and agile and insanely skilled, flitting around the field like a water bug.

Why isn't this guy on the varsity? I thought.

He schooled the opposing players almost every time he got the ball, not in a taunting, excessive way—just because he was at a different level. The opponents didn't like it, and on the few occasions they could catch him, they started getting dirty, kicking at his feet, grabbing his shirt, body slamming him off the ball.

"Knock it off," I told them. "One more foul and I'm sending somebody off."

Not even five minutes later, the little magician nutmegged somebody and that was it. The megg-ee caught up to him and jumped him, taking him to the ground and throwing a few punches for good measure. A teammate joined in. The poor kid was getting pummeled. I blew my whistle and ran toward the pileup, my outrage mounting as I went. I've got my own Injustice Meter, and almost nothing sets it off faster than a bunch of cowards beating up someone who is defenseless. The main offender—probably a 180-pound guy—was still on top of the little magician, still pounding on him. My friend, Stefan, a player on the men's team who was officiating on the next field, heard the commotion and stopped his game in case I needed help. I pulled the bully off the magician and threw him a few feet away. The bully started to get up and come at me and stopped. Stefan wasn't far away if I needed back up.

"The game is over. Now get out of here," I said, my words meant for the whole team, but mostly for the punk bully. He glared at me and skulked away.

Stefan looked at me in wonder.

"Bri, you just threw that guy through the air," he said.

"It wasn't a fair fight," I said.

"You're a badass," Stefan said.

Teammates and friends had called me a "badass" before. I didn't like it at first. I thought it was close to a racial stereotype; because I was Black and strong and had intense eyes, people were scared of me, so that qualified me as a "badass." But to me being a badass has nothing to do with making people scared of you. A badass is someone who is willing to dive into situations that are difficult and uncomfortable and do it with full intensity. It's someone who may feel fear about something but doesn't let it stop them. I was a one hundred forty-pound woman. I threw an angry frat boy who outweighed me by forty pounds through the air, and then stood over him as if he were my prey. Even with my green belt in taekwondo, this had a good chance of not ending well. But I didn't care. I think you must have some badass in you to be a top goalkeeper. There are times when you have to charge out of the goal knowing there's a good chance you are going to get slammed. Or that a skillful striker will maneuver around you and make you look like a fool. A badass goes for it anyway. She is true to herself. She does what she thinks is right, and if it doesn't work out, she accepts responsibility, and will do what she thinks is right again the next time.

You can call me a badass anytime.

"Thanks, Stefan," I said.

I was a badass again one Saturday night, on the steps outside an Amherst bar. If you've been in a college town on a weekend night, you know the scene. Packed bars, roving platoons of undergraduates, most of them happy, all of them well lubricated. I was with a group of teammates, and one of my friends had a disagreement with another young woman, over a guy. They started yelling at each other and then the other woman went after my friend, pulling her hair, punching her, the two of them tumbling down the steps. I had a front-row seat and wasn't going to let this go on. I forced my way in between them, pulled the other woman off my friend, hoping to calm things down. The other woman was really drunk and had no interest in calming down. She was screaming and cursing and trying to get at my friend, which wasn't happening, because I was holding her back.

"Get out of my way, bitch!" she shouted in my face. "Let us settle this."

"You're not settling anything," I said.

The other woman was still yelling and cursing when the cops arrived. People scattered as if someone had dropped a bomb. I had the woman pinned down on the steps when the cops hauled me off her. The woman kept dropping f-bombs and wanted to continue the fight. The cops handcuffed her and put her in the back of a squad car. She cursed them out, too. She was unhinged.

The cops then confronted me and asked me what was going on.

"I was just trying to break up the fight, officer," I said. "My friend was getting beaten up. I wanted to help her. That's it."

"That's what everybody says," the cop said, and then grabbed me, hard, turned me around and cuffed me.

"Please, officer. I didn't do anything. I wanted to protect my friend," I said.

My friend tried to intervene.

"You can't do this!" she said. "She didn't do anything wrong. If you take anyone in, take me. I was the one in the fight."

The cops stuffed me in the back of a squad car, even as a parade of people tried to explain what happened.

"It's too late," I heard one cop say. "She's already in the car."

They took me into the station and booked me on disorderly conduct charges. They took off my cuffs, demanded my belt and shoes, and marched me into a jail cell. The other woman was in the next cell, still cursing at anyone who would listen. The friend who I was trying to protect bailed me out a few hours later. When it came time to stand before a judge, the woman who started the whole thing and I were given the same probationary sentence: Stay out of trouble for six months and nothing will go on your record.

I didn't think it was fair but stifled my inner badass.

"Thank you, Your Honor," I said.

• • •

After my sophomore year, Coach Rudy and I met to talk about my game and areas that he wanted to see improvement. Thanks to his daily tutorials, my kicking game had gotten much better. As we wrapped up the conversation, Coach paused and looked at me. We were in his office in Boyden Hall, a drab, dungeon-like building with the charm of a concrete bunker. Coach had the chiseled good looks of an athlete, even in middle age, and a direct, almost pointed way of looking at you. It was one of the things I liked the most about him; he didn't play mind games or BS you. He told me how much progress I'd made, and how much he admired my attitude and hunger to get better.

"I think you have the potential to make the U.S. Women's National Team," he said.

"What's that?" I said.

He stared back at me, incredulously.

"Are you joking?" he asked.

"No, Coach. I don't know what that is."

He gave me a short history lesson, explaining that the USWNT—launched in 1985—was the pinnacle for a soccer player—a team that was comprised of the best players in the country and, moreover, the team that just the year before had won the first Women's World Cup. (That wasn't the official name at the time. FIFA, the world governing body of soccer, didn't want to sully its prestigious World Cup brand by associating it with women, so it called the competition the FIFA World Championship for Women's Football for the M&M's Cup.) I wasn't aware of this competition, either, though I did like M&M's. Coach, who was finding out just how sheltered a kid from Dayton, Minnesota, could be, had some educating to do. He walked me through the whole process of making the team, beginning with being invited to a USWNT camp to allow Anson Dorrance, the coach of the fabled University of North Carolina program and the head national team coach, along with Tony DiCicco, the goalkeeping coach, a chance to evaluate me. This was beginning to move fast.

Skye returned from her injury and was as good as ever, and as frustrated as ever. I had become her personal albatross. I started about two-thirds of the games my junior year and we had another impressive season, finishing with a record of 16–4, losing in the second round of the NCAA tournament, at which point Skye decided she was done with her albatross, and UMass, for good.

She transferred to George Mason University in Fairfax, Virginia.

It turned out brilliantly for all concerned.

• • •

Before I returned to UMass for my senior year, I was invited to San Antonio to compete in the U.S. Olympic Festival, which was basically a domestic mini-Olympics that gave promising athletes—mostly college kids—a chance to simulate the Olympic experience. Teams were divided by geography. Alex Rodriguez played shortstop for the South. Michelle Kwan skated for the West. I tended goal for the North. Before our first game, I was deep into my pre-game routine, walking the field, headphones on, checking the ground inside the eighteen-yard box when I felt a tap on my shoulder. When I had my headphones on, my teammates knew not to talk to me. I was annoyed by the interruption. I turned around to find a sturdy guy with black hair and black mustache standing in front of me. He was wearing a white U.S. Soccer polo shirt. I didn't know who he was, but the shirt identified him as someone important.

"Hey, Briana," he said. "I'm Tony DiCicco, the U.S. national team goalkeeper coach. Nice to meet you. We're going to be watching you today."

I hesitated for a moment. His words ran through my head a second time:

We're going to be watching you today.

"OK, cool. Thanks, Coach," I said. "Nice to meet you, too."

It was the first conversation I'd ever had with anyone on the national team staff. Tony departed and I went back to my preparation.

I hope I put on a good show for him, I thought.

What Tony DiCicco watched that day was not a good show. It was a horror show. In the opening minutes I had an inexplicable lapse in concentration and allowed a bouncing ball to go over my head into the goal. The other goals weren't so soft, but honestly weren't great, either. The score was 3–0 after fifteen minutes. In three years of college soccer my goals-against average was way below 1.00. At the rate I was going at the Olympic Festival, I was heading toward a GAA of 12.00. I got subbed out at halftime and deserved to get subbed out at halftime. The sad truth was that after the rocky start, I had a hard time letting go of how poorly I was playing.

From the North bench at the Virgil T. Blossom Athletic Center, I spent the entire second half in silent fury. Not at Tony. Not at my team. At myself. Three goals in a half, never mind one-third of a half, is an abomination. My teammates were supportive and so was my coach, but I stunk, and we all knew it. Everybody assumed the crux of the problem was that I tightened up and put extra pressure on myself because Tony was watching. I promise you that wasn't the case. If anything, the bigger the game, the greater the stakes, the better I played. My concentration wasn't close to where it needed to be. I just picked a bad time to have an awful game.

I wondered how bad a scouting report Tony might give to Anson Dorrance.

As disgusted as I was about my performance, though, it never occurred to me that I might've blown my big chance, that fifteen crappy minutes was going to prevent me from getting another look from U.S. Soccer. Call me naïve, or delusional, but I refused to believe that one poor half was going to define me. I would learn from my mistakes and get better. I'd go back to goalkeeping school with Jim Rudy and tighten up my game. If you work hard enough, and want it badly enough, you are going to find a way. Optimism is hardwired into me, what can I say? When my wife and I are on a beach vacation and wake up to a downpour, I'm sure the sun will be out by noontime. If it rains all day, I'm sure it will be better tomorrow.

The bottom line is that I don't give up. The road to success is not always a straight line. In fact, most times it isn't straight at all. There are wrong turns. There are potholes. There are detours that force you to reverse field and try a different route altogether. All kinds of things can knock you off course, but you keep the faith and you hold on to your destination. And you keep going forward.

Always keep going forward.

And always appreciate when someone (in this case Tony) has the open mind—and the wisdom—to give you a second chance; to realize that you may have a lot more to offer than you show in a single poor performance. I read a story once about the Oakland A's scout who signed baseball Hall of Famer Rickey Henderson. He was at an American Legion game in the Bay Area with another scout and saw Henderson strike out twice in the first four innings.

"I've seen enough," the other scout said, packing up his stuff. "I've got a plane to catch."

The A's scout stayed. Henderson homered in his final two at-bats. The scout pounded out a rave scouting report, telling the A's they had to sign this kid. And they did.

I didn't see Tony after the game and didn't really want to. By the time the Olympic Festival was over, I did not want to remember the Alamo or any part of San Antonio. I just wanted to get back to Amherst and get going on my senior year. With Skye at George Mason, there would be far less drama and far more starts. Both of those things appealed to me. So did getting back to work.

• • •

People make a big deal out of gays coming out of the so-called closet. I never saw any reason to come out at UMass or at any other time in my life, because I was never *in* the closet. So what need was there for a press conference or a team meeting or a family gathering? I was who I was and never wanted to be someone I was not. Even after my parents caught me with Kelly and had that talk with me, I wasn't going to stop robbing the bank. I was just going to make sure I didn't get *caught* robbing the bank.

All my UMass teammates knew I was gay. Some of them may have been gay, too; I honestly don't know. Either way, it wasn't a big deal. If there were friends I thought might be gay, I wasn't about to walk up and ask, "Hey, are you one of us?" Everybody is on their own path. It's a very individual decision to decide how public you want to be. Fear of being ostracized because of my sexuality was not a concern. If someone wanted to reject me because I preferred women to men, well, it was no great loss because that was not a person I would want to have as a friend.

In my junior and senior years at UMass, when I was 21, I would go to gay clubs and bars in nearby Northampton. Typically it would be a Wednesday night, when it wasn't so crowded, and in the company of players from the field hockey, softball, and basketball teams. We'd drink a little and dance a lot, and it was a blast—and for those who weren't out, it was a place where you knew you were safe and wouldn't be judged. One of the regulars in our group was a girl I'll call Darlene. We weren't dating but we got to be very friendly and I think she respected how comfortable I was with my sexuality. We were at a club named Diva's one night, standing by the bar between dances. Darlene was from a conservative Southern Baptist family. There may not have been Southern Baptists in Minnesota, but I still got an earful of conservative Christianity on Sunday visits to church with my parents. I was a regular for a while, but when the pastor started going off on homosexuality and how gay people were doomed and would spend all of eternity in a fiery hell, my attendance cooled off fast.

I had a good idea of what Darlene was up against.

"My family would kill me if they knew I was here," she said.

The more I got to know Darlene, the more insight I got into the depth of her struggle. She never said it in so many words, but I always got the sense that she was ashamed of being gay and would do almost anything to be straight. I knew other women who were the same way—who wished, desperately, that they could be someone else. After a while, Darlene stopped joining us on the outings to Northampton. I didn't know why and I never saw her again. I have no idea how she resolved the conflict she felt. Maybe it turned out that those Wednesday nights were just a phase she was going through, and she ultimately realized she was not gay. For her sake, I hope so. I'd hate to think that she went through life pretending she was someone she was not, just to assuage her shame and keep the peace in her family. Every time I meet someone who feels this sort of pressure makes me so grateful for my parents and their open-mindedness. Other than that one conversation after Kelly and I got busted, they never said another word to me. They accepted me for who I was and loved me for who I was. It's the greatest gift a parent can give a child.

• • •

The 1993 season unfolded much as I thought it would. Through our first seven games, we won six and tied one and outscored opponents, 19–2. We had a potent offense and a lockdown defense, and a team loaded with warriors. We finished the regular season 13–3–3, easily won the Atlantic 10 tournament, and moved into the NCAA tournament, crushing Providence, 5–0, in the first round, and holding off UConn, our archrival, 1–0, advancing to college soccer's final four. (It wasn't called the College Cup then.) Our opponent would be the University of North Carolina Tar Heels. All they'd done, under Anson Dorrance, was win seven straight NCAA titles. The last time they'd lost a game I was a fourteen-year-old Brooklyn Park Kicker. They were one of the greatest dynasties in all of sports. They had a roster loaded with superstars, led by Mariel Margaret Hamm, who went by Mia and was the leading scorer in NCAA history. The previous year, UNC played Duke in the championship game and won 9–1. The soccer world regarded them as goddesses outfitted in Carolina Blue, an overmatch for every college program on earth.

Jim Rudy wasn't buying it, and neither were my teammates and me. We were battlers. Competing is what we did best, no matter how hopeless the cause might have seemed to the outside world. I thought back to Coach Tank and his message to the Minnows about what was possible if we swam together. Through twenty-two games this season, we had allowed only eight goals, and my goal-against average—0.34—was the best in the country. We hadn't given up a goal in five straight games . . . 450 minutes. We knew how to keep the ball out of the net. I kept thinking about what drew me to goalkeeping in the first place:

We can't lose if I don't give up any goals.

The NCAA semifinal was being played on Fetzer Field in Chapel Hill (not exactly a neutral site, but what are you going to do?), a Works Progress Administration building that had been home for the North Carolina women since Dorrance founded the program in 1979. Coach Rudy came up with a superb game plan to cope with Carolina's famous high pressure, and the great Mia and all their other weapons, built on defensive discipline, careful positioning, and quick ball movement. We knew we couldn't match their technical skill, or athleticism. So we were going to bunker in, limit their chances, and hope we could get a goal or two on the counterattack. It's a time-honored soccer strategy, and that's because it can work. Let the other team have the ball. Let them knock it around for ten minutes at a time, if they want.

"It's not how much you have of the ball that matters," a smart commentator once said. "It's what you do with it when you have it."

• • •

The best coaches have a gift for not overcomplicating things, packing a lot into a few words. Jim Rudy is one of the best. In the locker room before the game, he said, "You've been facing challenges all season long, and this is just another one. You know who you are playing but let me just say this: They're not superhuman. You are playing a soccer game. Enjoy it. Stick together and leave it all out there. Now let's go."

We charged onto the field. I was more fired up to play than I could ever remember.

Carolina came out hard and fast. You can prepare all you want for their pressure, but when it's in your face it's a whole different deal. I was busy from the start. I punched away a corner kick and made a jumping catch of a cross. In the twelfth minute, Mia Hamm cut a defender, found space, and got taken down from behind. The whistle blew. I didn't even have to wait for the ref to point to the spot.

It was a penalty kick.

Mia stepped up to take it. The spot was twelve yards away and I had 192 square feet of goal to cover against the premier forward in college soccer. I never went for the arm-waving and jumping-jack routine the way a lot of keepers did. "Making yourself big," they called it. To me it was kind of gimmicky. I was five feet eight and no amount of waving or jumping was going to make me six feet two. I got in a slight crouch, knees bent, well-balanced and ready to break either way. I rocked back and forth almost imperceptibly. Coach Rudy, a goalkeeping savant, taught me cues to look for that often can help you get a read on where the shooter is going. Is her runup short or long? Are her hips open or closed? Is she looking to side-foot it, or pound it with her laces?

I didn't have any data on Mia's tendencies. She made a short runup and struck the ball with the side of her foot toward the right corner. I read it accurately and dove left, but her placement was too good.

Carolina 1, UMass 0.

"Let's go. Let's get it right back," I hollered to my teammates.

We picked up our play, but North Carolina was unrelenting. Rita Tower, another dangerous Tar Heel forward, blasted a shot on goal.

It had too much pace to catch, so I blocked it with both hands. Tisha Venturini, an All-American midfielder, drilled the rebound by me.

It was 2–0 not even halfway through the opening half, but I was almost defiant in my belief we could turn this around. Then four Tar Heels began zipping the ball around the box with the precision of Swiss watchmakers, until they found an opening and planted No. 3.

The scoreboard was an ugly sight, no doubt. So much for my fifteen shutouts and NCAA-leading goals-against average. But I was not backing down. At the half, coach challenged us.

"You have a choice. You can go out and compete and win the second half, or you can wind up the way Duke did last year. It's up to you."

I came out for the second forty-five and felt almost possessed. North Carolina continued to bring it. I was as locked in as I have ever been. Venturini hit a rocket toward the upper ninety, and I went fully horizontal, launching myself in the air, extending my arms and swatting it away with my left hand.

The Carolina players had already started celebrating.

On the sideline, Anson Dorrance told an assistant, "This goalie is brilliant."

I even started talking a little smack, which was not normal for me. A Carolina player took a shot that I saved easily.

"Is that all you got?" I yelled.

Nicole Roberts, one of our forwards, scored in the seventy-fifth minute to make it 3–1. I fought to the end. A late UNC goal made it a 4–1 final. It was not how I want to end my UMass career, but I was proud of the way we left it all out there.

In the postgame press conference, several reporters ask variations of a super-annoying question:

"Did you honestly think you could beat North Carolina?"

I rolled my eyeballs, doing a poor job of hiding my disdain for the line of questioning.

"Yes, we did, because why even go out there if you don't think you can win?"

I walked into the hallway when the inquisition was over. Mia and the Carolina contingent were waiting for their press conference. I saw Dorrance talking to someone about ten feet away. Mia waved me over. I was confused, even a little suspicious. I had no idea what she wanted.

"You played great, Keep," she said.

"Thanks, Mia," I said, hesitantly. The way she looked at me convinced me of her sincerity.

"Can you tell him that?" I replied, looking in the direction of the USWNT coach.

"He already knows," Mia said.

In the championship game two days later, UNC crushed George Mason, 6–0, for yet another title. Mason had advanced after outlasting heavily favored Stanford in the semis, a match that went to PKs after four overtimes. The George Mason goalkeeper, Skye Eddy, saved two of Stanford's PKs and was named the defensive player of the tournament. A few weeks later, the All-American teams were announced. Skye and I both made it. It wasn't always easy for either of us, but our competition made us both better players. Happy endings are nice.

CHAPTER FIVE

GOING NATIONAL

Our practice gear at UMass consisted of gray T-shirts and gray shorts that were the property of the school, a fact that the equipment managers in Boyden Hall reminded us of regularly. We called the gear the Boyden Grays. It was not a high-tech fabric or anything close to it. It was your basic gray cotton, and it might've dated to the Carter administration. Still, Tommy Bishko and Zaweeda Sahabdeen, the caretakers of all the athletic-department stuff, guarded them as if they were precious gems.

A few days after the disappointing end to our season, Jim Rudy called my dorm room and asked me to come to his office. It was a little before nine in the morning, a Thursday. The timing seemed odd. I wondered if there was something wrong.

Was there an academic issue? (Not that I knew of.)

Did I fail to turn in my uniform or my Boyden Grays? (No.)

Did he want to invite me over for Thanksgiving? (Doubtful.)

I hurried over to Boyden because I had political science class at nine thirty. I'd been in coach's office plenty of times, but this felt different. He told me to sit down. I looked at the assortment of All-America plaques and framed photos of former UMass players. Over his door, in front of his desk, was a quote that said, "When I walk on the field . . . I doubt defeat." I was curious and atypically anxious.

"Guess what?" he said.

"What?"

"You've been invited to U.S. National Team Camp. It's coming up soon, next week, in Florida. Congratulations, Bri. You've earned this."

I am not often speechless, but in that moment I came close.

"OK, cool. Thanks," I said.

It turned out Jim Rudy had much more to do with it than giving me the news. He and Anson went back a number of years. It was Jim Rudy, in fact, who brought Anson into the U.S. Soccer system to help him out with some men's teams in the 1980s. Anson had great regard for Coach, especially when it came to goalkeeping. Jim Rudy had been boosting my candidacy for a while and did again after we lost to UNC in the NCAA tournament.

"You saw what she can do," he said. "If you bring her into camp, I am telling you right now that she will be on the team for a long time."

Coach Rudy handed me a piece of paper with the number of a team administrator to make flight arrangements. The camp was being held at Cocoa Expo, near Cape Canaveral and Cocoa Beach. I called the administrator and booked a flight into Orlando. Even as I dialed the number, it was almost impossible to fathom what I was doing.

Before I left Amherst we had our end-of-the-year team banquet. We came up two games short of our goal, but we had much to feel good about. Finishing 17–3–3 and making it to the national semifinals is not too shabby. I was named National Goalkeeper of the Year by the Missouri Athletic Club. Paula Wilkins and I were named All-Americans, and Rebecca Myers was the Atlantic 10 Rookie of the

Year and Jim Rudy was Coach of the Year. Eager to celebrate my call-up, my teammates presented me with an American flag.

"It would be good to have one of these when you make the national team and want to display your patriotism," somebody said.

Coach wanted to have one more talk. He'd been around the best U.S. players on both the men's and women's side for a long time and knew that it was dangerously easy to go into camp for the first time and feel as though you have to completely reinvent yourself and be better than you've ever been.

"Don't do anything but be Briana Scurry," he said. "Remember that. Play your game. You can make this team. I don't have a doubt in the world."

One thing I knew about Jim Rudy was that he was no kind of smoke blower. If he didn't think I could cut it, he never would've lobbied for me to Anson Dorrance.

Cocoa Expo was built in 1964 as the spring-training home for the Houston Colt 45s (the original name of the Astros) and had since grown into a multi-sport facility. It had an enchanting name and was near a beautiful beach, and the fields were like golf greens, but it had not aged well. The place itself was drab and droopy, with weeds sprouting through cracks in the outdoor hallways, lizards popping out of overgrown vegetation, and the whole complex in bad need of a paint job. But I wouldn't have cared if camp had been held at an Interstate 95 rest stop. This wasn't a sightseeing trip or a chance to escape the late-autumn cold of Massachusetts. This was a business trip, and my business was to prove myself as a goalkeeper.

We did everything right there at Cocoa, and in the equally dingy hotel next door. It was where we trained, recovered, had meetings, ate meals, had more meetings, and slept. The days were planned almost to the minute. I wasn't just a newbie to this camp; I was a newbie to the whole U.S. Soccer developmental system. Typically, players will get discovered in their early to mid-teens and attend a succession of youth camps—U-16, U-17, U-18, and so on. I had never been U-anything, except maybe Who Are U? I didn't even make my region's Olympic Development Program (ODP) select team back in my Brooklyn Park Kicker days. I gained some recognition my senior year at UMass, but it's very rare for someone to be making her first appearance in a U.S. Soccer camp at twenty-two years old. Besides Anson and Tony DiCicco, I doubt that any of the other coaches and evaluators had any idea who I was.

When I walked on the field on Day 1, the first player I saw was Michelle Akers, whom Jim had coached at the University of Central Florida before he departed for UMass. She was thought by many to be the best women's soccer player in the world. After about two minutes of watching her play, I joined the many. Mia Hamm was there, of course. So was Kristine Lilly, her former North Carolina teammate and as good a flank midfielder as you will find anywhere. Tiffeny Milbrett, who played up front with Mia, was a tiny powerhouse on attack, and on the backline, the stalwarts included Carla Overbeck and Joy Fawcett. The core of the team had won the first Women's World Cup two years earlier in China.

You're with the big dogs now, I thought.

You would've thought I'd be completely intimidated and full of doubts whether I could cut it. That never happened. Not that I was cocky. I just had Jim Rudy's words—"You can do this"—running through my head on an endless loop. For reasons I can't fully explain, I had a core belief in myself that I could meet this challenge. I did not expect perfection. That would've been silly. Believing in yourself is not the same thing as feeling invincible. I did a ton of self-talk and went right at the challenge:

These are the best players in the world. How do I navigate this and show the coaches what I can do?

How? By keeping my focus one hundred percent on the shot that was coming at me in that moment. Whatever happened with that one,

I forgot it, and zeroed in on the next one, and the one after that. I was all micro, all the time. I'd never had to fish more soccer balls out of the back of the net in my life than I did in that camp. It was crazy. I stopped counting, but I didn't let myself get discouraged, and didn't betray any emotion, either. Jim Rudy used to tell me all the time that I was like a marble wall in the goal, not so much because I stopped every shot but because I never gave opponents anything to climb on. No self-directed anger, no defeatist body language. Even if I let a ball slip through my hands and let up a bad goal, I wouldn't reveal a thing. Coach loved it. He said that when a keeper starts to lose it emotionally, all it does is fire up the other team.

There were five keepers in the camp, and I was No. 5. They didn't keep official rankings, but I was the only newcomer, so I *had* to be at the bottom. Mary Harvey, who was in the nets when the U.S. won the inaugural World Cup, was there. So were Saskia Webber, Shelly Finger, and Kim Wyant, who had been the keeper for the first game in the history of the USWNT, back in 1985. I paid no mind to pecking order. I could see from the start the other keepers were technically more polished and better with their feet than I was, but I also knew I could get to shots the others couldn't. We worked on corner kicks and free kicks and did all sorts of drills, and I especially enjoyed getting into battles with Michelle Akers. Michelle had the hardest shot on earth—about seventy miles per hour—and she could put it anywhere she wanted. She was so good that she would sometimes tell the keepers where she was going with her penalty kicks and score anyway. I'd never faced a shot like hers, and I think she relished the competition, because she told me I made saves that she'd never seen a female goalkeeper make. One day we were going at it, just the two of us, and she hit a sick strike from the top of the eighteen, a rocket that was going to the upper right corner. She turned around after she shot it, her way of saying that she knew it was in; there was no reason to watch. The ball was veering away from me, but I read it well off her foot, sprung to my left, and leaped as high as I could, getting enough of the ball with my right fingertips to deflect it away.

As I jumped to my feet, Michelle turned back toward goal to find the ball not in the net but rolling away. I looked at her with hands on hips, smiling.

"What the hell?? How did you save that, you rat bastard?" she said.

Stopping a Michelle Akers shot was the greatest challenge a goalkeeper could have, and that is why I loved it. I loved her as a teammate and a competitor because even on a team full of warriors, she stood out as a person who would give as much of her spirit and body as anyone. I watched her sometimes and would think, *This woman would die on the field if that's what it took.* A few times she damn near did. It's easy to be ordinary. The world is full of ordinary. It's hard to be extraordinary. The way to get there is to embrace the *extra* work and pain and resilience that will take you there. Michelle did that every time she put on the uniform. She and I would continue to have these showdowns for as long as we were on the team together. She is without question the best player I've ever played with.

• • •

The best part of my days at Cocoa Expo was when we'd play small-sided games—4 v. 4, or 6 v. 6. The pace of play was insane, the shots nonstop. The coaches would form the teams and we'd have round-robin games, keep standings, and finally have a knockout tournament to determine the winner. It was competition at its fiercest—and where I think I showed my best form, flinging my body this way and that, batting down every shot I could. Anson joked that whoever had me on their team knew they'd get a notch in their belt, but I took nothing for granted. Not during the camp, and not afterward. I made it my mission to keep up my intensity every day, and to finish strong. Camps are a physical and mental grind. It's easy to have your level fall off toward the end. I looked at camps the same way I looked at games: I wanted to be at my best when it mattered most, so my goal was to start strong and finish even stronger. Peak to peak. When the camp ended, Anson and Tony met with me for what amounted to an exit interview. After Tony made suggestions about areas to focus on in my training—ball distribution and improving my kicking game—Anson gave me the bottom line.

"For your first camp, and playing against the best players in the world, I thought you did really well," he said. "We want to have you back in for our next camp."

When you are new, the No. 1 goal is to show them enough to get invited back. Obviously the Michelles and Mias of the world did not have to sweat this out, but the newbies did. For those who did not get invited back, it was crushing—sometimes even dream-ending—news. All I wanted to do was keep climbing the ladder. I upped my game again in my second camp, and my third. Before I left that one, Anson and Tony summoned me to the hotel again.

"You're going to be our starter in the Algarve tournament next month," he said.

"Cool, thank you," I said.

I walked out of the office, half-floating over the cracks in the sidewalks, trying to take it all in, without much success. I was about to embark on a whole new adventure. In three weeks, I would be leaving the United States for the first time in my life.

• • •

The Algarve is a dream destination on the southern coast of Portugal, full of majestic cliffs, crashing surf, and miles of Europe's best beaches. It was equally dreamy for a rookie goalkeeper making her first road trip with the U.S. Women's National Team. The Algarve Cup is now a

March fixture on the international soccer calendar, but in 1994 it was being rolled out for the first time. Comprised of a four-team field—the host, Portugal, and three global powers: Norway, Sweden, and the United States—the tournament provided elite competition and a good measuring stick for where you stood a year before the next World Cup. Anson had already announced he would be turning over the team to Tony when World Cup qualifying began later in the year and saw the tournament as way to begin the transition. He would still be the head coach, but Tony would gradually take on a more significant role.

Our first game was against Portugal in Silves, a picturesque medieval town that was inland from the coast, set amid citrus groves and vineyards, with whitewashed buildings and red tile rooves everywhere you looked.

You aren't in Dayton anymore, I thought, as our bus made its way through the thirteenth-century streets. When we arrived at Éstadio Dr. Francisco Vieira, we wound our way to the locker room, and as I entered, in the middle of a wall of lockers, I saw a bright yellow, long-sleeve jersey with the No. 1 and my name on the back, on a hanger. I went toward it as if drawn by a magnet. I touched the sleeve and held it up, the jersey and I having a moment to shake hands and get acquainted. We would be spending a lot of time together, after all.

About two thousand Portuguese fans turned out for the match—March 16, 1994—the opening day in the first Algarve Cup. Women's soccer in Portugal, as in most of the world then, was in its embryonic stages, but that was not even a blip on my mental radar. I was about to get my first cap—soccer parlance for a game appearance with your national team—and every bit of my focus and energy was on being locked in mentally for the occasion. If there were a gauge to measure adrenaline, I would've broken it. We went through warmups and huddled up one more time, and at 4:30 P.M., Silves time, my yellow jersey and I sprinted toward the goal I would be guarding and followed my customary ritual, jumping up and grabbing the crossbar, hanging for a moment or two, then dropping to a knee for a silent prayer in the center of the goal. When I was finished, I walked forward to meet with my defenders: Carla Overbeck, Megan McCarthy, and Tiffany Roberts. We were all arm in arm—a red, white, and blue sisterhood thousands of miles from home. Carla, the center back, a four-time NCAA champion for Anson's North Carolina teams and maybe the premier defender in the world, led the discussion. Carla was not a woman of many words, so the words she did say carried that much more weight.

"No sniff," she said.

She paused for a moment.

"No sniff," she repeated.

Everybody understood.

"No sniff" was the undeclared motto of the USWNT defense. It was shorthand for not merely shutting down the opponent but destroying its hope of getting even within sniffing distance of our goal.

It was shorthand for this:

> *Our defense is a fortress, and you are not penetrating it. You will look for openings and find nothing. You will look for headers in the box and we will beat you to them. We will win every loose ball, block every shot, protect our goalkeeper to the end. We will do whatever we have to do to beat you.*

I had been on the team for about two minutes, but the message was passed along to me with not just clarity, but with the force of Michelle Akers's free kick.

No sniff.

I got it.

Megan and Tiffany ran to their defensive positions on the flanks. Before I went back to the goal, Carla wanted a word with me. Carla Overbeck was royalty in our sport. She was a player and a person of impeccable character and quality. She clamped her hands on my shoulders. She looked me squarely in the eye.

"You deserve to be here," Carla said.

I locked eyes with her. I wanted to cry, to explode in some spasm of gratitude and shared belief, but there was no time for that. I nodded. Carla went back to her position, right in front of me. I looked at the No. 4 on her back with something approaching reverence. In two words she had given me my first true insight into the psyche of the National Team. I'd been blessed to be a part of some great teams with huge character and superb coaches. Without them, I knew I would not be where I was. I would not be even close to guarding a goal in Silves, Portugal, for the United States of America. You don't just show up one day and represent your country and make it to the highest level of your sport. If you think you do, you are deluding yourself. Yes, I'd been gifted with athletic ability, but so many others played a huge role in nurturing me and bringing that ability out. Pete Swenson and the Brooklyn Park Kickers. Dave Tank and the Anoka High School Tornadoes. Jim Rudy and the UMass Minutewomen. Every one of them taught me so much about being a good person, a good teammate, a great competitor. All of them poured strong, healthy messages and superb coaching into me.

And all of them lifted me up and put me in this Portuguese stadium, where I was able to take in Carla's message, and understand I was venturing into a competitive culture that was deeper, and altogether different. This, I was learning, was the essence of the USWNT, a mentality and a belief that no matter the circumstances, no matter whether the other team was more skilled or had more fans or had a two-goal lead . . . none of that mattered. We are coming for you, and we are going to beat you.

No sniff.

· · ·

Moments after Carla's shoulder-cupping affirmation, the Algarve Cup was on. Instantly my mind shifted to The Big Five Moments. This was another key part of our psychological agenda. The Big Five Moments are the first five minutes of the match, the last five minutes of the half, the first five minutes of the second half, the last five minutes of the match, and the five minutes after a goal is scored. Those are the times when scores are most impactful, the psychological balance of the match at its most delicate. I remember a game at UMass when we went up in the closing minutes of the first half. You knew that it was in the head of the other side all during the break. When the second half started, they mounted an immediate attack, leading to a point-blank shot. I saved it. In that moment, our 1–0 lead felt more like 2–0 or 3–0. Sometimes when you score—or when you deny a score—is almost as important as the goal or stop itself.

I got through the first five minutes against Portugal with no problem, and then the next five. Carin Jennings, another outstanding U.S. forward, beat the Portuguese keeper in the sixth minute. Lil made it 2–0 in the twenty-first minute. I had little to do and I didn't mind at all. My dream game was when there were zero shots on goal by the opponent, and I had enough free time to read a book. I like making a game-saving stop as much as anyone, but I go back to the ultra-logical wiring I got from my father. As much as he loved to tinker with engines, what he loved the most was when his car was running as if it had just rolled out of the showroom. When our team and especially our defense are well-tuned and in perfect harmony, I don't have to fix anything. The only stat I care about is a zero next to the opponent's score total. That didn't change over my entire career. Forget save totals and save percentage and all that garbage. When I see a zero, I am happy, because it means we won.

In Éstadio Dr. Francisco Vieira, the zero lasted for full time. The final score was 5–0. My career record for the U.S. was 1–0.

Our next opponent, a few days later, was Sweden, one of the top teams in the world. Mia scored in the opening minute, a beautiful thing, and that ended up being the difference maker. The match was taut throughout, and I was much busier, but I got my zero and now we were up against Norway in the final game with the trophy on the line.

In the big picture, the Algarve Cup is not a tournament with major international importance, but in 1994, a year before the second Women's World Cup, it had real gravitas. The U.S. was the defending world champion, and we wanted to make sure everyone knew we were still the big kid on the block.

Norway saw it differently. The Norwegians had beaten the Americans more than the Americans had beaten them. They were not buying into any sort of USWNT mystique. They were tough and talented and didn't give a hoot about what I'm sure they saw as red, white, and blue entitlement.

The Norwegians' attitude was "Let's go."

Our attitude was "Let's go."

So let's go.

From the first minute it was clear that the Norwegians wanted this as much as we did, maybe even more, because we had won the first World Cup and they had not. They were fighting for everything, backing off nothing. It was scoreless at the half and the drama was building like a tsunami. It was as intense a competitive cauldron as I had ever been involved in. Guarding the goal for my country for only the third time, and for the first time with a title on the line, I couldn't draw on any prior experience. The match went into the eightieth minute, still tied. Norway got a corner. Our whole game plan going in was to make sure that Ann Kristin Aarønes, one of Norway's top players, didn't beat us. Almost six feet tall, Aarønes wore a thick white headband and was as thin as a wafer, able to squeeze into tight spaces.

In the eighty-fourth minute she settled a cross and powered it past me into the corner. Her teammates mobbed her and successfully killed off the remaining minutes, and soon they were celebrating again, this time for winning the Algarve Cup. I allowed one goal in three games, but it was one goal—and one sniff—too many.

CHAPTER SIX

WORLD CUPPER

Whether you want to call it luck or serendipity or all part of God's plan, I have had impeccable timing ever since I was born. Arriving almost nine years after my nearest sibling gave me a more stable home life, my parents' resources and attention not stretched to the max the way they were earlier in their parenting careers. Arriving nine months before the passage of Title IX, the landmark legislation that ushered in an era of exponential growth of sports opportunities for girls, was clearly a stroke of genius on my part. By the time I got to middle school, there were girls sports teams popping up all over. Then I connected with Pete Swenson, just as his daughter, Denise, was being recruited by Jim Rudy, one of the top goalkeeper coaches in the country. At UMass, our run to the NCAA semifinals gave me a chance to show what I could do in front of Anson Dorrance—a chance that led to my invitation to USWNT camp.

And there, too, my timing was flawless. The U.S. was hosting the Men's World Cup in the summer of 1994, an event that would draw over three million fans and give the sport a higher profile than it had since the New York Cosmos signed Pele in 1975. And in just over two years women's soccer would be making its Olympic debut in the Atlanta Games. The U.S. was finally starting to get why soccer is the world's most popular sport. That coincided with the start of my USWNT career. I am such a good planner.

• • •

Looking to stay sharp and make a few bucks on the side, I accepted an offer from Tony DiCicco to work at his SoccerPlus goalkeeper camp in North Carolina in the summer of 1994. SoccerPlus was the premier camp of its kind, drawing hundreds of young keepers who aspired to play in college, the pros and/or the USWNT. The counselors were mostly of top collegiate goalkeepers, and a few pro and national-team imports. On my first day I met the other counselors, including an All-American from the University of Arkansas named Kerri Reifel. Kerri remembers our introduction vividly.

"I thought you were standoffish and arrogant. You barely even looked at me—like you were too good for the rest of us because you were on the national team," she said.

I don't remember doing that at all, and it doesn't sound like me, but I'll go with Kerri's take. Fortunately, she didn't hold it against me for long. We started to talk, did our demos. I really liked her. Kerri had a substance and presence about her that impressed me. She was studying criminal justice and sociology in college and wanted to be an FBI agent when she was done playing. She had big ambitions and demanded a lot of herself and seemed mature beyond her years. In goal, she had a polish and technical skill that exceeded just about everyone else in camp, including me.

This woman has definitely clocked the hours, I thought.

When Kerri watched me, she had a somewhat different impression.

"You would do so many things wrong and you'd still make the save," she said. "You were the most insanely athletic goalkeeper I'd ever seen, and honestly, it pissed me off."

Kerri and I had the same aspirations—she wanted to be on the USWNT, too—but our approaches couldn't have been more different. She was super-analytical, almost scientific, about her every movement. I was almost entirely intuitive; I'd see the ball and go get it. A strong friendship took root, anyway. Aside from training the campers, Kerri and I worked together in the camp store, where Tony sold jerseys, goalie gear, and USWNT clothing and miscellaneous items. Clerking together bonded us even more. Knowing I had left UMass, Kerri invited me to come down to Arkansas to train with her whenever the time was right.

"I'd like that," I said. Camp broke up on June 17. (I will never forget that because I watched O.J. Simpson and the white Bronco lead Los Angeles police on a long chase on a southern California freeway while I was waiting for my flight.) I hugged Kerri goodbye. I had a strong hunch that this wasn't going to be a summer-camp friendship, soon to be forgotten.

I was right.

• • •

Losing is no fun, but one nice thing about being on the USWNT team was that it didn't happen very often. I got overwhelmingly positive feedback from Anson and Tony after the Algarve Cup and, even more important, from my teammates. Having their trust meant everything to me. It was true with the Anoka High Tornadoes and the Brooklyn Park Kickers and the UMass Minutewomen, and it was true three games into my USWNT career. I wanted my teammates to know they could count on me, that I would always have their back, and that I would honor the crest, and their trust, with the way I went about my work. It's one of the foundational elements of the USWNT. You don't have to be best friends with every teammate. You don't even have to like them. But if you are going to get anything done on the pitch, you damn well better trust and respect each other, and be ready to lay everything on the line for each other.

My goal for the rest of '94 was to deepen that trust and make sure my performances kept me in the No. 1 spot heading into the World Cup in 1995 in Sweden. Our biggest test after the Algarve came in a stateside summer tournament called the Chiquita Cup between four of the best teams in the world: the United States, Germany, China, and Norway. Anson's handoff of the team to Tony was almost complete, and the transition was seamless. Tony was not just the goalkeeping coach, he was a former keeper who played briefly for the U.S. men's team himself, so as much as I liked Anson and was grateful that he gave me the chance, the change was positive for me. I now had someone at the helm who understood the challenges of goalkeeping implicitly. In our first game, against Germany, we drew a standing-room-only crowd of almost six thousand people (for about five minutes, it was the biggest crowd I'd ever played before; I told you Americans were finally getting it) at George Mason University in Fairfax, Virginia. We won, 2–1, and then we headed up Interstate 95 to Rutgers, where we beat China, 1–0. In the finale we had another shot at the Norwegians, and went on the road again, this time to Worcester, Massachusetts. More than 6,400 fans turned out, and we sent them home happy, giving Norway a 4–1 thumping and winning the Chiquita Cup. I was named the tournament MVP. It was my first individual accolade as a national-team player, and it meant so much. (If it entitled me to a lifetime supply of bananas, nobody ever told me.)

The tournament was a good tune-up for World Cup qualifying in the Confederation of North, Central America, and Caribbean Association Football (CONCACAF), which was held in Montreal and didn't include much competitive drama; we played Mexico, Trinidad & Tobago, Jamaica, and Canada and won by an aggregate score of 36–1. Ideally, you want to get pushed at least a little bit in qualifying, but most women's soccer programs in CONCACAF nations were still in their formative stages then. All we could do was play the side that was put up against us. It turned out our game against Norway in the Algarve Cup was our only defeat in all of 1994.

• • •

When the calendar turned to 1995, our entire focus was to peak in June and to defend our World Cup title in Sweden. After another bumpy go of it in the Algarve Cup—we lost to Denmark and dropped the third-place game to evil Norway on penalty kicks—we had won nine in a row as we flew to Sweden. It was only a twelve-team field and we had nine players back from the 1991 M&M's Cup winners, so we were the favorites. We opened against China, and it took six minutes for things to start going wrong. Michelle Akers went up for a header in our box, right in front of me, and took a blow to the head. She had to leave the game. We had a 2–1 lead at the half and extended it to 3–1 when Mia Hamm scored in the fifty-first minute, but China got stronger as the game went on, scoring two late goals for a 3–3 tie. I was furious. We had a two-goal lead with under twenty minutes to play and didn't get our three points. I was the keeper, and my job was to keep the ball out of the net. I did not do that.

All I could do was look forward.

Denmark was our next group opponent, and the unexpected draw with China made this a must-win match. Michelle was still out. We wore her No. 10 on our socks and tape to keep her with us. If we had taken the Danes a little lightly in Portugal, there was no chance that would happen again. We played a strong, tight defensive game, controlling possession and taking a 2–0 lead into the ninetieth minute when a long bouncing ball came back to me near the top of the box. I hadn't touched the ball in about a half hour. It was good to have something to do. I waited a few seconds for my teammates to get up field and eat a little clock, then punted. The ball landed about ten yards past midfield, and then the referee, who was not far from where my punt came down, blew his whistle. He was from Guinea, a man named Mamadouba Camara. He began marching toward me from half a field away. Nobody could figure out what was going on. As he approached the eighteen-yard line, he put his hand in his shirt pocket, clearly ready to pull out a card. A few steps outside the box, looking at me as if I were a criminal, he raised his right arm and dramatically held up a red card. I was standing near the goal, hands on my hips. I was so thunderstruck I didn't even argue or ask for an explanation. I just trudged off, silently and sullenly, like a kid who had been sent to the principal's office. I broke into a slow trot as I reached the sideline. The ref's action was based on a call by the linesman, who said that I had gone outside the box when I punted, and thus touched the ball with my hands in the field of play. The replay showed that I was, indeed, a bit outside the box, but it was completely inadvertent and I'd never seen this called—certainly not with a red card being the penalty—and neither had Tony. He was livid. Now there was another issue. Not only were we down a player, Tony had used all his substitutes, so he could not call on either of our backup keepers, Saskia Webber or Mary Harvey. Mia was the field player designated to play keeper in an emergency. On the sideline, I took off my gloves and yellow jersey and handed them to her. Mia put on the keeper jersey right over her white No. 9 USA jersey. She tucked it in, but still looked like a little girl wearing one of her father's shirts. She ran toward the goal, looking all business. I watched her the whole way, the surreal spectacle of five-foot, five-inch Mia Hamm wearing No. 1 and Scurry on her back.

Mia—"the deputy goalkeeper," a broadcaster called her—did fine. She handled a couple of chances and finished the game by smothering a cross with a Danish player charging at her and taking a monstrous goal kick that went about twenty yards beyond midfield. Camara blew his whistle three times and we were all but assured of moving into the knockout round. All that remained was to rip the referee in the post-match press conference. Tony, who filed a formal protest, acknowledged that I was slightly out of the box and could've been assessed for a hand ball, and maybe even yellow-carded had I been trying to sneak an unfair advantage, which I wasn't.

"It's naïve officiating," he said. "In the spirit of the game, it was an incorrect call. If she came out and handled the ball because somebody was breaking in, yes. If she takes somebody down, that's the correct call. But this was incorrect."

Even the Danish coach agreed.

I told reporters, "I really in all honesty don't understand what the call was all about. I think we have a very legitimate case (on appeal) because I didn't commit any serious foul."

The tempest was short-lived but it did impact our next game because the red card meant I had to sit for a game. Mia returned my jersey and went back to forward, and Saskia Webber took over as goalkeeper. After falling behind by a goal, we defeated Australia, 4–1, to move into the quarterfinals against Japan. Kristine Lilly blasted a brilliant free kick that beat the Japanese goalkeeper in the eighth minute, and we were on our way to a 4–0 victory. It was our best game of the tournament. Just as we'd planned, we were peaking at the exact right moment.

Next up: the hottest team in the tournament, the side that had scored seventeen goals and conceded zero during group play . . . that was now seen as the favorite to win it all. The game would be played in an old, lakeside city called Västerås.

Our semifinal opponent would be . . . Norway.

• • •

I was in our locker room in Arosvallen, a small stadium with World Cup history, having been the site of two group-stage games in 1958. Somehow I always knew it would be Norway. Four years ago in China, Norway had the better of the run of play but the U.S. won 2–1 on two Michelle Akers goals. The Norwegians were big and strong and more than any other opponent had a knack for disrupting our game. We'd been preparing for this game for months, paying special attention to the Norwegians' lethal set-piece ability. Typically, they looked for Ann Kristin Aarønes, the wafer in a headband who was the most dangerous player in the world in the air.

One huge plus was that Michelle was back in the lineup for the first time since the opening game against China. She was not one hundred percent, but just her presence gave us an emotional lift. In the eleventh minute, Norway forced us into a corner kick.

Here we go with the set pieces, I thought. It was the usual mayhem on the corner, everybody pushing and shoving and jostling, and trying to convince the ref they were doing nothing of the sort.

"Mark up. Get a man," Captain Carla Overbeck said.

I kept Aarønes in my sights. The corner was driven dangerously towards the center of the goal. Aarønes made a cut, knifing toward the near post. Someone must've gotten picked off because Aarones had space. I moved a few steps off my line and leaped for the ball, Aarønes alongside me. I was high as I could go, desperate to get a hand on it to knock it over the crossbar. Aarønes was way up in the air, too. The ball was on us now. Aarønes arched backward, snapping her neck forward, the ball powering towards the goal. I couldn't get it.

The ball slipped just beneath the crossbar. Aarønes was mobbed by her red-clad teammates.

Norway 1, U.S. 0.

Any ball in the air like that is supposed to be mine. That's how I looked at it. This was on me.

It was maddening that after all our months of making sure this didn't happen, it happened. The good news was that there were eighty minutes left to play. No reason to panic.

The Norwegians continued to press the action. Our offense wasn't generating much. Early in the second half, I made a couple of saves to keep it a one-goal game. The match moved into its final twenty minutes. Joy Fawcett ripped a shot off the crossbar. Bente Nordby, Norway's goalkeeper, made a dazzling stop from the ground, sticking up a hand to block Tiffeny Milbrett's shot. Just a minute or two later, Heidi Store, Norway's captain, got her second yellow card and was sent off. We had a man advantage and peppered Nordby with shots. Joy hit the crossbar again. Tisha Venturini struck a laser from distance that Nordby batted down. Time and again, we were a fingernail away from scoring.

And so it went right to the end. By then it felt as if Aarønes had scored her goal the day before. I was twenty-three and this was my first major tournament, and we were out in the semis. I was gutted. We lost to the one team we knew we had to beat. It didn't matter in that moment that my overall body of work in Sweden was good. Norway's keeper, Bente Nordby, played out of her mind. I played well and we lost. I would much rather play like crap and win. At this level, it's a zero-sum game.

One goal.

One stinking goal.

One goal that I allowed was the difference.

I didn't look at it like "Well, we should've scored two goals." I looked at it like "I gave up the goal that cost us the game." My plate was supposed to be clean. It wasn't clean.

After the game, the Norwegians celebrated by getting on their hands and knees, each of them grabbing the ankles of the person in front of her, forming a cleated conga line that looked like a cross between a caterpillar and a train. They were entitled to be happy, but the spectacle grossed me out. I made myself watch it the whole time, until the train stopped chugging. I wanted to feel the full burn. I wanted to remember what this felt like. I wanted it to still be burning when the 1996 Olympics kicked off in Georgia.

• • •

After we got home, I took Kerri up on her offer and stayed with her in Fayetteville, Arkansas. We trained together and talked goalkeeping shop and I continued to admire her disciplined, workmanlike approach to life. While I was in town Kerri introduced me to a friend, Lori Hodges, who I took a liking to and started to date. Knowing that our residency camp before the '96 Olympics was going to be in Orlando, I thought it made sense to stay in the South, and since I'd just signed an endorsement deal with Nike, I decided to buy my first house—a modest, suburban split-level in a new development in Fayetteville. The subdivision was located near the university and Walmart (a coveted daily double) and for a price of $96,000, I didn't think I could lose. (And I didn't lose.) Plus it kept me close to my new best friend (Kerri) and my new girl-friend (Lori), who helped with the down payment and moved into the house with me. All was good in my new life in Fayetteville until Lori and I took a twenty-mile drive one day. We were going to visit friends in Bentonville, corporate home of Walmart. We headed north out of Fayetteville on State Route 285 to the town of Rogers, in the northwest corner of the state, deep in the Ozark Mountains and not far from Missouri. As we approached Rogers, I saw a sign in the distance on the side of the two-lane highway. I couldn't make out the words. In another tenth of a mile or so, at the town line, I could read them very clearly.

N*****, *Don't Let The Sun Go Down On You in Rogers.*

I was aware of the history of so-called Sundown towns, about the lynchings and the violence that came with them. Their whole purpose was to discourage Black people from living there. Historians estimate there were as many as ten thousand Sundown towns in America at one point, many of them in the Midwest and West. Arkansas alone had hundreds of them. The rules were essentially the same in all Sundown towns: Black people could pass through and go to work or shop, but come sundown, if you were still in town, big trouble awaited you. If you were lucky, you might get off with a beating. If not, you would be lynched. In Mena, Arkansas, civic leaders took it even further, boasting about the community's assets in a marketing campaign: "Cool Summers, Mild Winters, No Negroes."

This Negro had never seen a Sundown town sign before. At first I was enraged. I wanted to pull off the road and find the person who wrote the sign and let him know I wasn't going anywhere and he could take his racist sign and shove it. But my other emotion was sadness. It was so pathetic, so paranoid and small-minded. Yeah, go ahead and keep the N****** out, it will solve all your problems. We were handy to have around when you wanted to have your cotton picked and crops harvested and your wealth built, but now you wanted us hanging from a tree?

OK, I get it.

I was an Arkansas homeowner in a nearby town and a woman who within months would be representing the United States in the Olympics, but I better get my Black ass out of Rogers before dark, or else?

Yeah, I get it.

If you think your obscene sign is going to run me off, you don't know me very well.

"I'm sorry you had to see that. It's awful," Lori said to me gently.

I thanked her. "Nobody has to tell me there's racism in this country, but to see it advertised on a road sign is disgusting."

We continued on to Bentonville and didn't spend any more time in Rogers than necessary. On the ride home we took a different route so we could avoid it altogether.

• • •

We finished the 1995 season with a record of nineteen victories, three defeats, one tie, and a lockout. The lockout came in December, five months after we finished our year by beating Norway in the U.S. Cup in August. Toward the end of the year, prior to a December training camp in Chula Vista, California, U.S. Soccer sent us contracts for 1996 that included Olympic bonus money, but only if we won the inaugural women's soccer gold medal. A silver or bronze would get us nothing but the medal itself, and probably a dirty look from Hank Steinbrecher, the CEO of U.S. Soccer. The U.S. men's team was getting bonuses for any finish that resulted in a medal. We didn't understand why there should be a double standard. We didn't understand a lot of things, so nine of us—Michelle, Mia, Kristine Lilly, Joy Fawcett, Carla Overbeck, Julie Foudy, Carin Jennings, Tisha Venturini, and I—declined to sign the contracts as written. Julie and Michelle, our captains, got us together on a call to talk about the importance of being united. Julie had been in regular touch with Billie Jean King, who not only was a founder of the women's tennis tour but was (and is) an iconic figure in the gender-equity movement, and the person more responsible than anyone for women tennis players getting equal pay with men. Billie Jean kept reminding Julie that this fight wasn't so much about getting more for ourselves now, but for plowing the ground for future generations of female athletes to be compensated fairly.

Julie got it, and so did the rest of us. We loved playing for our country but didn't understand how U.S. Soccer could justify giving every U.S. male player who qualified for the 1990 World Cup a $10,000 bonus and give the women who qualified for the 1991 Women's World Cup a few tee-shirts with a Budweiser logo. (Budweiser was a U.S. Soccer sponsor.) Julie asked Billie Jean what strategy to pursue to rectify the medal incentive matter. Billie Jean said it was simple: Don't play.

It's the only leverage you have. That's when we elected not to sign the contracts that had been sent to us. Steinbrecher did not take kindly to being challenged this way by a bunch of upstart girls, going into full pit-bull mode, canceling our plane tickets to California and saying that the contracts were now off the table and the only way we could come to the camp was on a per diem basis, at Tony's invitation, and if we said, "Pretty please." (OK, I made up that last part.) He went on to talk about how U.S. Soccer had invested $3.4 million in the women's program and that we were the best-compensated women's team in the world, which wasn't saying much, since most players on the team were making about $2,000 per month.

"We cannot reward mediocrity," Steinbrecher told the Associated Press. "It seems some players are more concerned about how green their shoes are, instead of bringing home the gold." Pressed to comment further, Steinbrecher said, "Bonuses are paid for superior performance. Our expectation is to be playing for the gold and winning it. That's where the bonus should go."

I learned quickly upon joining the USWNT that from the earliest days it seemed to be viewed by most of the men running U.S. Soccer as somewhere between an annoyance and a high-maintenance stepchild. When he took over as U.S. Soccer president in 1990, Alan Rothenberg admitted that he didn't even know the U.S. *had* a women's national team. That we won a whole lot more matches than the men didn't seem to matter. Nor did it matter that we always represented our federation and our country with class and dignity. Julie told me how on international trips they would almost always be in the middle seats of commercial flights, and often in the back, when they still had smoking sections there. In the year they won the first World Cup, the players earned $10 a day.

Ten bucks.

Per day.

Make it last, girls.

Of course we knew that the sport was young, and the economic engine behind it was not all that robust, but even so, the underlying attitude of U.S. Soccer never strayed far from You Should Be Thankful You Are On The Field.

I was extremely thankful to be on the field. But I also knew when I was being screwed. So we refused to sign the contracts, and then Hank told us we weren't welcome in Chula Vista. With the Atlanta Olympics coming up, we were certain that U.S. Soccer didn't want the impasse to imperil the Games. Michelle said in an interview that an Olympic boycott was a distinct possibility but hoped it didn't come to that.

"If we medal or win, the opportunities for our sport will be wide open," she said. "We understand how big the Olympics are. We hope the federation keeps that in mind."

The standoff lasted a for a couple of months, until U.S. Soccer backed off and agreed to award bonuses for gold and silver. It wasn't a total victory, but it was a start. There was a long way to go (and there's still a ways to go as I write this twenty-five years later), but as the calendar flipped to 1996, Hank Steinbrecher and gender equity were not our foremost priority. Women's soccer was in the Olympic Games, and the singular mission of everyone on the team was to finish in first place.

CHAPTER SEVEN

DEBUTANTES

If you ask most footballers, they will tell you the greatest achievement in the sport is to be a World Cup champion. It is the prize that confers the most meaning and does more to define you as a player than anything else. I am not most footballers. I did not grow up with soccer. I didn't come through the U.S. Soccer age-group pipeline. Remember, I was so naive I didn't even know what the U.S. National team was until my college coach enlightened me.

Julie Foudy told me not long ago that one quality (apart from skin color) that differentiated me from the rest of the team was that soccer was who they were, whereas for me, soccer was just something I did. I took no offense at all, because she was right.

Don't get me wrong. I came to love the sport and loved competing in the World Cup. But the Olympics stole my heart when I was eight years old and it never let go. There was something about the size and scope of the Games, the pageantry, that resonated with me. In the

Summer Games, there are typically more than ten thousand athletes from over two hundred countries. You meet people who are from places you've never heard of. It's a teeming international bazaar of elite athletes. You aren't just part of your national soccer team; you are a member of Team USA, and that somehow enriches the importance of what you are doing.

With our labor dispute resolved, we holdouts reported to Olympic Residency Camp in February 1996 in Sanford, Florida, and got to work, training hard over the ensuing months in preparation for Atlanta. On the final day, Tony and his staff posted the Olympic roster outside our locker room. It consisted of just sixteen players, two of them goalkeepers, along with four alternates. I had been the No. 1 keeper for almost a year and a half. I had no reason to sweat making the team, but I was taking nothing for granted, especially after our labor "action." I saw the list from a distance as I walked out of the locker room. My pulse quickened as I got closer. It had been sixteen years since the Lake Placid Olympics in 1980 and the start of my infatuation. I wondered if Jim Craig felt this way when Herb Brooks posted *his* roster. Soccer is completely different from the timed and scored Olympic sports, in that the rosters are subjectively chosen by the coach. In track and field, if you finish in the top three of your event at the Olympic trials, you make the team. In wrestling, if you win your weight class at the trials, you make the team. I believed I had a strong track record to fall back on, but if Tony thought that two other keepers in camp had outplayed me, the closest I'd get to the Olympics would be the television coverage.

The list was typewritten and taped to a wall. Now I was close enough to read it. Goalkeepers are usually placed at the top. I looked at the first line.

It said: GK Briana Scurry.

I paused for a second, looking up and down the hallway to make sure nobody was watching. I reached out with my hand and touched my name on the piece of paper. It was an out-of-body experience. I was a poor kid from Dayton, Minnesota, who wanted to play in the NFL before switching dreams after a bunch of college hockey players (mostly from Minnesota, by the way) went to Lake Placid and wound up doing the unthinkable. Just beneath my name was the next person on the roster: GK Mary Harvey. I was so happy for Mary, a 1991 World Cup champion and a great teammate and a woman who was classy to the core, even when I took her job. Not everyone would be so gracious. I was happy for all fifteen of my teammates. We had made it. I had made it. I was a United States Olympian, and I was going to be in goal for Team USA. when women's soccer made its debut.

I went back to my room and packed up my stuff. As much as I tried, I couldn't fully process what it meant to me to see my name on that roster. That's sometimes how it is with me, deep emotions coming on tape delay. I flew home to Arkansas that night. I walked down the center aisle of the plane, passing the rows and looking at my fellow passengers and wondering how people would react if they knew there was an Olympian on their flight.

At thirty-five thousand feet, I sat by a window in the back of the plane. I looked out into the night and the image of the roster list with my name at the top came back to me. I thought about my eight-year-old self, and two of us had a quiet, joyful cry.

• • •

One of the first things you do as an Olympian is collect gear. Lots of gear. I really like gear, so this was no problem. About ten days before the Games, we took the short trip from Orlando to Atlanta to get out-fitted for the Olympics. The flight felt like a Magic Carpet Ride. At the end of it, we were whisked to a massive convention center, where the U.S. Women's National Soccer team was greeted as if we were royalty. The place was Olympic heaven. The logos, the signage, the mascots, the red, white, and blue Team USA motif everywhere you looked—we might as well have been in Oz. Even the veterans on the team—Mary Harvey, Carin Gabarra (she got married), Michelle Akers— had never experienced this before, so they were as in awe as the rest of us. This was our appointed time to get all our stuff, and it started with your credential. It was a four-inch by six-inch laminated card on a lanyard that was your golden key to do anything and go anywhere for as long as you were in Olympicland. As athletes, our credentials had a big"A" on them, which put us on top of the five-ring food chain. Your credential was the ultimate validation of your right to be there. I cherished it and still have it hanging in my office today. The other goodies were also cool . . . pins, bags, jackets, Opening Ceremony outfits, and, most important of all, our Presentation uniforms. This was what we were to wear on the medal stand. We submitted measurements beforehand, but just in case, they had a squadron of seamstresses with sewing machines in an adjacent room, to make any needed alterations. The U.S. Olympic Committee wanted us to look our best on the medal stand. The person in charge of gear distribution made it clear that these outfits were strictly for the medal ceremonies.

"You are not to wear your Presentation uniform at any other time," she said. "You are not to wear it in the Village, or when you are out and about. It is strictly for the medal ceremony."

I got the memo and I didn't mind. I grew up wearing hand-me-down clothes until the pants were six inches above my ankles. I had no issue with abiding by the rules.

The first outfit I wore over my new panther tattoo, naturally, was for the Opening Ceremony in Centennial Olympic Stadium, an hours-long procession of national delegations, in alphabetical order, except for the host country, which always goes last. Marching behind our flag bearer, freestyle wrestler Bruce Baumgartner, we were greeted by a thunderous ovation as we were introduced, beginning our long, slow lap around the track, 646 athletes strong, men in blue blazers and white pants, women in red blazers and white pants, and every one of us wearing a white hat. We were supposed to be in formation, but good luck with that. I was deliriously happy and there was no shot at me marching in a straight line. I danced and waved and laughed with my teammates. I felt strong and alive and grateful. Red is my favorite color, a power color. The blazer was perfect, and so was the climax of the ceremony. The last runner in the months-long Olympic torch relay was Janet Evans, the legendary U.S. swimmer, who carried the torch around the track and then up a long ramp to the rim of the stadium, where she handed it to the person who would light the Olympic cauldron—a person whose identity had been a closely guarded secret for months. I gasped out loud when I saw him . . . the Cauldron Lighter . . . Muhammad Ali. I was too young ever to have seen him box, but when I watched the footage of him, I just thought he was one of the most beautiful athletes I'd ever seen, a glorious blend of grace and strength. I loved that he stood up for his beliefs and wouldn't let the hate and vitriol that rained down on him dissuade him. He was dressed all in white, with a red and blue design on the right side of his shirt. I could see his right arm, and much of his body, trembling from his Parkinson's as he clutched the torch. I felt like running up the ramp to steady him, let him know he would be able to do this. From the infield of the stadium, I silently willed him on.

Ali leaned over and touched the torch to a small flame, sending it on its way upward, a dramatic, diagonal climb that reached its summit and then ignited the Olympic cauldron, a bursting orange-yellow lamp that would not be extinguished until the Games were over, sixteen days later.

• • •

Our attitude about big tournaments was that the first and last games were the most important. The last, for the obvious reason . . . if we win it, we are champions. But the first game in the group stage also carried a lot of weight. We not only wanted to get the three points, we wanted to send a message—to get into people's heads that we were going to be their worst nightmare. We wanted to get every advantage we could, even if it was nothing more than injecting into our opponents a sliver of doubt. It was one of the important lessons we learned from Dr. Colleen Hacker, whom Tony hired to be our sports psychologist at the start of 1996.

One of Colleen's core points was that elite-level, multi-round competitions often come down to one or two plays—to a percentage point or two or three of improved performance. If you can give yourself even a minuscule advantage, it could mean the difference between gold and silver. Look at the 1995 World Cup. How much did I miss Aarønes's game-winning header in the semifinals by? A fingernail, maybe? What if I had coiled my legs a bit more and gotten another inch or two of elevation on my jump? What if I'd made a quicker read on the corner kick and broke off my line and punched it away before she could get her head on it?

Colleen used to show us a video she called "Red Car, Blue Car." It was the end of a Daytona 500–type event, hours of full-throttle racing coming down to a final sprint and the two cars separated by an inch or two. When you are competing, you don't know when you might gain that difference-making inch. As a goalkeeper, it made me much more conscious about my fundamentals and how I went about my training. I worked on moving my feet and covering as much ground as possible, then collecting myself and exploding to the ball. If I collected and exploded a nanosecond too late, the ball often would be in the back of the net. Only through hundreds, even thousands, of repetitions did I get a sharper sense of how long I had to move my feet before collecting. The same number of reps went into learning when I could catch a ball—always my preference—as opposed to deflecting it. Even though Colleen was no goalkeeping expert, she did so much to make me better at it, sharpening my game by paying attention to every detail, and understanding that even incremental improvement can make all the difference.

The red car/blue car device melded seamlessly with another of Colleen's beliefs: the power of visualization. I already had a positive experience with this as a Minnow, but Colleen took it and ran with it. She would splice together individual, two- or three-minute videos for us, taken from game footage. It would show a play unfolding but left it to us to visualize the ending. So my video might begin with a corner kick coming high into the center of the box; it would be up to me to see myself coming off my line and snagging the ball out of the air. The video would show a penalty-kick shooter striking the ball; I would see myself making a diving save to punch it away. Colleen's video would cover most every scenario I would face in a game, and by consciously, uber-intentionally, seeing myself make a positive play, it heightened my mental awareness and confidence. In the heat of a real game, it helped me stay calm and perform the needed task as I'd done so many times before, even if it was on the field of my mind.

I'd do most of my visualizing in the day or two before a game, but when I woke up on game day it would typically take a different form. I'd relax in my room, watch some TV, and chill. As the day went on, I'd be thinking more and more about the game, reminding myself what I needed to do and how I needed to feel. I'd think about my feet being strong and solid beneath me, my attention on the ball unwavering. I'd see myself in the stadium we would be playing in, in the goal I'd be protecting, not feeling any nerves or pressure, just resolving to not let a soccer ball inside it. A couple of hours before the game, when it was time to get on the bus, I'd put my headphones on and listen to Nine Inch Nails or Whitney Houston's "It's Not Right, But It's Okay," and that's when everybody knew: Do not even think about talking to Bri. I was in what Colleen called my inner performance zone, or IPZ. We all had our own IPZ, and they were all different.

Julie's was the funniest, because her IPZ amounted to trying to disrupt everybody else's IPZ, walking around, doing crazy dances, laughing, a locker-room standup comic. She knew better than to mess with my IPZ, though. The closer I got to game time, the more my visualization switched to energy-gathering. I could see it. I could feel it. It was as if I were collecting all these dispersed, random beams of light, shooting in all directions, somehow catching them and containing them and then in the pre-game moments on the field, they would forge into a single, searing source that would course through my body like a laser. I could feel all slack and lethargy draining from my body, replaced by the purest form of power, an adrenaline rush times a million. That was the state I played the entire game in.

• • •

Soccer was a so-called satellite sport at the Atlanta Games, played at five venues outside of Atlanta to accommodate larger crowds. Like the World Cup, the competition began with a group stage. There were two groups of four teams each, every team playing three games, with the top two teams advancing to the knockout round, which in this case, was the Olympic semifinals.

Our first game was against Denmark, at the Citrus Bowl in Orlando. On the short ride from our hotel to the stadium, I sat alone on the left side of the bus, halfway back, leaning my head against the window, headphones on, the world blocked out. I was deep into energy-gathering mode. Ninety minutes before kickoff, my whole world was my IPZ. The beams, the energy, kept building. We pulled up to the stadium and I looked up at it and gaped, probably like a farm girl making her first visit to Chicago or New York City. I couldn't believe the size of the place, a two-tiered concrete bowl with a capacity of sixty-five thousand people.

I had played two games in the Metrodome with the Minnows, of course, but somehow the Citrus Bowl, in that moment, looked as if it could hold ten Metrodomes. I can tell you this with total candor: I almost thought I was hallucinating. I smiled. I made sure nobody could see it.

This is where we are playing? Seriously?

The place wasn't full when we came out for warmups, but there were still more people in the Citrus Bowl stands than I'd ever seen—over twenty-five thousand. We had played Denmark in Orlando about five months before, at a much smaller venue, winning 2–1. The crowd was a little over two thousand fans. We were in the same city, but in a whole different universe.

Denmark was a good team that we had a weird history with. We had crushed them, 7–0, in February 1995, and then lost to them three weeks later at the Algarve. I wish I could tell you how that could happen. They were physical and feisty, and you took them lightly at your own peril. Of course, even if we had been playing a U-10 club team from Orlando, I wouldn't have taken them lightly. I was locked in and ready, and we took care of business, winning 3–0. I didn't have a lot to do. As you know, those are my favorite kind of games.

Next up was Sweden, another difficult Scandinavian opponent. We'd beaten them in a pair of 3–0 decisions leading up to the Olympics, but we knew we were the team the Swedes wanted to beat more than any other, and that's how they played. We went up two goals before a free kick ricocheted off Carla Overbeck's leg for an own goal, making it 2–1 with over twenty-five minutes left to play. It wasn't anyone's fault, just one of those freak things that can happen in soccer. We finished the game with an advantage of 22–4 in shots, but that was irrelevant. We dominated the run of play, and it remained a one-goal game with under ten minutes to play, at which point, increasingly desperate to equalize, a Swedish player chopped down Mia Hamm. This was nothing new. Mia was used to it, and we were used to it. If you want to stop a speeding car, you slash the tires. It was a time-honored soccer strategy; go after the opponent's best players and see what happens. I'm not saying the foul was committed with an intent to injure, but it was hard and it carried a message that the Swedes were not done fighting, and it left one of the premier players in the world with a very painful ankle.

Three-quarters of a field away, my alarm grew when Mia did not get up. It grew even more when she was taken off on a stretcher. Now I was furious. *You can't beat us fair and square, so you are going to take out one of our best players?*

We held on for the victory, which ensured our advancement to the semifinals, no matter what happened in our third group-stage game, against China. China was also assured of advancing, so there was little at stake when we squared off against them in the final game before the knockout round. Because we knew we would very likely see China again, our coaches were in no rush to show them too much. Mia sat out the match, which ended in a 0–0 tie. It was on to the semifinals, where our opponent would be Norway.

This is perfect, I thought.

CHAPTER EIGHT

GOLDEN GIRLS

Norway is a lovely country of 5.4 million people that is famous for its fjords, salmon, and cross-country skiers. Two years before the Olympics came to Atlanta, it hosted one of the most beautiful Winter Games I've ever seen, in the small town of Lillehammer. I have nothing against Norway the nation. It was just its women's soccer team—the *Gresshoppene* (the Grasshoppers), as they were known—that I didn't care for, and the reason was simple: They were the only team in my early years on the USWNT that beat us more than we beat them. I respected their talent and skill, and how passionately they played, but I didn't care for their swagger (of course, lots of countries said the same thing about us), and I despised their choo-choo train celebration ritual.

From the day the Olympics started, I could not wait to play them. The semifinal round was fitting, since that was when the Norwegians beat us in the World Cup the year before. This was the perfect time and place to change the ending.

The final three games of the Olympics—the two semifinals and final—were held at Sanford Stadium in Athens, Georgia, home of the University of Georgia. The other semifinal was China vs. Brazil. The crowds by now had grown to almost sixty-five thousand, another mind-boggling number. The best part for me was that Ernest and Robbie Scurry, the two people who were most responsible for me being there, were among the multitudes. I flew them down from Minnesota with money I made from my contract with Nike. They sat in the designated Friends and Family section, were looked after by everybody, especially Mia's parents and Lil's parents. Having them there evoked the same feelings I had when I was a kid. I felt completed, lifted up. I felt that I would do great things, that I could do whatever I set my sights on, because that's what they always told me.

I was more fastidious about my kit (soccer slang for uniform) than I was when I got dressed for a big night out. It was part of my mental preparation. The process, and the order, was unwavering: skids (spandex-type undershorts), shorts, socks, shin guards (taped to keep them in place), boots, and, finally, the jersey. I was fanatical about my boots. Our equipment manager kept a shoe-polish kit ready, and before every game I'd put new polish on my boots and buff them until they were glossy and perfect. I never put them on until they looked like that. Before a game was the only time I'd ever polish my boots. It was another psychological alert that it was almost time to compete. I'd closely examine my gloves and dampen a towel and then dab a little water into the palms to make them a little bit sticky. You couldn't use too much water, or else the gloves would be slippery. Once they were ready, they'd go into my glove bag. And once I was ready, I'd go into the bathroom and stand in front of a full-length mirror. Everything had to be straight, neat, shirt carefully tucked, as crisp and tidy as a soldier in her dress uniform. I never wanted to walk out on the field without my kit in perfect order.

• • •

The semifinal against Norway started cautiously, like two heavy-weights feeling each other out, throwing an occasional jab and not much more. Mia and Michelle almost connected on an early corner kick. Tiffeny Milbrett stole the ball in the Norwegian end and had a breakaway on the left side, but her centering pass to Mia missed the mark and the opportunity went for naught.

Norway seemed to feed off the reprieve and went on the attack. Forward Linda Medalen took a well-placed chipped ball and came in alone on me. I sprinted out, crouched low, trying to pressure her and cut down her options. She went low to the left side. I dove but the ball missed my fingertips by the width of a blade of grass.

Norway had a 1–0 lead.

I immediately channeled another Colleen Hacker strategy, one of her best. The worst thing you can do after the other team scores is to second-guess yourself or beat yourself up or lose even one percent of your concentration.

"All you can do is box it up, and put it on the shelf," Colleen told me.

Medalen's goal was on the shelf before we even kicked the ball off.

Mia was generating threats and Lil was carving up the Norwegians with her runs on the left flank, and nineteen-year-old Tiffany Roberts, our youngest player, was doing yeoman defensive work blanketing Norway's Hege Riise, one of the world's top players. But we weren't as consistent as we needed to be against a quality opponent.

We ramped up our urgency in the second half and played nearly all of it in Norway's end, the Norwegians smothering Michelle and especially Mia, who got hacked down—hard—three times in the first ten minutes of the second half.

They're really slashing the tires now, I thought.

The game passed the three-quarter pole and urgency morphed into desperation. In the seventy-seventh minute we were on the attack again when the ball appeared to graze the hand of a Norwegian defender. The ref awarded us a penalty kick. Minutes earlier, the ref missed a much more obvious hand ball by Norway and the crowd booed. A makeup call? I don't know and I definitely don't care. Michelle buried it to make it 1–1.

We stayed on the front foot, and Mia burst into space off a misplaced Norwegian header, racing toward the goal when Agnete Carlsen, a defender, grabbed her shirt from behind and wrestled her to the ground. This time slashing the tires didn't work; Carlsen was given a red card, and with four minutes left in regulation, we were up a man.

When regulation ended, we stretched and drank water, and Tony kept saying, "Sudden victory, sudden victory." Officially there would be two fifteen overtime periods, but the next goal would end the game. "Golden goal," they called it. It's beautiful when you score it and godawful if the other team scores it. We dominated the extra period from the start. Mia spun a defender with a sharp cut to force a corner kick and made another run on goal before losing her footing in the box. Down a player, Norway was just trying to hold on and get to a shootout. Six minutes into overtime, Tony subbed Shannon MacMillan for Tiffeny. The college player of the year at the University of Portland the year before, Shannon was probably our fastest player, and absolutely our freshest at the moment. Shannon made a long run to catch up to a long ball from Carla Overbeck, forcing Nordby to come out of the box and kick it back into our end.

Tiffany Roberts got her head on Nordby's kick, steering it directly to Julie Foudy, who had plenty of space on the right side. She surged forward, still unmarked. On the left side, Shannon made a darting, diagonal run to the center of the box, Julie pushing a perfectly weighted through ball that landed right on Shannon's foot. Nordby broke from goal, but Shannon tucked the ball deftly into the left corner. An explosion of ecstasy ensued, Shannon buried in a pile of white jerseys, while the gutted Norwegians collapsed to the ground. One hundred minutes of soccer concluded with ten or twelve seconds of exquisite play: a well-directed header, a superb pass, and a clinical finish.

There was no Norwegian choo-choo this time. We were in the gold-medal game. Our opponent would be China.

• • •

In the days leading up to the final match, I had this profound feeling of lightness and relief. Of course we had a job to finish, but we had beaten our archrival and were right where we wanted to be. Now we could put it all out there in one winner-takes-all match, and I knew if we did that we stood a good chance of coming away happy. For me there was something totally liberating about that.

My parents came to see me at our team hotel the afternoon before the final. They were surprised by the armed guards with big machine guns who were posted in our hotel lobby—the Olympics do not mess around in security matters, especially after the bombing in Centennial Park earlier in the Games—and also by how loose and playful I was. They knew I wasn't the worrying kind, but the day before the biggest game of my life I don't think they were ready for their daughter to seem so chill.

"Hey, Pops, are you going to give me $25 if I get the shutout?" I said.

He laughed.

"If you get the shutout, don't you think the gold medal will be enough?" he said.

The lightness I felt extended to training, too. The three goalkeepers—Mary Harvey, Saskia Webber, and I—would normally go out on the practice field forty-five minutes before the position players. Tony was out there with us. The three of us warmed up by skipping down the field and wheeling our arms, looking like kids at recess, but the training sessions themselves were as intense and focused as ever. I dove and ran and went 1 v. 1 with Michelle on PKs, the same as always. I couldn't wait for kickoff.

The night before the game, I made sure I got my mind right with Colleen. We looked at the film she made for me, and we went down my fundamental checklist . . . my feet, my hands, my positioning . . . being intentional about all of it in the hope of bringing that extra two or three percent against China. Long after our session was over, I was in bed, still going through my fundamentals, and now visualizing myself back on the Sanford Stadium pitch. I saw myself flying, diving, exploding off the line, grabbing every shot I could reach with two strong hands and deflecting or punching out those I couldn't. It was no night to count sheep; I was counting saves. The visualization went on for a long time. It was a short sleep.

• • •

It was a few minutes before eight o'clock on Thursday night, August 1, 1996, when we took the field and I ran toward my goal in Sanford Stadium. I hung on the crossbar, dropped to a knee, and said my prayer. I wondered whether the match would unfold cautiously, the way things did in our semifinal with Norway. I did not wonder for long. A few minutes in, Mia hit a rocket that sailed high. Gao Hong, the Chinese keeper, made a brave save as Carla crashed into her after taking a chip from Shannon MacMillan, who earned the start after her golden-goal heroics in the semis. Gao was busy again minutes later, sprinting way out of her box to clear a through ball Shannon played for Mia.

Soon China got on the attack, too. I charged out to my left to defuse a chance for Sun Qingmei. Sun was on the go again, playing a clever back heel to Sun Wen, China's captain, who was stripped by Joy Fawcett. Suddenly we found ourselves chasing the game, China dominating possession with nimble attacks and deft ball movement. There are times in matches when you just have to absorb the pressure and wait to counter. This was one of them.

I scooped up a through ball that was a bit heavy, and then threw the ball to Joy on the right side. Michelle wound up with it in midfield, and with the outside of her foot knocked a seeing-eye ball twenty-five yards on the ground to Lil, who was making a run on the left. Lil took a few dribbles and lifted a textbook cross into the box, where Mia ran onto it and one-timed it, drilling a low, hard shot to the left corner. Gao dove and got a hand on it, but Shannon was right there and left-footed the rebound into the net.

U.S. 1, China 0.

Over one hundred yards away, I had the worst view on the field of what just happened, but I saw enough to know it was glorious—one of those goals that made me love soccer, a goal created by skill and will, by gifted players doing their thing. Michelle's pass to Lil, Lil's cross, Mia's one-time strike—they were all practically flawless. Shannon's finish was also flawless, and the result was that against the run of play, we had the lead.

I love when that happens.

Not even ten minutes later, Mia took a pass from Tiffeny and attacked. Mia was playing on a bad left ankle and had been dynamic anyway, and now she eluded a defender and smoked a shot at Gao, but not with the direction she wanted. China pressed forward, solving our pressure, and played a long ball to Sun Wen, who got a step on Carla. The ball was bouncing, not rolling. I bolted from my line to secure it, but Sun got there first and chipped it over my head. It trickled into the goal, despite Brandi Chastain's hustling effort to catch up to it.

U.S. 1, China 1.

We had scored a goal that came out of nowhere. Now China had done likewise. I was sick about it. I hadn't played it well. Bouncing balls are far easier to chip than balls that are on the ground. I should've read it better, stayed in goal, and let my defender defend. Instead, I came out, I got chipped and gave up a goal I should not have.

The first gold-medal game for women's soccer in Olympic history moved into the second half. I was not thinking about history. I had waves of highly skilled, insanely determined Chinese players in red jerseys who were trying to get another ball past me.

China continued to be the aggressors, pressure that made me hypervigilant. I was acutely aware that any mistake, any letdown, could be the difference between gold and silver. I thought again about one of Colleen Hacker's core points . . . that it may all come down to one or two or three percent. We had played China twice at the Olympics and here was my takeaway: This was one hell of a team. The so-called experts talked endlessly about the U.S. being heavy favorites on home soil. I guarantee you that the experts had no idea how good China was.

More skillful, tic-tac-toe offense from the Chinese sprung Sun Qingmei loose, directly in front of me. I ran off my line and smothered it before she could get there. For almost twenty minutes to start the second half, they were carving us up. In the sixty-fourth minute, Carla launched a goal kick beyond midfield, giving us some much-needed respite. Michelle won the header and flicked it on to Mia, who left two defenders looking as if they were glued to the grass, and was now racing toward the goal. The crowd roared in anticipation of a break-away and a potential game-winning goal. Gao hustled out. She went low to try to strip her, but Mia veered by her with a quick right-footed touch, nudging the ball ahead. She had an open net in front of her, but from nowhere Chinese defender Xie Huilin made a remarkable recovery run, catching up to the play and shouldering Mia off the ball to force a corner.

The close call energized us and we started to create more chances. Joy Fawcett, our right back, stole a pass near midfield and the ball caromed to Shannon, who found Mia near the right sideline. Joy saw a channel and never stopped running. Mia slid a pass to her and now Joy had no defenders—only Gao—in front of her. Gao broke out to stop her but as soon as she did Joy centered the ball to Tiffeny, who slid it into the open goal. A blast of noise rocked Sanford Stadium. It got even louder when Tiffeny did a celebratory forward roll. It was the sixty-eighth minute.

U.S. 2, China 1

Twenty-two minutes plus stoppage time remained. Tony subbed Tiffany for Tiffeny—Roberts for Milbrett—to get an extra defender, and Roberts almost instantly made a seventy-five-yard run down the right side to force a corner kick. Ten minutes now. The goal I was defending was in the closed end of the stadium. At the other, a huge scoreboard was directly in front of me.

I tried not to look at it but it was impossible, yellow numbers on the black board, ticking off minutes and seconds against a pink-purple sky.

"C'mon, hurry up," I said silently to the clock.

Now there were five minutes left, and I reminded my defenders about our mantra.

"Big Five, Big Five. Let's stay tight," I said.

Three minutes turned to two, and two to one, and the Chinese, who attacked with such skill and effectiveness for much of the game, were stuck in neutral. We mostly had them pinned in their own end. In the eighty-ninth minute, a "USA, USA" chant rumbled through the stadium. In the ninetieth, Mia got plowed into by a Chinese defender and went down hard, grabbing her tender left ankle. She was in extreme pain and got carried off on a stretcher, and it was somehow fitting, because Mia hadn't only been wonderful at these Olympics; she had all but given her body to the cause.

Carin Gabarra came on to replace her. A couple of minutes of stoppage time passed. The referee looked at her watch. Still the game continued. I could barely stand it.

An errant ball rolled to Carla in the center of our defense, and she boomed it high and far downfield, and before anyone could touch it, the whistle finally blew, and I ran out of the goal as fast as I could to join the building scrum of U.S. players, coaches, and staff in the center of the field. The crowd sounded louder to me than a hundred jet planes taking off. I jumped on the pile, a goalie and a gold medalist, just like Jim Craig.

• • •

A half hour later, we were finally allowed to put on our Presentation uniforms. Mine felt crispy and new and perfect. We lined up to get our medals, and when I bent down to receive it, I couldn't believe how heavy it felt around my neck. The International Olympic Committee didn't skimp on production quality, that was for sure. They played "The Star-Spangled Banner" and the American flag went up the pole in Sanford Stadium, and I cried the whole time. I cried more when I saw my parents at our team party, held in a University of Georgia sorority house. I let them hold my new gold medal, like a kindergartener during show-and-tell.

"I told you that you could do anything you put your mind to," my mom said.

The night was a long, happy blur, but I didn't forget to honor my word. I had told a writer from *Sports Illustrated* that I would run naked through the streets of Athens if we won the gold. The writer and *SI* photographers were at the party and they kept asking me when I was going to do it and if they could shoot it.

I said, "Yes, I am going to do it, and no, you can't shoot it."

About two in the morning, my girlfriend Lori and I sneaked away from the party and drove a few blocks to a dark, deserted side street. I got naked, covered certain areas of my body with my hands, ran about twenty or thirty yards, and turned around and ran back. The only thing I was wearing was my gold medal.

CHAPTER NINE

FULL HOUSES

I could write a separate book about how great my teammates were as competitors and athletes. They were no less impressive as people. Here I was a Black lesbian with a completely different background from any of them, the only "out" person on the USWNT, and I never felt anything but respected and loved. Nor did I ever feel judged. When I expressed this to a friend once he accused me of being in denial.

"It's hard to believe you weren't an outsider in some way," he said.

"Sorry, but your preconceptions are wrong," I said.

Not only was I accepted, so were my parents and my girlfriends, when I showed up with someone at a game or a tournament. I can't even provide an example because that's how it was every day. It was one more thing for me to treasure about the culture of the USWNT.

Shannon MacMillan, one of my closest friends on the team, remembers it the same way I do. "I think it speaks volumes about who you are as a person that you were embraced and respected by everyone," Shannon says. "You were strong and confident and so comfortable with yourself. We knew there would be differences among some of us, but when we came together and we crossed the white line, we put all that aside and were ready to do anything for each other."

That truly was the essence of the USWNT. We demanded a lot from one another, but we didn't judge and I think almost all of us looked for each other's positive attributes instead of things that might tear us apart. I thought some other players on the team may have been gay, but the last thing I would ever do is press the issue if they were not comfortable being public about it. We're all on our own journey.

• • •

The 1995 World Cup had about as much of a big-time feel to it as a regional AYSO tournament. That's probably unfair to AYSO because at least those tournaments have enthusiasm, signage, and a sense that you are at a significant event. I don't blame our hosts, the Swedes. I blame FIFA and the old men's club that runs it. About the only upgrade from the first Women's World Cup in China in 1991 was that FIFA actually lent its storied name to the 1995 event and ditched the "M&M's Cup." The stadiums were mostly small and the fields second- or third-rate, and the publicity and marketing campaigns were nonexistent. I didn't expect a kickoff parade in Stockholm, but even a poster on a telephone pole would've been an improvement.

We were the defending champions and we drew a bit over eight thousand fans in our three group-stage games combined. Another group-stage game had an attendance of 650.

So, when the U.S. won the right to a host the 1999 World Cup, FIFA was thinking less about imaginative ways to build its brand and tap into the sport's burgeoning popularity in the U.S., and more about how not to take a financial bath. Originally, FIFA's plan was to hold the entire event in five small sites in the Northeast. That all changed when we drew over seventy-six thousand fans in the 1996 Olympic gold-medal game. The Women's World Cup Organizing Committee pushed hard to get FIFA to think bigger and the old boys finally relented, going along with a reconfigured plan that would include eight big-time venues, from Foxborough, Massachusetts, to Portland, Oregon, with the championship set for the Rose Bowl.

For two years leading up to the World Cup, we weren't just soccer players. We were a roving band of grassroots promoters and marketers, crisscrossing the country, doing clinics, making appearances at club events and tournaments, playing games, signing autographs, doing media spots . . . anything and everything to raise awareness that the world championship of women's soccer was coming to the U.S., and the home team was the favorite. We focused most of our energy on areas where the games would be played, and we were relentless—dogged, door-to-door saleswomen. I never handed out so many flyers in my life, but I didn't mind it at all. In our own way, we were like the owners of a start-up business. We had to sell our product, show people the value of our product, get them to believe it was worth their time and money. Doing all this spadework gave us ownership of the coming World Cup, and when you have ownership, it doesn't feel like a burden being imposed on you; it's an investment in yourself.

We felt like this World Cup was ours to put on, and ours to win, though I had had a separate agenda, too, which was to try to help grow the game beyond the mostly affluent suburban communities where it was most popular. I'm all for anything that popularizes the sport, but more and more it seemed that highest levels of youth soccer in the U.S. were becoming the exclusive domain of the well-to-do. To play on a top travel club, get individual training, work with a fitness instructor, attend a major showcase tournament—all of it can up to thousands of dollars. I never forgot that I probably never would've gotten close to the USWNT without Pete Swenson quietly laying out money to cover for me. One of our promotional stops around this time was in Chicago, at a Boys & Girls Club in a predominantly Black community. We had a clinic, did some drills and handed out our flyers, and then signed autographs and met with the kids. One young African American girl who looked to be about ten came up to me when we were winding down.

"I didn't know Black people played soccer," she said.

I winked at her and smiled.

"Well, I guess now you know, right? Soccer is a fun game and it's a great option for you if you like it."

From the beginning of 1997 until the World Cup kicked off in mid-June 1999, we played sixty-three games against international opponents, going 55-4-4. We were good on the field and we were also darn good promoters, I have to say. It wasn't easy to do both. Imagine if an NFL or NBA team had to devote time and energy to traveling the country to promote their sport in the runup to the Super Bowl or the NBA Finals. Maybe it's not a perfect analogy, but you get the point. Our sport was still a toddler. Our hope was that a successful World Cup would give women's soccer a massive lift, and potentially lead to the launch of a women's professional league. That was our mission, and the big reveal on how successful we were would come on June 19, 1999—the date of the opening game of the third Women's World Cup.

It would be played in New Jersey at Giants Stadium. The generic name for the area was the Meadowlands, which makes it sound like some bucolic family vacation spot. The reality is that the Meadowlands was built on what Bruce Springsteen describes as "the swamps of Jersey." The New Jersey Turnpike runs right through it, and it's impossible to tell where real earth ends and landfill begins. For the USWNT, the only concern was that there was a stadium amid those swamps, and from everything we heard, it was supposed to be a sold-out stadium that day. Aaron Heifetz, our PR guy, told us that they were expecting a sellout—upward of seventy-eight thousand people—which would be even more than the New York Giants drew for NFL games. Aaron—known as Heif to all—said that the only time the stadium had a bigger crowd was when Pope John Paul II attracted almost eighty-three thousand people in 1994. (With all due respect to the pontiff, he was allowed to have worshippers on the field, and we were not. It's apples and holy oranges.)

We left our hotel about two and half hours before the game. We did not get far. The Meadowlands has a spiderweb of highways and ramps surrounding both the stadium and the adjacent arena, and all of them were choked with traffic. I looked out the bus window and said out loud, "Why would they schedule something else on a day of our first World Cup game?"

"Umm, I think this traffic is for us," Brandi said.

And sure enough, when I looked closer at the cars sitting in traffic, many of them had U.S. Soccer-related writing on the windows, or U.S. Soccer flags. We passed a car with a big No. 9 and the words "We Love You, Mia" scrawled on the back window. Car after car had similar messaging. When a big SUV loaded with young girls with their faces painted red, white, and blue pulled alongside us and discovered who was in the bus, they went crazy, cheering and blowing kisses and half hanging out the window, the way I did that day I forgot my Tornadoes uniform. We were cheering them right back. It was mind-blowing. Sure, we had played in front of those big crowds in the '96 Olympics, but somehow this felt different, maybe because the excitement wasn't stoked by the Olympics and its global brand, but solely by the sport of women's soccer. That made this more powerful to me, the impact deeper.

We needed a police escort—a convoy of state troopers on motorcycles and a small fleet of squad cars—to blast our way through traffic to get to the stadium on time. Following the cops' lead, our driver steered the bus onto the shoulder. We finally arrived, and as far as I could see there were tailgating clubs and families, and young girls kicking soccer balls around the Giants Stadium parking lot. When we took the field to warm up, we were greeted by the sweetest, most high-pitched cheer I've ever heard in my life. It sounded as if the average age of the seventy-eight thousand plus fans was about ten. It was going to be a big day for the cotton-candy and ice-cream vendors—for the beer guys, not so much.

• • •

We'd worked our tails off to promote this World Cup and now that we had a full house to show for our efforts, we had to play a soccer match, against a strong Danish team that had steamrolled the competition in European qualifying. The underaged crowd wanted Mia, and they got Mia. In the eighteenth minute, she settled a well-placed cross by Brandi Chastain, cut her defender, and ripped a left-footed shot into the net, just under the crossbar, and then took off at full speed for the bench. The cheer was so loud it felt as if the swamp was shaking. About fifteen minutes into the second half, Mia ran onto a ball on the right and crossed it into the box, where Julie Foudy drilled a high, left-footed shot, squeezing it just inside the near post. By the time Kristine Lilly took a pass from Joy Fawcett and carved up the Danish defense along the eighteen, and tucked a shot in the corner, the prepubescent party was in full swing. I had a low-stress day in goal, which was fine by me; it allowed me to take the whole spectacle in.

Our goal for the day was to not only get the three points that accompanied a victory, but to make a statement to the rest of the field that we weren't messing around. We checked both boxes and didn't let up. From there we traveled to Chicago, where we played before another sellout crowd—over sixty-five thousand people—in Soldier Field against Nigeria. The game began disastrously for us. A botched clearance led to a prime chance for Nigeria's captain and midfielder, Nkiru Okosieme, who booted it by me in the second minute. The crowd was stunned and we were, too. The Nigerians, an attacking group to begin with, became even more emboldened. They had us scrambling and when we did go on the attack, they turned to the slash-the-tires strategy, cutting down Mia with a couple of hard fouls in the opening ten minutes or so. Mia doesn't say much or emote much, but I could see by her body language that she was getting ticked off. It wasn't that she ever wanted or expected special treatment; it was just that she hated dirty play. When she was chopped down for a third time, Mia was furious. This was not a good thing for the Nigerians. In the nineteenth minute, she blasted a free kick that a Nigerian defender deflected into the net for a tie game on what was officially an own goal. Twelve minutes later, Mia scored again and then set up Lil for another goal. The floodgates were as wide open as Lake Michigan now. We scored three times in one four-minute span, and didn't let up, walking off with a 7–1 victory.

We wrapped up group-stage play against North Korea in Foxborough, Massachusetts. Tony rested some starters because we'd already locked up a spot in the knockout round, and that provided opportunities for Shannon MacMillan and Tisha Venturini, two main-stays of our 1996 gold-medal team. North Korea packed the box to stop us, hoping to catch us on a counterattack. It made for a dull, slow-paced first half, but Shannon smoked a shot into the net early in the second, and Tisha followed with a flying header, and a second header off Shannon's free kick. We were up 3–0, and this time I had to sweat to earn the shutout. I sprinted off the line to smother a breakaway and turned away two other dangerous attempts with full-extension dives.

In three games, we'd outscored our opponents, 13–1, and seemed to find deeper belief in ourselves every time out. We would need every bit of that belief when we started the knockout stage against Germany, one of the premier teams in the world, and a group that wasn't going to be in awe of us.

"We are no more afraid of the Americans than they are of us," German goalkeeper Silke Rottenberg said. "We don't want to hide from the Americans."

• • •

After the huge turnouts and strong results during our group-stage games, we were beginning to become low-level rock stars. People recognized us and asked for autographs if we were out and about. When we traveled, we started to put our rooms under assumed names. If you called our hotel and asked for Briana Scurry, you would've been told there was no guest by that name. That's because I was either Shaniqua or Logan. Media attention started to build, too. I wasn't the most requested player—that would've been Mia, followed by Julie—but being the fly in the milk gave me a curiosity factor. I remember sitting down with a reporter in the days leading up to our first knockout stage game, against Germany, at Jack Kent Cooke Stadium in Maryland.

As we were getting started, the reporter wanted to know more about my off-field life.

"Have you thought about what you want do with your degree after you are done with soccer?" the reporter asked. "Are you still thinking about law school?"

I hated it when this topic came up.

"I'm not really sure," I said, giving my boilerplate answer. "Right now, all I'm thinking about is being a goalkeeper."

I never lied to anybody about my academic resume. However, I wasn't fully transparent either. I never got my degree. I was a student in good standing for close to four years at UMass. I especially liked the business and psychology courses I took and planned on taking more of those to finish my twelve remaining credits, but then everything changed when I was invited into my first USWNT camp late in the fall semester of my senior year. At the start of the spring semester, I was invited back for another camp. By late February, I was the No. 1 keeper. When I should've been on spring break in 1994, I was in goal for the U.S. in the Algarve Cup. When I should've been preparing to get my cap and gown, I was in Port of Spain, Trinidad, helping us qualify for the 1995 Women's World Cup. As much as I enjoyed my time at UMass, I had been invited to play soccer for my country and be part of the best women's team in the world. The decision, to me, was a no-brainer. School would always be there. When would another opportunity like this come along?

Everyone in my life—my UMass teammates, coaches, and friends—was ecstatic for me. The only person who wasn't fully on board was my mom. She wanted me to get my degree on time and graduate with the rest of my classmates in May 1994. Growing up poor in Texas, dropping out of high school to have a baby, my mom saw a college diploma as much more than a piece of parchment; it was proof of how far our family had come, a validation of our collective intelligence, and a means to a better life. Some of my older siblings went to college, but none of them had a four-year degree. I was her last chance.

I totally understood where she was coming from. But still . . .

"I want to get my degree as much as you do," I told her. "But how can I pass on this opportunity? There's an Olympics coming up in a couple of years. How long have I been talking about being an Olympian in 1996? Remember the sign in my room? This is my best chance."

My mom wasn't happy, but I think she came to understand my point.

I told her that whenever my time with the USWNT was finished, I'd go back and get my degree. And I meant it. How long would my stint on the team last? A year? Two? Three? I never imagined I'd set records for most caps by a goalkeeper. I piled up a lot of victories and shutouts, but never managed to knock off those twelve credits, which would've made me a college graduate and spared me some pangs of guilt when I misled reporters.

• • •

I wore my favorite red jersey—my power jersey—for the quarterfinal against Germany. In the fifth minute, I felt much more helpless than powerful, after Brandi scored an own goal for Germany. An own goal is the most demoralizing thing that can happen to a soccer team. It's even more demoralizing when it happens in the opening minutes. Brandi was covering a run by a German forward and didn't hear me yelling, "Mine!" as I came out of goal. She tapped a back pass to me but broke the cardinal rule of back passing—to always direct it outside the goal. The ball was squarely on goal and neither I nor any of the other defenders could do a damn thing to stop it. I watched it roll in and stood there, almost frozen, looking up at the stands. We'd just handed the Germans a 1–0 lead on a platter. I needed to put this on the shelf, fast. I didn't say a thing to Brandi. Nobody felt worse about it than she did. I would yell at teammates if we escaped a close call—"C'mon, we've got to tighten up on her!" or "You need to drop faster"—but never when the opponent scored. I knew they were trying their best. By venting your anger at someone after a mistake, all you are doing is adding to their load and running the risk of losing them mentally. We needed Brandi to be at her best. Captain Carla made sure Brandi wasn't going to a dark, self-critical place.

"Don't worry about it. There's a lot of game left. We're going to win and you're going to help us," Carla told her.

Ten minutes later, we had a flurry of chances and had the Germans scrambling when Michelle Akers teed up a shot from about twenty-two yards out. A German defender deflected it and a teammate failed to clear it. Tiffeny Milbrett beat everyone to the ball and slid it into the left corner to level the score at one. It looked as if the half would end tied and we could go into the break and make some adjustments and seize control, but in the first minute of stoppage time, Bettina Wiegmann, a German forward, pivoted away from pressure just outside the eighteen and launched a left-footed strike into the side netting of the far post.

The Germans went into the half not just with a 2–1 lead, but with belief, having been the better team for most of the opening forty-five minutes. They were stretching our defense with their technical skill, and doing a remarkably effective job of not allowing Mia or Michelle much space to operate in.

We pressed Germany hard and created some possession in the opening minutes of the second half, forcing a corner kick. Mia curled it toward the far post. The ball bounded in front, and Brandi anticipated it perfectly, going to the ground to hit a stunning half-volley past Rottenberg, before sliding on the grass and sprawling on her back as everyone raced to mob her. Carla was one of the first to arrive. Brandi had stayed in the game mentally, and here was her just reward.

Wanting to inject energy into the offense, Tony subbed out Julie Foudy for Shannon, who was the leading scorer for us in the 1996 Olympics and now was a tremendous weapon off the bench. Shannon's first touch of the game was a corner kick in the sixty-sixth minute, a low, driven ball to the near post, where Joy Fawcett was stationed. Joy, the mother of two young children and a USWNT stalwart seemingly forever, jumped and redirected a header past Rottenberg. We took a 3–2 lead and joked with Tony later that Shannon had made him look like the most brilliant coach of all time. After a few adventures with our backline possession over the final twenty minutes, we closed it to move into the final four, where we would face Brazil.

• • •

Our semifinal at the 1999 World Cup was scheduled for the Fourth of July, just four days and a cross-country flight after the Germany game. It didn't make for fresh legs, but both teams were in the same beaten-up boat as we took the pitch before over seventy-three thousand fans in

Stanford Stadium in Palo Alto, California. We had fallen behind early in our previous two games, and that was getting old. It adds so much more stress when you have to play from behind.

In the fifth minute, Julie lofted a cross near the left end line, a looping ball that slipped through the hands of Maravilha, the Brazilian keeper. Cindy Parlow was right there to head the misplayed ball into the goal. The Brazilians didn't go on the attack much over the first twenty-five minutes or so, but we knew that, more than any other team, they could use their sublime skills with quick and devastating effect, and that's what happened in the thirtieth minute, when Sissi, their center midfielder, played a ball into the box that floated dangerously toward goal. I burst off my line and was able to punch away a shot by a Brazilian forward, both of us sprawling to the ground.

We took the lead Cindy gave us into halftime, but as soon as the second half started, Brazil swarmed us. After a foul near the center circle, Brazil's Formiga did the fastest restart you will ever see, and the ball went out to Nenê on the right. Nenê lifted an arching ball that I thought was going to be a cross, but was heading straight for the upper left corner. I scrambled back as fast as I could, jumped and tipped it over the crossbar.

Brazil kept the pressure on. A snappy series of passes changed the point of attack, and left Nenê with room on the right. She fired a low, hard shot toward the far post. I flung myself to the right and batted it away with my right hand. We had over a half hour yet to play.

If Brazil keeps this up, it's going to feel like half a day, I thought.

The clock moved past sixty-five and then seventy, and we were starting to possess the ball more, but Brazil did a better job defending us than I'd ever seen them do. We had no combination plays and practically no serious threats. The Brazilians had done their best work of all on Mia, marking her closely from the outset. Finally, in the seventy-ninth minute, Michelle went up with two Brazilians just past midfield, the three of them battling to get a head on Carla's goal kick, the ball flicking ahead into Brazil's final third. Mia read it instantly and made a run, dribbling into the box, where Elane, a Brazilian defender, shouldered her off the ball and sent Mia to the ground. The ref blew her whistle and pointed to the penalty spot. The Brazilians argued vehemently, but a minute later Michelle, the greatest PK taker on earth, took a one-step runup and smashed it by Maravilha, who guessed right and still couldn't stop it.

I knew the feeling.

The Brazilians were not done, though. Pretinha put a move on Carla and blistered an angled shot on goal. In a deep crouch, ready to dive, I punched it away with two hands, the ball rolling towards the far corner. It turned out to be Brazil's last gasp; we managed the final minutes without further excitement. No host team had ever been to a World Cup final, until now. After getting mobbed by my teammates, I ran to the side of the field and found my parents. I pounded on my heart and jumped up and down and pumped my arms up and down, too, my own display of emotional fireworks on the Fourth of July. I was named "Player of the Match."

CHAPTER TEN

"THIS IS THE ONE"

While we were playing an uninspired semifinal against Brazil, advancing with a highly misleading 2–0 score line, the great Sun Wen and her teammates were taking Norway to the Chinese woodshed. Sun scored the first of her two goals in the third minute and the rout was on. In the most stunning and impressive result of the whole World Cup, China handed the Norwegians as bad a loss as they had ever had, a 5–0 thumping that happened largely because the Chinese punished Norway—masters of set-piece play—with four goals off corner kicks and free kicks. They attacked with dazzling creativity, doing it so emphatically that Hege Riise, Norway's star midfielder, offered a prediction.

"If China plays the way it did today, with all their speed and with the way they attack," Riise said, "they will beat the U.S. team . . . The Americans are good, but it's hard to imagine anyone stopping them."

The ninety thousand plus fans in the oval steam bath known as the Rose Bowl came with their painted faces and red, white, and blue regalia, but if they were expecting a stress-free coronation for their girls, we in the locker room knew differently—knew that this was a world-class opponent at the top of its game that was going to give us an epic challenge. China had beaten us in two of our previous three meetings and had only gotten better since it pushed us to the limit in the 1996 Olympic gold medal game. The Chinese were, undeniably, the most in-form team at the World Cup, with a single game left to play. I knew they would have more of the ball than we would, because that almost always was the case when we played. We just needed to be smart and seize our opportunities when they came.

The Chinese did, indeed, have a lot of possession in the final, but I noticed early on that they weren't attacking us the way they did against Norway. Maybe their coaches thought it best to be more measured in the final, I don't know. Every game of soccer is unto itself, like a chess match on a much bigger board. I think the Chinese were concerned about our counterattacking ability and didn't want to get caught with too many players forward. I know *we* were concerned about how dangerous the Chinese could be, which made us conscious of staying compact and organized and not giving them any cracks to exploit with their rapid-fire ball movement. The result was that most of the game was played between the eighteen-yard lines, the bulk of the shots not terribly menacing and coming mostly from distance.

In the twelfth minute, shortly after Mia made a strong tackle at midfield to gain possession, Michelle let a shot rip from forty yards out. If anyone else had done that, I would've considered it a wasted possession, but not with Ms. Thunderfoot. I'd seen her score from there more than a few times. Her shot came in high and hard and right on target. Gao Hong, China's keeper, reached up and grabbed it with both hands.

Michelle's shot produced the loudest roar of the match to that point, and not even three minutes later, she was in the thick of it again, stripping a Chinese defender with a surgical tackle, freeing the ball to Cindy Parlow, who went one v. one on a Chinese defender and looked as if she might be in on goal when she was taken down in the box. No call was made, and the Rose Bowl rocked with boos that there would be no penalty kick. The Chinese defender made contact with Parlow, but she got the ball first; it was a good non-call and superb marking, which both sides displayed throughout the match, the game dominated by strong, unrelentingly organized defense in the final thirds. Every time there looked to be space and a legitimate scoring opportunity, it got closed right down.

The lock-down defense continued in the second half. Ten minutes in, Julie played a through ball to Mia, who was making an overlapping run on her left, the crowd roaring as she went. China covered the run like a blanket, and no threat emerged. In the fifty-ninth minute, Chinese midfielder Liu Ailing threaded a gorgeous pass to Bai Jie, a defender making her own overlapping run. Bai managed to turn the corner on Joy, and tried to cross before Carla raced over, blocking the ball over the goal line for a corner. Carla had a sensational World Cup from start to finish but was never better than in the final.

The corner was taken by Liu Ying, a twenty-five-year-old midfielder. She drove it low and hard toward the near post, where Sun Wen got on the end of it and flicked it on, a laser of a header that whistled just wide. Sun grabbed her head with both hands. I exhaled.

And so it went. The pressure kept building as the game went into the final twenty minutes. It was going to come down to a moment of brilliance, or a mistake, or the slightest lapse in concentration. I had a strong sense that this was going into extra time, and maybe beyond—into penalty kicks.

Moments before the end of full time, China had one last corner. Liu Ying took it again, this time hitting it higher and more centrally.

A cluster of red jerseys and white jerseys jostled for position as I came off the line. It was a dangerous ball and I wanted it out of there. I went up strong and punched it out, but in the process clobbered Michelle, our best player, in the head. She went down and stayed down. When the ref stopped play, I went over to check on her. It didn't look good, even for a player as fierce and tough as Michelle. She lost track of how many operations she had. She suffered from a horribly debilitating disease, chronic fatigue syndrome, and still summoned the strength to be one of the very best players on earth. She was technically superb and physically overpowering, and it was a hybrid nobody could match. She was a peerless ball-winner in midfield, a lethal scorer, a savvy quarterback of the attack. And now she was down, and seriously woozy, because I had accidentally clocked her while clearing a ball. After getting to her feet, Michelle, predictably, tried to convince the training staff to let her keep playing, but there was no chance of that. She finished the game hooked up to an IV bag in a training room in the bowels of the Rose Bowl.

I felt terrible about what happened but couldn't spend a second thinking about it. We had two fifteen-minute extra-time periods in front of us, and it was the golden-goal format; if one team scored before the thirty minutes were up, the game was over. All that did was ratchet up the pressure even more. Extra time began and it was obvious from the start that Michelle's absence made a big difference. China had much more success building through the midfield, and in the one-hundredth minute, the player I was most concerned about, Sun Wen, found space and rifled a shot from twenty-five yards that was deflected for a corner.

Liu lined up to take it. On the near post Kristine Lilly reached down and took a drink from the water bottle that was just outside the goal, and sprinkled some water on her head, too, anything for a moment's respite from the heat. The corner came in maybe seven or eight yards out from the goal. Without Michelle, our tallest player and best header, we were much more vulnerable in the air. China's Fan Yunjie went up and sent a hard, well-angled header toward the goal. I had taken a step or two out and had no play on it. When I saw the ball go by me, I was sure the World Cup was over. And the next thing I knew, Lil, who read the play perfectly and edged toward the middle of the goal, headed the ball off the line. Brandi bicycle-kicked it out of the box, and we were saved, and the game went on.

It was a Rose Bowl miracle, but nothing Kristine Lilly did ever surprised me. This was her one hundred eighty-sixth game wearing the U.S. crest, and her experience, skill, and work ethic showed in everything she did on the field. Without a doubt, it was the greatest clutch defensive play in the history of the USWNT. It left me not just grateful to her, but with a surging, spiritual belief.

There's no way we are losing this game.

The Chinese continued to have the better of it for the rest of extra time. Our best chance came in the final minute or two, when Mia drove a free kick high into the box. Gao, supported by two defenders, came out and punched it away and nobody was there to pick up the second ball. The referee blew her whistle. After two hours in withering heat in the California sun, the 1999 Women's World Cup winner would be decided by ten kicks taken from twelve yards out, five by each team, from what soccer players call the penalty spot.

It was time for a penalty-kick shootout. Winner takes all.

I hadn't been in a shootout since the Minnows beat Park Cottage Grove in my senior year of high school to win the Minnesota state championship. The stakes were a wee bit higher now. As we huddled on the sideline and the coaches settled on the final order of our kickers, their biggest challenge was to decide who would replace Michelle, the GOAT of PKs. I had nothing to do with any of that. I was sitting by myself on the ground, knees bent, focusing on the challenge ahead, gathering the energy beams so I was at peak readiness, gearing up to go into goal feeling like the most intensely coiled spring ever, ready to unlock and unleash when the kick came. Lil came over and playfully slapped at my legs.

"Catlike reflexes, Bri. Catlike reflexes," she said.

"I'll get one," I said. "You do the rest."

• • •

I was inside my 192-square-foot rectangle now, oblivious to the electrifying buzz from the ninety thousand who surrounded me. I took a minute to go through my PK checklist: Make sure your feet are solid beneath you, that you are balanced and slightly crouched, your hands strong yet supple, your body ready to fire, left, right, up, down. It sounds basic, but going through it helped lock me in.

Our coaching staff, especially Tony's top assistant, Lauren Gregg, put a ton of energy not just into executing our PKs, but researching our opponents' tendencies. Do they like to go left or right? High or low? They built on the work I used to do with Jim Rudy, looking for cues that might help me make an educated guess where the ball is going. I reminded myself to study each kicker carefully, to pay attention to her hips and the angle of her foot, and where she was approaching the ball from.

I took a deep, calming breath. It helped me settle in. I did it before every kick. China won the coin toss and went first. As Xie Huilin, a Chinese defender, approached the spot, I did not look up. I never watched a player's walk up to the spot. I never watched my own team's kicks, either. The crowd would let me know what happens. There was no good that could come from my mind processing all that was going on with our kicker and the other keeper.

All I wanted to do was see the ball and stop the ball. Keep it simple.

An instant before Xie kicked, I got a little deeper in my crouch. On contact, I sprung forward a couple of steps. I did that on every kick, by design. Tony coached me this way and we practiced it every day in training. Technically, keepers were not supposed to come off their line, but Tony knew most of them did it and it was one of those rules that just wasn't enforced. On NBA free throws, players aren't supposed to enter the lane until the shot hits the rim, and everybody has done it for decades. Tony believed we were well within the spirit of the rules. Xie's strike was hard and beautifully placed, in the upper left corner. China took a 1–0 lead.

First up for the U.S. was Carla Overbeck. She had scored only seven goals in her long career as a center back, but Carla was money in the clutch. She heeded the advice from the coaches to not look at Gao, who was an effusive, almost goofy person and would often smile at kickers to try to get into their head. If she smiled this time, Carla never noticed. She pushed the ball comfortably into the left side of the net.

U.S 1, China 1.

Qui Haiyan was China's second shooter. She came on as a sub so she would be in the game for PKs. Qui lined up straight behind the ball, a good six or eight feet deep. She ripped it towards the same upper left corner Xie did. I dove and got close, but not close enough. China was two for two.

Joy Fawcett, who rarely made a fuss about anything, playing with surpassing skill and no theatrics, drilled her shot into upper right, Gao never moving and almost seeming as if she were caught off guard.

U.S. 2, China 2.

Liu Ying, whose corner kick almost ended the game in the one-hundredth minute, made the walk from where her Chinese team-mates were lined up, and something—who knows what?—told me to look at her. My eyes were fixed on her the whole way—the only kicker in years I can remember watching during her walk up. Her body language wasn't good. She didn't look as if she wanted to take this kick. She seemed hesitant. She put the ball down and stepped back.

This is the one, a voice told me. I had no clue where the voice came from either, but it was powerful, and even audible inside my head . . .

This is the one.

Liu lined up straight behind the ball. Her hips opened as she reached the ball and side-footed a low, hard shot toward the right. I knew where she was going because her hips tipped me off. I bounded out two steps again and dove to my left, horizontal to the ground, extending my arms. Everything slowed down. I saw the ball heading toward the goal and thought I could get. The shot was on me now. I was stretched out as far as I could go, my eyes locked in on the ball. I got a lot of my left hand on it, and a little bit of my right. The ball bounced away. The Rose Bowl erupted and so did I, jumping to my feet and screaming and pumping my clenched fists like they were pistons, over and over. It was the most emotion I've ever shown on a soccer field by a multiple of a thousand. (Predictably enough, there was a lot of talk afterward about my forward movement. I had done it on the first two kicks and the referee never said anything or warned me at all. Maybe because of my quickness, my movement seemed more glaring, but either way Tony and I thought it was very nitpicky.)

Lil stepped up next. She hit a bolt into the upper left corner. Gao guessed correctly but didn't get close.

U.S. 3, China 2.

Zhang Ouying, a forward, followed with China's fourth kick. Under insane pressure, she did a good job disguising her direction, driving a low shot to the left that I couldn't touch. It was tied at 3, but we had two shots left, and China had only one.

Next up was the reluctant superstar, Mia Hamm. Though she was the all-time leading scorer in women's soccer, Mia wasn't keen on taking one of the first five PKs, and told Lauren Gregg so. Lauren wasn't buying it. "We need you," she said. Mia walked up to the spot, put the ball down, and took a second to move a few wisps of hair from her eyes. She buried her shot in the lower right corner, then turned around and ran back to the team, jumping into the arms of Shannon MacMillan and everyone else.

Making the decisive stop in the 1999 World Cup final shootout against China. I don't think this was the best save I ever made, but it was the most famous. (Credit: John Todd/ISIphotos.com)

China's fifth kicker, Sun Wen, the top scorer and probably the top player in the World Cup, had to score or it would be over. She kissed the ball as she walked up, took a long runup, and rocketed a shot into the upper left corner.

So now we were down to our fifth kicker, Brandi Chastain. Brandi had made a spotless sliding tackle at the top of the box in extra time that robbed China of a great scoring chance. Now she had a chance to be a hero again. The coaches were initially undecided whether Brandi or Julie Foudy should take the kick, but Tony's thinking was to have Brandi change it up and take the PK with her left foot. In a loss to China in the Algarve, Brandi shot right footed on a PK against Gao and hit the post. Tony figured Gao wouldn't be expecting this at all. Brandi was all for it. She walked so briskly up to the spot you would've thought she was late for a meeting. She planted the ball on the grass, retreated a few steps. It was just a tick over three minutes since I'd made the save on Liu. I was still not looking when Brandi prepared to take her left-footed kick.

There was no reason to change now. The crowd would let me know.

Brandi ran up and powered her left foot into the ball, the contact strong, the direction even better. The ball ripped high into the side netting behind the right post. Gao Hong, as formidable as she was, had no prayer. No keeper on earth would've had a prayer. We were not just five-for-five in our PKs now. We were World Cup champions, and the instant Brandi's shot dropped into the back of the net, she ripped off her No. 6 jersey, twirling it overhead and dropping to her knees with her fists clenched, an American hero in a black sports bra, as the entire U.S. Women's National Team sprinted to engulf her, the Rose Bowl rocking so hard and loud I thought it might leave the Pasadena earth.

I always wondered how it would feel to be a World Cup champion. Now I knew.

Celebrating with my teammates and 90,000 good friends in the Rose Bowl after winning the 1999 World Cup. (Credit: J Brett Whitesell/ ISIphotos.com)

150

CHAPTER ELEVEN

SIT AND WEIGHT

There is no tactful way to put this. In the heady aftermath of the World Cup triumph, I ate myself out of a job. I didn't realize it at the time. It certainly wasn't my intention. But I went from being a World Cup champion who made an epic save in the decisive shootout, from a player my coach called the best goalkeeper in the world, to Siri Mullinix's backup.

This is nothing at all against Siri, who was a two-time national champion and All-American at North Carolina and wound up setting a U.S. Soccer record of fifteen shutouts in a calendar year. Siri was a topflight keeper who got an opportunity and ran with it, all the way to the Olympic medal stand, and deserves nothing but kudos for that.

But I opened the door for her, did everything but escort her over the threshold. I did it by gaining thirty pounds in near-record time and being almost clueless about it. I ticked off my coaches and my teammates, and, maybe worst of all, I dishonored the U.S. Soccer crest.

I was proud to wear that crest from my first cap to my last, and yet here I was practically pissing on it.

It's embarrassing—even humiliating—to cop to this, but it's the truth. I was almost blind with anger for much of that year. I felt like a victim. I felt like they kicked me to the curb six months after I played a big part in winning the World Cup.

This is so unfair, I thought. *How can they have such a short memory?* I pouted. I had nonstop pity parties for myself. My energy was crap. The biggest problem was me, but it took me a long time to realize that.

The trouble started in the late summer/early fall of 1999, when we went on a victory tour to celebrate our success and help grow the women's game in the process. We played in indoor arenas around the country, against an opponent we called the World All-Stars. We drew good crowds and made decent money. Between the tour and promotional appearances, I was on the road almost nonstop. I made seven separate trips to New York. I was on with David Letterman, Jay Leno, Rosie O'Donnell. I took off my soccer boots and kicked up my heels and had a ball. Traveling this much is usually not the best thing for your routine, or your diet. It's not that I ate cheeseburgers, pizza, and French fries nonstop for six months, but it's also not as if I was careful, or minded calories, or stuck with my workout regimen. I lived it up, pursued fun at every opportunity. At the age of twenty-eight, my metabolism was slowing down a bit. Put them together and here's what you have:

Scurry weight, July 10, 1999: 145 pounds.
Scurry weight, January 10, 2000: 175 pounds.

I rolled (almost literally) into residency camp in Chula Vista in January, the first under our new coach, April Heinrichs, who took over after Tony retired. April wasn't thrilled with her newly enlarged No. 1 goalkeeper. You can't blame her. She was even less happy when I developed shin splints in training, a painful and notoriously slow-healing condition.

At the close of camp, April asked me to meet her in her hotel room.

"I'm disappointed that you came to camp unfit," she said. "You didn't come ready to play."

The term "unfit" in soccer is the universal code word for "fat." April told me I better get to work on getting fit, which was now going to be harder because of the shin splints.

"OK," I said. "I get it."

But I didn't truly get it. I knew I wasn't in my best shape but didn't think I was that far gone. I rationalized it by telling myself that it was not realistic for a coach to expect players to be always in peak fitness. I also convinced myself that this would not have happened if Tony were still the coach. Tony was a goalkeeper coach, after all. We spoke the same ball-stopping language. We had a long and successful history, and he would've given me more runway. April was overreacting.

Isn't the whole purpose of residency camps to get into game shape, as opposed to arriving in game shape? I thought.

Siri got most of the reps in training, and virtually all the starts in games. Sitting did not sit well with me. I was working myself back into shape but still getting little playing time. The USWNT played thirty-eight games in 2000; I played 270 minutes total—or three full games. I spent many more minutes getting annoyed whenever April or one of my teammates would rave about how good Siri was with her feet, and how she was a new-school goalkeeper—a sweeper-keeper, some called it—who would range far out of the net and at times play almost like a sweeper back.

By the time spring turned to summer, I was close to my "fit" weight, but the writing was on the whiteboard. I hadn't started a game since February. April had her goalkeeper and she wasn't named Briana. All I could do was bring my best form to training every day. About two months before the Sydney Olympics, we had a five-game

European swing through Germany and Norway. Our last game in Germany was in Braunschweig, a medieval city in the central part of the country. April asked me to come to her room. It was one of those typical European hotel rooms, a little bigger than a walk-in closet. Her window looked out on a thousand-year-old cobblestone street. It was gray and rainy. The discussion didn't last long.

"I've decided to go with Siri in goal at the Olympics," she said. "I know you'll work hard and stay ready when we need you."

I resisted the urge to say something snarky, like "Thanks for the news flash." I thought about asking April if there was anything I could do to change her mind, but it was clear the decision had been made. I heard her out, said OK, and took the gut punch. It was a little ironic that five days after receiving the worst news I'd ever gotten in my six years on the USWNT, April named me the starter and gave me the captain's armband, not as a consolation prize but to recognize my one-hundredth cap. It was supposed to be a festive occasion, a salute for becoming the first U.S. female keeper to reach what was, and is, a cherished milestone. I received U.S. Soccer's traditional gift to commemorate the feat: a Rolex watch. We tied Norway, 1–1, in that game. I didn't feel very festive.

• • •

I had a decision to make as we headed toward the Sydney Olympics in September 2000. I could be a good teammate or a selfish jerk. As brutal as it was to watch from the bench, I resolved to conduct myself with professionalism and class. I had too much respect for my teammates to do otherwise. I trained hard and stayed ready and I think April noticed. Being a backup in any sport is not easy. A No. 2 quarterback in the NFL trains all year, learns the playbook, runs the scout-team offense, and knows the only time he'll get on the field is if it's garbage time or the No. 1 quarterback gets hurt. You can't allow yourself to think of how little you might get in return for your diligence. You are on a team, and your job is to help the team. Athletes with integrity do everything they can toward the end.

And that's how it was with me.

Our Olympics began with our old friends from Norway.

"You've got this, Siri," I said to the starter after warmups.

And indeed she did. We shut out Norway, 2–0, in our first group game, and followed with a tie with China and a victory over Nigeria. Having won our group, we advanced to the semifinals against Brazil. It was a raw and rainy day and one of the nastiest games I've ever seen, with a total of fifty-one fouls and eight yellow cards. Three of the yellows were for crunching, late fouls on Mia, as the Brazilians spent almost the entire game in slash-the-tires mode. They wound up paying for it in the sixtieth minute, when Brazilian stalwart Formiga chopped Mia down from behind, leading to a free kick by Brandi Chastain from forty-five yards out. Brandi sent a high ball into the box. Tiffeny Milbrett and the Brazilian keeper got tangled up. It was chaos in the box, and then the ball came to Mia, who was virtually alone on the left side of a net that was unguarded. Mia slotted it into the right corner and we had a lead we would not relinquish.

It was on to the gold-medal game—against Norway.

I was thrilled we would get to defend our Olympic title, but I'd be lying if I said I was as charged up as I was in 1996. Of course I wanted the same outcome, but when you aren't on the battlefield—when it isn't your ass on the line—it's hard to feel the same degree of ownership deep in your soul.

Still, we had business to take care of, and we took that business seriously. We were defending World Cup and Olympic champions. We were the No. 1 team in the world and every one of us knew that Olympic and World Cup titles do not happen by chance. An insane amount of work goes into those trophies, and even more character and courage. We certainly never doubted the Norwegians on those counts.

We just believed that when it came down to it, there wasn't a team on earth that would dig deeper than we would.

• • •

It was a Thursday in Australia, gold-medal day. We were in Sydney Football Stadium. The crowd was not even a third of what it was in Athens, Georgia, four years earlier, but the home team wasn't playing, so it was understandable. We came out flying, buzzing all over the Norwegians, making them look as if they were playing with ankle weights. In the fifth minute, Mia directed a perfect cross to Tiffeny at the six-yard line. Tiffeny buried it, and we were on our way. The Norwegians spent almost the entire half chasing, trying to put out fires, and barely succeeding. When you have the run of play the way we did, you always want to have more than one goal to show for it. We did not. And then a minute before halftime, Norwegian defender Gro Espeseth knocked in a header off a corner and the game was tied.

From a psychological standpoint, this was the pits. We went into the locker room with the game tied, and the scoreboard didn't give a damn that we had played a better forty-five minutes by far. Soccer is the greatest sport on earth, but it can also be the cruelest. I learned that a long time ago.

Norway beefed up its midfield and defense in the second half and came out with much more intensity. The longer the game stayed tied, the more it seemed to embolden Norway. In the seventy-eighth minute, Norway played a long, high ball into the box. Siri came out to play it, twelve yards off the line, but collided with Joy Fawcett as she tried to smack the ball out of danger, and Norway's Ragnhild Guldbrandsen headed it into the open goal.

We had twelve minutes plus stoppage time to defend our gold medal. We kept pressing forward, trying to build an attack, but Norway continually turned us away as the game clock hit ninety and we moved into stoppage time. Only two minutes were added and we were down to seconds when Cindy Parlow directed a masterful header to Mia, who was out wide on the right. Mia lifted a cross into the box, and Tiffeny, all five feet, two inches of her, rose and nodded it into the left corner of the goal.

All of us on the U.S. bench were in joyous disbelief. About twenty yards away, the Norwegian coach collapsed to his knees, hands to his face. We had tied the gold-medal game in almost unimaginable fashion. The game went to extra time. It would be golden goal over two periods, but if nobody scored, we would be back into PKs again. We knew the Norwegians had to be psychologically reeling after our stoppage time goal and aimed to take care of business quickly. We had been all over Norway from the start. Extra time would be more of the same, I was certain.

Before the extra session began, April came over to me.

"Start warming up. If we go to PKs, you're going in," she said.

"OK," I say.

I was stunned by April's words. I never saw this coming but was thrilled that she believed in me enough to entrust the shootout to me. I took off my warmups and started stretching and getting loose. An assistant coach knocked balls at me to warm up my hands and simulate game action. I scooped up low balls, jumped for high ones, dove left and dive right. I wanted us to score and win it outright in overtime, but I would be ready if it came down to a shootout.

Tiffeny, who already had two goals, was giving Norway fits, and opened extra time by sending a dangerous cross into the box. A few minutes passed and the game opened up a bit, weary legs unable to chase the way they had an hour earlier. Norway picked up two yellow cards in its effort to slow us down. In the twelfth minute, Norwegian midfielder Hege Riise settled a ball near midfield and sent it toward our box. Forward Dagny Mellgren, a late substitute, went up for it, covered by two defenders. Joy had the best read on it and jumped to head it. The ball caromed off Mellgren's left arm and dropped to the ground. Mellgren squeezed through a double-team and poked a shot toward the right side of the goal. Siri dove. She got her hand on it, but not enough to stop it from rolling into the net.

On the field, on the bench, we were almost catatonic, eyes glazed, hands on hips, unable to grasp that a game we were sure would be ours had gone the other way. I stopped warming up. The finality of the moment hit me like a sledgehammer.

Our locker room inside Sydney Football Stadium had the look and feel of a funeral parlor as we waited for the medal ceremony. We hadn't lost a match of this magnitude since the World Cup semifinal in Sweden in 1995. We forgot how crappy it felt. The locker room was cramped and thick with the smell of sweat and grass. The silence was interrupted only by the occasional sound of sobbing. Mostly heads were down, the talk at whisper level. The reserves took the lead on offering words of solace to the starters.

"You left it all out there. You've got nothing to hang your head about."

"I know you are hurting now, but there's no shame in winning a silver medal in the Olympic Games."

"We showed the world our fight and our character and don't lose sight of that."

"We're going to be better because of this."

The words were well-intentioned but they can't be absorbed in a moment like that. I walked over to Siri's locker and put my hand on her back and patted it a few times. I'm sure nobody felt worse than she did. I knew better than anybody in the room what a shitty feeling it is as a keeper when you get your hand on a ball and don't save it. You second-guess everything. Did I react fast enough? Was my arm fully extended? Why didn't I get lower? Why didn't I get higher? You think of twenty things you possibly could've done differently that might have kept the ball out of the net. It's self-inflicted torture. Most every goalkeeper does it.

When it was time for the medals to be awarded, I was the first out of the locker room, because the lockers go by number and I wear No. 1. It was fine with me. I just wanted to get out of Australia. The Norwegian flag was hoisted up the pole, and its national anthem, *Ja, vi elsker dette landet* (Yes, we love this country), was played in Sydney Football Stadium. It's a lovely song and I loathed every note. We just won a silver medal and I felt hollow.

CHAPTER TWELVE

LOSING POPS

"Most men would rather deny a hard truth than face it," wrote George R.R. Martin, the novelist and screenwriter whose work was the inspiration for *Game of Thrones*. Most women are the same way, me included. Through much of 2000 and the early winter of 2001, I would've won gold if denial had been an Olympic sport. I had no peer in fooling myself, until a package came in the mail.

It was flat and cardboard, and the "Do Not Bend" stamp alerted me to the presence of a photo or some sort of artwork. I opened it up and looked at a photo of me jumping to grab a cross in January 2000. My face was as round as a pumpkin. My body was all but bulging out of my uniform. I looked as if I'd bulked up for a movie role. I stared at the photo for fifteen or twenty seconds. I was so . . . so . . . unfit. And that was it, the death of my denial, of the self-righteousness and bitterness that at times consumed me in 2000. I knew I had gained weight. My uniform was snugger, and I wasn't as quick and couldn't jump as high, but as weird as it may sound, it wasn't until I saw the photo that the full, plus-sized truth hit me.

This had nothing to do with April not knowing me as well as Tony, or April treating me unfairly. She wasn't fat-shaming me. She wasn't doing anything but letting me know when you are an elite athlete you can't take a few months off and expect everything to be hunky-dory. This was one hundred percent self-sabotage. I didn't keep my focus on what was important. I didn't take care of my body. As epiphanies go, it was extremely painful, and what made it worse was that I had full confidence that I could've helped the U.S. win its second straight Olympic gold medal in Sydney, had I been fully fit . . . had I given April that option. The only positive takeaway for me was that I knew I would never let this happen again.

The team had already had a number of camps in 2001, none of which I'd been invited to. Every time I was passed over, it stung a little more. I'd look at the rosters and note the goalkeepers invited. In almost every camp it included Siri Mullinix, Hope Solo, and LaKeysia Beene, a former All-American from Notre Dame. All three were a good deal younger than me, and it seemed clear that April was ready to turn the proverbial page on me. All I could control was my own preparation and my own performance. I had a new team to do that with—the Atlanta Beat of the new Women's United Soccer Association (WUSA). I agreed to join the Beat after my first three allocation choices—Boston, D.C. and the Bay Area—were taken by Lil, Mia and Brandi. The Beat coach, Tom Stone, had been a scout for Tony DiCicco and had seen me play a lot in 1999. After the draft, he was approached by a team official who said he had a chance to get Michelle Akers in exchange for me.

"Would you make that trade?" the official asked Stone.

"I love Michelle Akers, but I would not trade her for Briana Scurry in a million years." Stone said.

I knew there was one person for me to reach out to if I truly wanted to work harder and prepare better than I ever had before:

Kerri Reifel.

One of the things I cherished the most about Kerri from the start was her honesty. So many people sugarcoat their feelings or avoid them altogether. I thought I worked hard in my early years on the USWNT, but when I trained with Kerri she essentially called me a slacker. She wasn't being mean at all.

"I know you think you are training hard, but you can do more and you need to do more if you want to raise your game," she said.

Kerri wasn't just a high-level keeper; she was also, by now, a high-level coach who had an uncanny ability to motivate and teach. She was an assistant coach at the University of South Carolina in 2001. We hadn't been in touch for a while. She was disappointed that I'd let the starting job slip away. Kerri knew April well and knew how much value April placed on a player's work habits.

"When April got the job, I had a strong feeling that it wasn't going to go well," Kerri said.

So I called Kerri out of the blue.

"I know what I need to do now. I'm ready to put in the work and do whatever I have to do," I said. "Can you help me?"

Kerri had been waiting—hoping—to hear this from me for years.

"I just stood there, dumbfounded. It was like I was watching a movie," Kerri said. "I was so happy for you and so grateful you called. A million emotions came up for me. I could hear in your voice how much you wanted it. I knew if you committed yourself you would get your job back and be better than ever before."

I flew to South Carolina and got after it. The bulk of our work was in the weight room. Kerri set up a lifting regimen tailored to goal-keeping. We did tons of squats, strengthening my legs for increased explosiveness. We worked on core and lateral movement and building up my quadriceps and hamstrings for quick firing. Kerri also tutored me on reading game situations and finding out the optimal position to be in for each one. When I was done working out and studying, I was eating better than ever—tons of fresh fruits and vegetables, chicken, and fish—and started taking so many supplements, I carried around my own little pill box.

I was all in on my new regimen. I felt a difference almost immediately. Within a month or two, I wanted to get in the net and show April the new me. In the meantime, I met with Tom Stone and Chris Peet, the Beat goalkeeping coach, as we began our preseason training. As big a fan of mine as he was, Tom Stone didn't know what sort of player he was getting from a motivational standpoint.

"Not long ago you were the best goalkeeper in the world," Stone said. "Is that what you want to be again?"

"That's why I'm here," I said. "That's what I'm going to put my heart and soul into."

The coach smiled and said, "We're totally on board with that."

Before I reconnected with Kerri and made these changes, I was squatting 185 pounds. Now I was squatting 245. I was moving better than I ever had, covering more space, hitting my head on crossbars again. I loved playing for Tom and Chris. Tom appreciated the intensity I brought to the team and was a constant source of encouragement. Chris was a beacon of calm and a wonderful teacher of technique, especially with my kicking game. With talents like Cindy Parlow and Sun Wen, the Chinese star, the Beat won the regular-season title and gave up the fewest goals in the lead. We made it to the finals and, except for losing a penalty-kick shootout in the championship, it couldn't have gone any better.

I was a thoroughly reimagined keeper, and found a wonderful social circle in Atlanta, as well. I made friends in the local lesbian community, and as an openly gay athlete for the home team, found myself being sought out by gay opposing players who were coming to town for a game. I was always open to helping them, which is how I came to be known as the "Gay Welcome Wagon." That's a stretch, for sure, but I *did* know where all the gay clubs and bars were, and was happy to introduce them to visiting players who were looking to unwind. It wasn't uncommon for us to all go out together after games.

Unbeknownst to me, Tom was in regular touch with April and keeping her abreast of my resurgence.

"Bri's better than she ever has been," he told her. "What are you waiting for?"

I didn't know what she was waiting for, either. Playing for the Beat was a godsend, but my overarching goal was to regain my starting spot with the national team. Not getting invited to camp through all of 2001 didn't fill me with optimism. You can't be in the conversation if you are not in camp, and you won't be in camp unless you can convince the coaching staff that the team would be better off if you *were* in camp.

Early in 2002, I decided it was time to be proactive. I knew the team was coming to Charleston, South Carolina, in January for a friendly against Mexico. I called April and asked if I could meet with her.

"Sure," she said. "Tom has been telling me great things about how you are playing."

We met in her hotel for a half hour. I owned everything about the runup to the 2000 Olympics.

"By not being fit, I know I didn't just let myself down. I let the team down," I said. "I didn't give you a choice about who to play. That's on me, and I'm sorry." I told her how hard I'd been working and that I'd learned an important lesson about complacency.

April thanked me and smiled.

"Goalkeeper was the one position I didn't think I had a decision to make," she said.

She also said, "I don't believe in closing the door on any player."

My long-awaited return to USWNT training camp came in the late spring. It was like my first camp all over again, being four or five deep on the depth chart. That didn't concern me in 1993 and it didn't concern me in 2002; this was the ultimate meritocracy, and whether it was Siri, Hope, LaKeysia, or me, whoever did the best job of keeping the ball out of the net would move to the forefront. We had a busy fall schedule that year, and that was good with me. The more games we had, the more opportunity I figured I'd get to show April what I could do. On September 29, 2002, we played a friendly against Russia in Uniondale, Long Island. It wasn't a game of much consequence, or drama (we won 5–1), but it was a turning point for me. For the first time in over two years, I was the starting goalkeeper for the USWNT.

The starts came more regularly by the end of the year, and as we edged closer to the 2003 World Cup, I was regaining April's trust. I was in goal when we won the Algarve in Portugal in March, and as we began to prepare for the World Cup in earnest, it was clear to me I was the No. 1 keeper again. Much less clear was where the World Cup would be held. It was supposed to be in China, but an outbreak of SARS made the idea of hosting an international sports event inconceivable. In early May, FIFA announced the tournament would be relocated, and three weeks after that, it announced the site of the relocation: the United States of America, the same country that had successfully hosted the 1999 Women's World Cup.

Though I was relieved not to have to travel to the other side of the planet during an epidemic (I'd never heard the word *pandemic* in my life at that point), it was also bittersweet. My parents were there in person for my last two major tournaments that had been held stateside. That was not at option this time. My father's health was on a long, downward slide. He had a fall a year earlier, hitting his head. He had a mini stroke. Complications from his diabetes necessitated the amputation of his right leg below his knee, and ultimately forced him to go on dialysis. My mom was a nursing assistant when they were courting and my father drove the blue Busy Bee Taxi almost forty years before, and now she was a full-time nurse as she struggled to help my dad get some vitality back. It was hard on both of them. Losing part of his leg took a heavy emotional toll on my dad. He had a prosthesis, but it wasn't comfortable and he didn't like wearing it. His world was shrinking fast. He spent more and more time in bed, where he'd prop himself up and watch TV, always with his right arm folded behind his head, elbow out, pointing to the Olympic silver medal that was on his bedpost. I gave it to him after I came back from Sydney, and for some reason it seemed more special to him than the gold medal we won in 1996. I never asked why, but I think he was proud of the way I responded to the disappointment of losing my job. He knew it wasn't easy to accept responsibility and make the necessary changes. He and my mother saw a dedication from me they had never seen in me before, and it was a direct line from that dedication to getting my job back. To my father, that was as good as gold.

• • •

As the 2003 World Cup began, I was thirty-two years old and as confident as I'd ever been. In my USWNT starts dating to April 1999, the U.S. was unbeaten in thirty-one games—twenty-seven victories and four ties. We cruised through three qualifying games, scoring eleven goals and conceding just one, and moved into the quarterfinals against our old pals from Norway—still the only country that had a winning record against us. Every time we played them, it seemed to come down to one or two plays. I'd seen it over and over. The record books show a W or an L, distilling the competition to a few immutable digits, but so often whether you wind up with the W or the L, whether you are holding the champion's trophy or the runner-up trophy, is determined by the smallest of things. Not getting the explosiveness I needed to knock down a hard strike heading toward the far post. A defender losing her mark for a second or two, giving a forward time and space to work a little magic. A midfielder not tracking back hard enough to help with our coverage in the box. A forward with a clear look at goal, leaning back on a shot to get more on it, and launching it over the crossbar. A single action, or inaction, amid the fast flurry of play, can alter everything. It is the beauty of the game, and the harshness of it. If Kristine Lilly hadn't headed the ball off the line on that corner kick in extra time in the 1999 World Cup final, China would've scored the golden goal, and we would've finished second. I never would've made the save in the shootout because there would not have been a shootout. Brandi would've kept her shirt on because she would not have had a PK to kick. I would never have been on a Wheaties box, and the cover of *Sports Illustrated* probably would've been a New York Yankee or a San Francisco 49er, not Brandi and her black sports bra and her rippling six-pack. The WUSA might never have gotten off the ground. The whole arc of my life would've been different. You get no advance notice about when that decisive moment might come. I don't believe what happens in life is random, ever, but the idea that you have no clue what is going to be the pivot point that changes everything is, from a goalkeeper's perspective, both exhilarating and terrifying. It demands hyperalertness from the first moment to the last. It was why I would come off the field feeling like I'd played twelve hours of chess.

· · ·

I started my international career in earnest getting my heart shredded by a six-foot Norwegian heading in a corner kick. Eight years later, in the twenty-fourth minute of our quarterfinal in the 2003 Women's World Cup, the towering game-changer was on my side. Her name was Abby Wambach, and she was a force of will and nature, and everyone who was paying attention in Gillette Stadium in Foxborough, Massachusetts, knew it. Abby was as good in the air as anyone I'd ever played with, not just because of her height, but because of her cunning and her absolute refusal to let anybody stop her. Cindy Parlow, our star forward and my Beat sister, had been fouled by a Norwegian about forty yards out from goal. Cat Reddick immediately launched the free kick into the box, where Abby outjumped all of Norway and headed the ball into the net. The usual warfare went on for more than hour, but Norway had no answer. I only had to make one save, and it was no big deal.

We moved into the semifinals against Germany, the hottest team in the tournament. The Germans had blown through their group with no problem, and then annihilated Russia, 7–1, in the quarterfinals. Several of the top German players were standouts in the WUSA, so we knew how good they were. They took little time to give us a reminder. Kerstin Garefrekes, a jumbo midfielder, got on the end of a corner kick in the fifteenth minute, and knocked it into the upper ninety at the near post. We had multiple chances to equalize. Silke Rottenberg, Germany's keeper, made a diving catch of Lil's left-footed strike to preserve the lead. Mia and Tiffeny Milbrett both got taken down in the box, but no penalty was called. Rottenberg turned away everything we threw at her, and I knew I had to do the same. I made my two best saves of the day off another German set piece, parrying two shots in rapid succession from point-blank range, but the longer the game went, it just felt that there was a cement wall in front of Germany's goal. We pushed forward and hoped to find Abby in the box, but the Germans marked her superbly, and in stoppage time, our hope ran out along with the clock when Germany scored twice on breakaways. It was a most deceiving 3–0 score line, but that offered no consolation; we did not defend our title. Germany went on to beat Sweden to capture the World Cup. We rallied to defeat Canada to win the bronze medal. I was really proud of the way we rebounded from the semifinal, but it didn't make the loss any less crushing. It's a hell of a long wait when an event only comes around every four years.

• • •

The WUSA was a phenomenal league and a noble experiment. Launched and bankrolled by John Hendricks, founder of the Discovery Channel, and a group of his rich cable-TV pals, the league began in 2001 with eight teams and apparently unlimited funds. It hired a Quaker Oats executive to be its CEO, and Tony DiCicco to be commissioner. Those of us on the National Team were tagged as Founding Players and paid $85,000 a year. The perks, the playing conditions, the travel—all were first-rate. In Atlanta, we had the same doctors the Braves and Falcons had. We had a superb training facility at Georgia Tech. When visiting teams came to town, they stayed at the Westin downtown. League headquarters was in Rockefeller Center in New York City, where office space was about a million dollars per square inch.

When I heard that, I thought, *Hello? We aren't the NFL quite yet.*

I loved the WUSA and I am not sure my comeback ever would've happened without it. From Day 1, it was by far the best women's soccer league in the world. The problem was that the business model wasn't sustainable. The WUSA was like a jet plane that burns so much fuel on takeoff that it doesn't have enough to complete the journey. We were in training camp in Philadelphia in September 2003, not even a week before the start of the Women's World Cup when we found out the league had folded after three seasons. I was crushed but I can't say I was shocked. Hendricks acknowledged that the staggering success of the '99 Women's World Cup had fooled him.

"I was intoxicated by what I witnessed in 1999 with the corporate sponsorship. I mistakenly assumed it would overflow onto the league," he said.

It wasn't until 2009 that another women's soccer league—Women's Professional Soccer—was formed. WPS was also a great league, but its foremost problem wasn't spending too much money, but spending too little. It was a league on a shoestring. It, too, lasted three seasons. The current league, the National Women's Soccer League, has far surpassed its forebears and I believe it is here to stay (that's why I purchased a small stake in the Washington Spirit in 2020), but only if it addresses the toxic and even abusive workplace culture that was linked to several of the league's male coaches during the 2021 season. With the players united in demanding change and full transparency and accountability, I believe the NWSL will find its way forward.

With no more Beat to play for, I packed up my place in Atlanta and moved to Rhode Island to live with a friend, but my heart and soul were in Dayton, Minnesota, as my father continued to slip. I made several trips back late in 2003 and early in 2004, and every time he seemed to get a little worse. One day I went for a walk on a wooded path near where I was staying in Rhode Island and my mind turned into a highlight reel of memories and images of my father. I saw him in his overalls, wrench in hand, leaning over the engine of his Mustang, tinkering to his heart's delight. I saw him on the porch at the grill, making his famous ribs. I saw him cleaning up the Nacirema Club on Saturday mornings, telling me I could keep the hundred-dollar bill I'd found. And of course, I saw him next to my mother in his folding chair along the byline, near the corner flag of a thousand different soccer fields, and eating fish and chips together at Arthur Treacher's after the game.

"Thank you, Pops," I said out loud. "I love you." The thought of losing him was crushing, but in that moment, on that woodsy path, I was beginning to process it, grieving and celebrating him all at once. I was close to the end of my walk.

"It's OK, Pops," I said. "When it's time, I'll be ready. I'll be sad because I love you so much, but it's OK."

• • •

My parents traveled to Galveston to visit family in the winter of 2004, but getting away from the Minnesota cold didn't help my father's health. He had some heart issues and wound up spending a month in a Houston hospital. I was in Costa Rica for CONCACAF qualifying and asked April if I could leave for a few days to go see my dad. She said of course. My father looked frail and sad. He was always thin, and now he was forty pounds thinner.

He might not even last until the Olympics, I thought.

My mother continued to be a world-class nurse, but she was swimming against the tide and I'm sure she knew it. In June, during a short break from the USWNT, a group of former WUSA players organized a nationwide barnstorming tour, one of the stops being the National Sports Center in Blaine, Minnesota, fifteen miles east of Dayton. My dad was back in the hospital. I stayed at home with my mom and we went to visit him in the hospital on a Saturday afternoon. My dad had just gotten out of the intensive-care unit and looked to be on the upswing. His eyes were brighter, his energy better. When we walked in the room he was sitting up in bed, right arm behind his head, bent the same as always. The Olympics were seven weeks away. It would be just like him to hold on so he could catch a few more games.

We had a lovely, tender visit.

"Thanks for coming, honey," he said.

"Love you, Pops. See you soon," I said.

My mom and I had a quiet evening at home, dinner and a movie. A few minutes after eleven o'clock, the phone rang. My mom answered. It was a nurse from Mercy Hospital, where my dad was, just across the Mississippi River in Coon Rapids. She said my dad had taken a turn for the worse and we should get to the hospital as soon as we could. It was only five miles away and we got there in under ten minutes. My dad was on a ventilator, his heartbeat faint. His eyes were open but looked glazed and distant. My mom was on one side of the bed, and I was on the other. It was shocking to see how fast he'd declined. It made me think he had waited for me when I saw him earlier, that he wanted that visit before it was time. We each held his hand. My mom spoke to the nurse. The machines he was hooked up to were keeping him alive. That wasn't what he wanted, or what she wanted.

I was crying. My mom was crying. We kept holding his hands.

"You don't have to fight anymore, Pops," I said. "Don't worry about anything. I love you, and I will take good care of Mom."

My mom stroked his head and spoke to him so softly it was almost a whisper.

"It's OK, Ernie," she said. "You can go now."

A minute or two later, Ernest Scurry took a shallow final breath. His eyes stayed open. My mother reached up to his face with her index fingers and gently shut his eyes. The clock had moved past midnight. It was Sunday, June 20. It was Father's Day.

CHAPTER THIRTEEN

GOLD NEVER GETS OLD

I bought two shirts and a tie for my father before he died, but never got the chance to give them to him. I did the next best thing. I had him dressed in one of the shirts—a fuchsia-colored Pierre Cardin—with a complementary, diamond-patterned tie for the funeral. He looked smashing. Everybody thought so. I delivered the eulogy without writing down a word; it was straight from my heart so there was no need to put anything on paper. Mostly I talked about his character and quiet dignity and how he never played the victim or blamed other people if he had a problem. He and my mom were the first African Americans in Dayton, Minnesota, as far as I know, and yet my dad always said the only "N" word he ever heard was "neighbor." I hope that was true. His outlook on life poured into me. My dad always told me to try to be the best, so that's what I did.

On Friday, the 25th of June, 2004, we buried him in Fort Snelling National Cemetery, in honor of his Army service in Korea, with his favorite keepsake—the silver medal from Sydney—around his neck. Planes rumbled overhead as they lowered his casket into the ground, which was inevitable, since Fort Snelling is about a corner kick away from the Minneapolis–St. Paul Airport. Two days later, I was on one of those planes, off to rejoin my team for the final preparation for the Athens Olympics. Our first game was August 11. There was no time to fully grieve my loss; that would have to come later. Winning in the other Athens—Georgia—seemed like an achievement from another century. (It actually *was* an achievement from another century.) My dad treasured his silver medal, but I was going for an upgrade to gold and I knew exactly who was going to be my inspiration to get it done.

We started our Olympics against the host country, which earned an automatic spot because they were, well, the host country. The Greek team was mostly comprised of U.S. college players of Greek ancestry, and they got a robust cheer when they took the field in Heraklion, the

Sharing a quiet moment with my parents at their grave, Fort Snelling National Cemetery.

capital of Crete, in a new stadium on the coast. It was as beautiful a setting as I had ever played in, mountains on one side, azure waters on the other, and archaeological ruins dating to 3000 BC in between. The fans quickly became aware of a much more contemporary attraction, Mia Hamm. About fifteen minutes in, Mia juked and stutter-stepped a defender so badly that she fell, then placed a perfect cross to Shannon Boxx, who planted it for a one-goal lead. The defender was so aghast she pulled her shirt over her head, and probably wanted to do it again when the referee told her to go off the field and remove her necklace. She complied, but in the brief time that Greece was a woman down, Kate Markgraf served a nice ball into the box, which Abby Wambach headed in for 2–0. Mia finished the scoring with a goal late in the second half. Greece took the first shot of the game, and it turned out to be its only shot of the game. Harder workdays were coming.

Our second group game was against Brazil, a team that had restocked with insanely gifted young players who could samba you into submission, making moves you'd never seen before. They played with huge flair and emotion, which sometimes helped them but also sometimes hurt them. When they were cooking, connecting, stitching together passes as if they were making a quilt, it felt as if they had twenty-two players on the field. But if they fell behind or someone made a bad mistake, the energy would drain out of them in a hurry. You were never quite sure which Brazil would show up. We found out in Game Two that it was the quilt-making Brazilians. They came out with energy and totally had the run of play in the first half. I walked off the field after forty-five minutes and saw a 0–0 scoreboard and felt grateful for that. I had been busy, but also lucky; Brazil hit the post twice. I wasn't complaining. I'll take luck when I can get it. At halftime April lit into us, appropriately so, asking for more energy and commitment, or did we just want to see the samba routine continue?

The second half was a different story, and as I watched it unfold, I had an almost out-of-body experience. The dominant player in the half, competitively and theatrically, was Abby Wambach, and it was almost as if I were seeing the goal-scoring torch being passed to her from Mia. The all-time leading goal scorer, male or female, in international competition, Mia had announced this would be her last major event. She had probably done more to popularize our sport than any player, before or after. Mia was only thirty-two years old and still a dynamic player (see Game One), but it was clear to me that twenty-four-year-old Abby, as different from Mia as black is from white, was the future. It was almost comical how dissimilar they were. Mia was small—listed generously at five foot five and 120 pounds—and was almost allergic to attention and media fanfare. For years Mia was the face of U.S. Women's Soccer—really, all of U.S. Soccer—and she hated it. It wasn't fake humility. She wanted somebody else—anybody else—to be the center of attention. She would practically holler at people, "Don't you see how great Kristine Lilly is? And Carla Overbeck and Joy Fawcett, too?" When interview requests would come in, she'd do it for the good of raising the profile of the women's game, but her preference truly was to suggest the journalist go find somebody else more worthy. I always admired this quality in Mia, and still admire it. These days people actively cultivate celebrity and spend a lot of time—and money— figuring out social-media metrics that will get them there. Mia was a sensational soccer player who wanted nothing more than to be "just" a soccer player.

Abby was close to six feet tall and if Mia's MO was to beat people with her technical skill and change of pace, Abby's was "You want a piece of me?" She was so strong she could shed tacklers as if she were swatting away a mosquito. Abby loved the spotlight, the heat, the drama, the competitive fray. She was every bit as authentic as Mia; it was just that their authenticity came from profoundly different places. Abby didn't set out to hog headlines for her own benefit. She loved her teammates and fought for her teammates. She was simply a massive extrovert and a reporter's dream whose approach with the media was basically "I will talk, and you tell me when to stop."

Abby was at the center of everything in the second half. She got a yellow card (her second in the group stage, which meant she had to sit out our next game) in the first few minutes. It didn't stop her, or us. In the fifty-fifth minute, Abby was taken down in the corner of the box by Brazil's Monica. Mia converted the ensuing penalty kick to give us the lead, and a little over twenty-minutes later, Abby made a brilliant run, toasted two defenders, and tucked a shot inside the right post to make it 2–0. That was how it ended, but the story pivoted sharply afterward when René Simões, Brazil's coach, called us a "dirty" team that won the game because the referee didn't do his job, because we elbowed and pushed and bullied our way to a victory, going on to talk about the huge "swellings" that were inflicted on the ankles of Brazilian stars Formiga and Cristiane, and the eighteen-year-old prodigy, Marta.

"It is not the way we Brazilians see the game," Simões said.

It's a good thing I wasn't at the press conference when he said that because I might've thrown up. I love the Brazilians' skill and the artistry they bring to the game, but his characterization of what happened was laughable. For sure, we ramped up our intensity and physicality in the second half; there was, however, nothing dirty about it. We didn't target his best players and send them to the hospital, as Simões contended. The Brazilians are gifted players, but they also are masters of the well-placed elbow and knee, the ankle kick, the jersey tug, the invisible blow that knocks you down when nobody is watching. Abby came off the field after the game with a ripped shirt, and enough bruises and abrasions to suggest she'd been in a boxing match. So don't give me this garbage that you are soccer artistes and the rest of us are thugs.

The victory over Brazil assured us of a spot in the knockout round. In our next game, against Australia, all we needed to win our group was to tie, and tie we did, Australia—the Matildas, as they are known—scoring a late goal to get a result against us for the first time in seventeen years—a span that included fifteen straight losses and a goal differential of 58–9. The Matildas celebrated as if they'd won gold, for the point they earned moved them into the knockout round, as well. I admired their fighting spirit. I wasn't thrilled with the cautious and at times passive way we played, but these big tournaments are all about pacing yourself, getting the results you need, and peaking at the right time.

• • •

It was two days before our first knockout game—a quarterfinal against Japan—and out of nowhere a flood of memories of my father washed over me. Grief has its own timetable, and its own process. I was learning that in a hurry. Some days I would feel OK, and others I felt as if the pain and sadness would never end. This was one of the other days. I was sitting in the corner of the hotel lobby, softly crying. I was thinking about going back up to my room in case I started bawling when Cindy Parlow spotted me and seemed to know exactly what was going on. She came over and put an arm around me and reached out for my hand. If she said anything in that moment I don't recall it, but she didn't have to say a word, because compassion and kindness were all over her face.

"Just thinking a lot about my dad," I said.

She nodded. "I'm sure it's really hard."

"Yeah, it is. I've never been through anything like this before."

Not a lot of people are comfortable dealing with death. They don't know what to say or do, and don't want to be insensitive or make you feel worse, so they tap dance around the subject. I knew my teammates felt for me, but throughout the Olympics it was kind of the elephant in the team room. Our massage therapist, Naomi Gonzalez, whose powerful, intuitive hands could feel the depth of my grief, was my greatest source of comfort, but more than any player on the team, Cindy was there for me. I felt understood, cared for, somehow not so alone with my loss. What a gift Cindy Parlow gave me. I have never forgotten it.

• • •

An interesting lineup change came with the quarterfinals, when Brandi replaced Cat Reddick as the starter at left back. Brandi hadn't played a minute in the group stage. Brandi and April didn't see eye to eye on many subjects, and the relationship frayed further when Brandi met with U.S. Soccer president Robert Contiguglia and secretary-general Dan Flynn in the wake of the 2003 World Cup disappointment to let them know that a number of veteran players were not happy with the team's direction under April. Was Brandi's benching April's way of getting payback? Rumors swirled that April was forced by the higher-ups to play Brandi. I had no idea about any of this, and honestly couldn't afford to let any energy get siphoned off thinking about it.

I was twenty minutes into my warmup before the quarterfinal when somebody told me to look up into the stands. About halfway up in the middle of the field, standing in an aisle with blue shorts and a white top, waving to me, was Robbie Scurry. It was the best moment of the Olympics. I sprinted out of the goal, climbed into the stands, and ran up the steps like I was being chased. I was in a sweaty yellow goalkeeping jersey and still had my goalkeeper gloves on. I wrapped up my mom with a big, long hug.

"I'll see you later, Meresie. Hopefully after we win."

I worried that the trip might be too much so soon after losing my dad but she insisted she wanted to come. U.S. Soccer had someone meet her at the airport and get her to the stadium, with all the other family and friends. The Hamms and the Lillys said they would look after her, which was so comforting to know. As I made my way back down the steps, I imagined my mom yelling the same thing she used to say at Brooklyn Park Kickers games:

"Kick it! Get that ball out of there."

Every time my parents saw me play in person at a major tournament, we won. It would be nice to keep the streak going. The Hamms and Lillys and Robbie Scurry had a good day of rooting. Mia was the best player on the field in the first half. We carried the play and did quality marking on Japan's Homare Sawa, one of the premier attacking midfielders in the world. Just before halftime, Lil, playing her 280th international game, more than any soccer player in history at the time, hammered in a goal in a scrum in front of the Japanese goal to get us on the board. Japan equalized on a fluky bounce off a free kick not even four minutes into the second half, and then Mia took a free kick from the left side in the fifty-ninth minute. Craziness ensued. Japan worked an offside trap, all its defenders stepping forward, succeeding in putting Julie, Lil, and Abby all in offside positions. But Shannon Boxx saw it unfolding and stayed onside. She got on the end of Mia's kick and then slid it over to Abby (who was OK to play it because now she was back onside). Abby punched it in and we had a lead we kept to the end.

This moved us into the semifinals against Germany, a rematch of the World Cup semifinal from a year before. The game took us back to Crete, and paradise by the sea. The next day in the hotel lobby, I visited with my mom. I got her a cup of coffee and I drank water and we sat at a small table near a window. She had sadness in her eyes, but she was also excited to be in a beautiful, exotic place, watching her daughter play soccer the same way she did in Anoka or Champlin.

"Your dad loved that save you made the other night when the girl made you dive," she said. She was talking about the Japan game. I smiled even though I wasn't sure what save she was talking about. The details didn't matter. I was on a Greek island before an Olympic semifinal with my mom, the person who always told me I could do anything. And here we were. She was a teenage mother from Galveston, Texas, who loved to sing and was about to turn seventy and had just buried her husband and raised nine kids with limited means. She spent her life giving and giving, and she was talking about saves in a soccer game. People always made a fuss about my strength and character. I looked at my mom and her sweet, light brown face, sipping her coffee, and all I could think was *You are the strongest woman I've ever known. You inspire me in ways I can't even express.*

I never wanted to go global with my thinking in the middle of a major event—keeping balls out of the net was hard enough—but in this case rolling waves of larger emotional forces overtook me. My five teammates who won the first Women's World Cup in 1991—Mia, Lil, Julie, Joy, Brandi—the so-called 91ers—were playing together for the last time. Along with the legendary Michelle Akers and a few others, they were the people who laid the foundation of the USWNT. Without them, there are no World Cup titles or Olympic golds. Greatness did not happen by accident. It happened because gifted and committed athletes gave everything they had. So now it was on us, the 2004ers. Were we going to give them the sendoff they deserved? Were we going to honor the legacy they had built? We'd fallen short in the 2000 Olympics and the 2003 World Cup. A narrative was taking root in some places that the USWNT wasn't what it used to be.

Our job was to change it.

More personal questions weighed on me, too. *Would my mom ever see me play again in person? Is this my last Olympics? Whatever happens here, would my dad want me to continue playing? Should I start sending my resume out?* I hoped and prayed for clarity on all of this. The clarity was slow in coming. I was in full grief mode and trying to take in all these other things left me feeling like a human kaleidoscope.

• • •

Lil had a phenomenal tournament from the start. Her consistency was as mind-blowing as her fitness, which was saying a lot. She defended like a barracuda and created havoc with her runs. It was no different in the semis against Germany. In the thirty-third minute, she took a pass from Abby and knocked it past Silke Rottenberg, the German keeper, to give us a 1–0 lead. We were on our game, and my defenders were having their best match of the tournament, suffocating the main German attacking threats, Maren Meinert and Birgit Prinz. Prinz, their captain and top scorer, was in the middle of winning three straight FIFA World Player of the Year awards. She had won both the Golden Ball and the Golden Boot at the World Cup the year before. Meinert was the reigning Most Valuable Player in the WUSA. At five feet, ten inches, Prinz was basically Abby's size and, like Abby, demanded your complete attention. Both Prinz and Meinert had this efficiency about them, so you couldn't let your guard down for a second when they were on the ball in the box. On a semi-breakaway in the World Cup final a year earlier, Prinz took a touch and drew me out, then made a deft cut around me to elude my dive and slide the ball in. It isn't a happy memory.

Neither Prinz, Meinert, nor any other German had a shot on goal in the first half. We carried the lead into the second half, but fifteen minutes in Julie went down with an ankle injury. When April had to sub her out of the game, I knew it was even worse than I feared. Julie wasn't just our captain and most vocal player, she was an inexhaustible wellspring of positive energy, no matter whether things were going well or going haywire. As much as anybody on our team, she understood that in late stages of a World Cup or the Olympics, the margin of victory so often doesn't come down to transcendent skill or highlight-reel heroics, but the willingness to grind it out just a little harder than the opponent. It could be winning a ball in midfield, making a forty-yard run to support your defense and defuse a threat, getting all ball on a sliding tackle an instant before an opponent unleashes a shot. In my decade on the national team, we weren't always the best side on the field, but we almost always were the most determined and the most resilient. Julie epitomized those qualities.

Aly Wagner came on to replace Julie, and we continued to connect and have the better of the play. Mia carved up the German defense again and again. She'd carefully watched film of the 2003 World Cup match with Germany, and found that she was not aggressive enough, too often deployed out wide and sending mostly harmless crosses into the box. To break down the Germans' tight and disciplined defense, she knew she had to hold the ball more, take people on, and beat them to draw the defense out of shape. The Germans, meanwhile, finally had their first shot on goal in the seventy-seventh minute but weren't generating any consistent threats.

The clock moved to the eightieth minute, then the eighty-fifth. We hit the ninetieth minute and now only a couple of minutes of stoppage time were separating us from the gold-medal game. We hadn't been in one since Sydney four years earlier. The Germans, in full desperation mode, sent everyone forward, hoping for a miracle. In the second minute of stoppage time, Germany's Isabell Bachor had the ball and waited for an opening to shoot. The ref was going to blow her whistle to end it any second. Bachor found a little space and fired her shot. I was tracking it the whole way, but then it smacked into Joy Fawcett's hip, changed direction, and whistled past me into the net.

I couldn't comprehend what had just happened. The Germans jumped for joy, literally, the improbable equalizer entitling them to every bit of their happiness. The whistle blew.

A little late, I thought.

As we came off for a five-minute rest period before extra time, I had already put it on the shelf. Sometimes with goals like that it's easier; you can't second-guess yourself or pinpoint a glaring error. The ball took a crazy deflection and went in. What can you do? I drank water and stretched and as I looked around I was loving what I was seeing and feeling from my team. We'd just suffered a crushing turn of events and there wasn't a trace of despondence. The game was tied and it was up to us to outwork and outgrind one of the hardest-working, toughest-minded teams in the world. We ran back out and we were ready. I was struck at how different my feeling was from the semifinal a year before.

We're going to do whatever we have to do to win this thing, I thought.

• • •

We came out hard, unyielding. Heather O'Reilly, who entered in the seventy-fifth minute, went at the German defense from the start, flying around like a teenager who had had too much Mountain Dew. HAO—her nickname, short for Heather Ann O'Reilly—was nineteen years old and a sinewy live wire of energy. About two minutes into the extra time, she created space on the left wing, cut in toward goal, drew Rottenberg out, and then deked her. HAO (pronounced HAY-o) took another touch and had an open goal in front of her—and hit the post.

The game was still tied. HAO was aghast that she hadn't buried it (she said so later). Even at her tender age she had the maturity and poise to forget it and put her rampant energy to something more productive. Like Mia and Lil and Carla (and April) and about a thousand others, HAO came to the USWNT out of UNC, where Anson Dorrance won so many national championships the NCAA should've just renamed its tournament the UNC Invitational. HAO grew up in East Brunswick, New Jersey, with a Mia Hamm poster on her bedroom wall. Now, in the Olympic semifinal, if she looked to her right, HAO could see the real Mia Hamm with the ball. About five minutes after HAO hit the post, Mia took a pass from Abby and made a run down the right side. True to her film study, she took a defender on, pushing the ball into the final third, drawing defensive attention, pulling the Germans a little bit out of shape. The defense stretched to cover her. HAO saw some space and made a run. Mia, the poster girl, slid an artful pass to her. HAO got on the end of it, took a gentle touch, and was alone with Rottenberg again. HAO slid the ball past her, and we were in the finals, thanks to the sublime skills of a young Tar Heel and an old Tar Heel.

Meanwhile, Brazil got by Sweden, 1–0, in the other semifinal. So the gold-medal game was going to be a rematch of a group-stage game that had stirred up hard feelings all the way around. The Brazilians were loaded with motivational ammo for the final. First, they had dominated possession and outplayed us in our first game and lost. Second, their coach told the whole world we were dirty and won only because we cheap-shotted his best players. He went on a rant and April called him out for the inappropriateness of his rant. My own motivation was much simpler: I hadn't won an Olympic gold medal in eight years. I probably would never get another chance. I wanted to win it for Pops.

• • •

Twelve days before my thirty-third birthday, I sprinted into the U.S. goal in Greece, ready for my third Olympic gold-medal game, but my first as a starter since 1996. I was at my athletic pinnacle. I was stronger, fitter, smarter, more explosive. I appreciated the position I had now more than I ever had. The dots were not hard to connect. Not long ago I'd lost that position because I was lazy and complacent. I had to work my ass off to get it back. When you have to empty the tank every day to achieve something, it always feels more rewarding.

Because you know you've earned it.

"There's not a goalkeeper in the world who can make some of the saves you make," April told me.

Before I left the hotel to get on the bus, I had a talk with myself:

You are about to leave this room to play for an Olympic gold medal. When you return, you will have a medal around your neck. Will it be gold? Or will it be silver? Think about what you have to do today against Brazil. Pour everything you have, mentally, physically, spiritually, to get the outcome you dream of. Later tonight you will be back here. Imagine yourself getting off the elevator and arriving at the room. You open the door. You walk in and you're so happy you can't even find the words. You have celebrated with your mom at the postgame party. You have honored your dad. You put your new medal on the nightstand next to you. Its color is gold. You are an Olympic champion, again.

The U.S. had never lost to Brazil in games that I've started (10–0). I didn't know whether that was in the Brazilians' heads, but I hoped it was. We got the best possible news before the game: Julie was going to start. When she hobbled off in the semis, I thought she was done for the tournament, but our crack training staff did wonders. Julie wasn't one hundred percent, but knowing her she would've played on crutches.

In the second minute, Lil, who had goals in three straight games and been our best player the whole tournament, made a sliding interception of a pass deep in Brazil's end. Her momentum carried her into Elane, who stumbled over her and on the way to the ground, stepped on Lil's arm with her right cleat. Mia came over right away to tell the referee that it was a cheap shot and the ref shooed her away. I wasn't shocked that Brazil put a hurt on one of our star players so early in the game. Four minutes later, Elane was on the right side, pushing the attack. She hammered a low drive to the far post. I dove right and made a fingertip save.

Elane was in the middle of everything. She took Lil down in the tenth minute and, right after, wrapped her arm around Abby, taking her to the ground and then falling on top of her. It was ridiculous that there was no yellow card. Brazil also flashed its incomparable skill, especially Marta, its eighteen-year-old wunderkind, who made a fifty-yard run, slaloming through us like a skier zipping in and out of gates.

The half moved into its final fifteen minutes, and the brutally physical play continued. Abby went in hard on Formiga, and no foul is called, and moments later, Mónica just destroyed Abby from behind, with a takedown worthy of a linebacker.

Brazil has again carried the play, but in the thirty-eighth minute, Brandi won a ball at the midfield circle and nudged it ahead to Lindsay Tarpley, a junior at North Carolina. Tarpley took a couple of dribbles, before blistering a shot from twenty-five yards out, across the flow of play. Andreia, the Brazilian keeper, dove but couldn't stop it.

Lindsay Tarpley had given us a 1–0 lead.

The Brazilians came right back at us. A scramble in the box followed an indirect kick, and Cristiane ripped a left-footed rocket. I dove right and knocked it away. We took our 1–0 lead into halftime. I'd only had to make two saves, but they may have been the best ones I've made in the tournament.

The second half brings no letup in intensity. In the forty-seventh minute, Mónica continued to play the heavy, throwing a cross-body block on Mia, earning a richly deserved yellow. Marta seemed to be on the ball more than every other Brazilian combined. She hit a low drive on a free kick that deflected off somebody in the wall and was running to the far corner. I raced to my right, and sprawled to grab it. With under seventeen minutes left, Cristiane outran our defense, beat a double-team, and crossed it. I stepped out of the net to cut down the angle and got a hand on it. However, Pretinha, on the doorstep just behind Julie, knocked it in.

Tie game.

Brazil was flying now, attacking in yellow waves. Cristiane fired a shot inches outside the right post. In the seventy-seventh minute, she carved us up and curled a shot to my right. It ricocheted off the post.

Thanks, Pops, I thought.

We were like a staggering fighter trying to stay on her feet. In the eighty-eighth minute, here came Marta, attacking on the right and slipping a sweet ball to Pretinha, who had a wide-open look in front of me. She drove a left-footed shot to my right. I dove but couldn't get it.

This time, the ball ricocheted off the left post.

You are coming up big, Pops, I thought.

Pops and the left post got us to the end of regulation. We needed to get our stuff together, fast. This was the first international tournament to be played without a golden goal, meaning we would play out the full thirty minutes no matter what. The Brazilians weren't slowing down at all. Pretinha got on the end of a cross, but I grabbed her header in the second minute of extra time. Marta put on a spin move to elude two defenders, rifling a cross that produced a low drive by Daniela. In the final minute of the first extra time period, Cristiane escaped our defense and came at me on the left side. I slid over to cover the near post. I wanted to make her go wide, a tougher shot. Cristiane went for the near post but missed to the left.

The Brazilians were mentally exhausting for me to play against because they could create magic in an instant. Yet I feel as energized and determined as I was when we started. Midway through the second extra-time period, Cat Reddick sent a long ball into the box where Abby and Mónica, the two tallest players on the field, were running toward goal in lockstep. Mónica defended it brilliantly and headed the ball over the byline for a corner kick. Lil took it and dropped a left-footed ball to the center of the box, about seven yards out. Abby was closely marked but rose up and headed it toward the upper left corner, driving it past Andréia, into the net.

We were up a goal with seven minutes remaining, and the moment the ball landed, Abby took off running, zigging and zagging, raising her fist, swarmed by her teammates. We stayed compact and did a good job killing off the remaining time. Soon there was another swarm, an even bigger one, and I was in the middle of it, a green jersey in a sea of red, after the ref blew her whistle and the Olympic soccer tournament ended. Eight years after we'd won in Athens, Georgia, we got the same outcome in Athens, Greece. The first one was out of this world, this one even more so. We gave the 91ers—Joy Fawcett, Julie Foudy, and Mia Hamm—the send-off they deserved. As I stood on the medal platform and sang the national anthem, all

With my mom after winning gold at the 2004
Olympics in Greece. She always told me I could be
whatever I wanted to be. She was right.

I could think of was how much my father must be loving this. At the
postgame party, my mom was equal parts exhausted and ecstatic. In
the wee hours of the morning, I walked back into the hotel room I'd
left ten hours earlier. I put my new gold medal on my nightstand. I
returned a champion.

CHAPTER FOURTEEN

TEAM TURMOIL

While I was in the process of winning a gold medal, another major event was unfolding in my life. I was falling in love with Naomi Gonzalez. Naomi was the massage therapist for the USWNT. As this was a workplace romance, we had to be discreet about it. We met when she came to the team from the Boston Breakers of the WUSA, on the recommendation of Kristine Lilly. Naomi was probably the most gifted massage therapist I've ever had. She had a deep and intuitive understanding of physiology, with a healer's heart and hands. The sign on her office door said "House of Pain," and yes, sometimes it hurt like hell to get a deep-tissue massage from her, but you always came out feeling so much better. I have little doubt that the work she did, along with our training staff, was why Julie was able to play 120 minutes in the gold-medal game against Brazil.

Naomi and I started our relationship following my father's passing. I was hurting and vulnerable and being with her gave me such comfort. Together with Cindy Parlow, Naomi helped me through the greatest loss of my life. I wanted to be with her every moment I could, but our first quality time together came the day after the gold-medal game. We went to the open-air markets and visited ruins and had a lovely al fresco dinner overlooking the Parthenon, where we were served a heaping platter of lamb and various Greek delicacies. It was perfect, and even the bird that decided to drop some doo-doo on my shoulder couldn't ruin it. I washed it off and went right back to Naomi. We walked for a while after dinner and then stopped by a hotel to see if we could get a room for the night. The hotel was booked. We stopped at a second hotel, and a third, and a fourth. They were all full. At the sixth hotel we tried, a small place on a side street, Naomi asked the front-desk clerk if there was any hope at all of getting a room—maybe if there was a cancellation.

'I'm sorry, but we are completely full," the clerk said. "There's only one room that isn't occupied and they are supposed to check in later." Not one to give up easily, Naomi asked the clerk if fifty euros in his pocket, on top of the cost of the room, might help find a vacancy.

"A room just opened up," the clerk said. Naomi handed him his fifty euros and we checked in, delighted to continue our Athenian adventure.

We checked out early the next day and decided it was time to go public with our relationship. Naomi loved her work—she dreamed of being in the Olympics from a young age, too—but it was clear that her personal and professional code of ethics would not permit her to continue working for the team if she was my girlfriend. She resigned at the end of the year.

Not long after, in February 2005, came another resignation, this one from April Heinrichs. She was replaced by her assistant, Greg Ryan. I didn't know Greg well—I was much closer to Phil Wheddon, our goalkeeper coach—but even before the coaching change happened, I was already pondering my future. I was only thirty-three years old, but I'd been with the team for eleven years and part of me thought it might be a good time to retire. We had just won the gold and I still hadn't fully processed the loss of my dad. The WUSA had gone belly up. Naomi and I had moved into a cool apartment in the Castro District in San Francisco, one of the epicenters of American gay culture, just two blocks from the Harvey Milk Civil Rights Academy, a public school named for the late San Francisco city supervisor and gay activist who was murdered by a homophobic political opponent. We lived on Eureka Street and we found something better than gold: a rich life together full of love, laughter, and community. Our place wasn't fancy—a second-floor walk-up—but it had two bay windows that let the light pour in and was in the heart of everything. As completely comfortable as I was with my sexuality, I'd lived as an extreme minority for my whole life. In the Castro District, I wasn't a minority at all and it was liberating. I never wondered if people were looking at me funny or judging me. Naomi and I made friends, hit the bars, marched in parades, and joined a gay softball league. I played shortstop and hit a lot of home runs. One night we had a game in fog so thick over San Francisco Bay that fly balls literally disappeared into it. I hit one into the fog that night and have no idea where it landed.

"When Bri got up, we basically waited to see how far it would go," Naomi said.

And then there was an annual lesbian soccer event called Festival of the Babes. Many of the players dressed up in costumes. I didn't wear one and was wary about the whole thing, as I really didn't want to have my soccer future jeopardized by an injury incurred at the Festival of the Babes. That would be a tough conversation to have with Greg Ryan. But Naomi was into it and said we'd have fun. And we did have fun, for a time. I was playing the field and was on the attack, dribbling at the opponents' defense, when someone came in hard and ankle-high, slide-tackling me to the ground, getting no ball but a lot of Bri. It was a vicious play, plain and simple. Pain surged through my left ankle. They didn't do red cards at the Festival of the Babes, but this definitely warranted one.

"What the f*** is wrong with you?" Naomi screamed at the opponent who took me down.

I don't know if I was a trophy for this imbecile, who could brag about taking out a World Cup and Olympic champion and didn't care. I got helped off the field and was tended to well by the medical people on hand who iced it, elevated it and told me to see a doctor. I got it X-rayed and it turned out I had a ligament tear and a hairline fracture. They sent me home with crutches. I had physical therapy and rested it and iced it, but it was still a couple of months before it felt right again.

All because of a fast and loose lesbian who wanted to show how tough she was.

It was my one and only appearance at the Festival of the Babes.

The one positive about the injury was that it gave me more time to think about the future. I'd never thought of soccer as something I would do until I couldn't play anymore and had to be hauled off the field. There were other things I wanted to do. Real estate was interesting to me. For years I'd read books about money and finance, and that was a potential direction, too. Naomi had a connection at First Republic Bank in San Francisco and I applied for a position there. The person who interviewed me knew about my soccer career and I took that as a good thing. She explained that if I got the position, I would start as a teller to get a solid grounding in the retail part of the business and build up from there. I got the job and on Day 1. I wondered if this was really it: Was I going to leave the goal forever to be a San Francisco banker?

I had an open mind. I made an earnest attempt to acclimate to being a teller, thinking about what it might lead to, but life in the window didn't really do it for me. Hours of looking at the glaring green of the computer screen gave me headaches, and the sameness of each day wore on me. It wasn't the bank's fault; it didn't hire me to make diving saves, after all, but to learn the banking ropes as a teller and work my way up the ladder into the wealth management group with First Republic. I found out I was not a cubicle/window sort of person. It was just too small a world.

I was still trying to figure it all out. After years of traveling the world and moving all over the country—in a dozen years since leaving UMass, I'd lived in fifteen different places—I yearned to settle into my life with Naomi, to take a deep dive into the Castro District. I did that, but the truth is that I was still lost. In the hypercompetitive world I'd lived in, pressure was a constant and urgency was almost a given. You had to be the best, work the hardest, stop the shots that nobody else was stopping. I signed up for it, and I loved it, but I also knew life wouldn't be like that forever, even if the competitor in me was in denial about it. It's one of those strange parts of being an athlete. You are blessed with these physical gifts and they help take you on an extraordinary journey. But bundled with all that is a feeling of invincibility, a misguided belief that you will be able to perform at this level for as long as you want. It's a sweet concept. It's also a lie. I knew I would not be able to make a diving save like the one I made on Cristiane in Athens forever. I wasn't ready to move to Florida and start playing shuffleboard, but I was trying to come to terms with my athletic mortality. So that was my quandary in the spring of 2005. Was it time to move on, to make sure I would not be another athlete who fools herself that it will last forever? Or was I ready to plunge back into the competitive fray?

I wasn't sure. Greg called in March 2005 and asked what my plans were, and if I would be coming back to camp right away. I thanked him for reaching out but said I needed more time. I did *not* tell him that when my dad passed, it almost felt that some of my passion for the game did as well.

Greg didn't seem thrilled about my response, but I wasn't going to change my decision and rush back. I wasn't sure if I was coming back at all. As months passed, I discovered that the endorphin rush you get when you compete, and compete well, at a high level gets into your system, and withdrawal does not come easily—especially when your teammates want you to come back.

The calls came early in 2006, from various teammates, and all carried the same message:

"Please come back, Bri. We need you." It's not as if I was holding out to have people beg me to return, but I was moved that my teammates would reach out. I called Greg and told him I wanted to come into the next camp. I hadn't done a good job at all of staying in touch with Greg, keeping him apprised of my thinking. In fact, I'd done a terrible job. I just kind of disappeared. For all he knew I might've still been a bank teller. My first camp back was in the summer of 2006. Greg seemed to be happy I was back, but not *that* happy. One of the first things he did was fill me in on where I stood.

"Hope's my keeper. I want you to know that," he said.

"OK," I said, taken aback.

My gut feeling was that Greg was ticked off that I'd rejected his overture early in 2005 and felt disrespected that I had been so out of touch. To me, clearly, this was his payback. I thought it was odd. I knew Hope Solo was a talented, young goalkeeper who had shown promise. I knew that her kicking game and her feet were superior to mine. I certainly didn't expect to be handed my job back. I just wanted to compete and push each other to get better. That's how it works. As far as I know, neither Tony nor April ever told Mary Harvey or Siri Mullinix or anyone else, "Bri is my keeper." I didn't even *want* to be their anointed keeper. I wanted to earn it . . . to train hard, compete hard and ultimately be the goalkeeper who the coaching staff thought gave the team the best chance to win. But from the day I came back, Greg told me, in so many words, that there would be no competition.

I went about my work the same way I always did. I had nothing against Hope. We got along well and I supported her in every way I could. Hope got almost all the starts for the rest of 2006 and into 2007. She was playing well, and we were winning games. I may not have cared for how Greg "welcomed" me back, but the greater good of the team, and upholding our team-first culture, was more important than anything.

I got a start in the Four Nations Tournament in China to begin 2007, and another in one Algarve game, but the big games were Hope's and the results were impossible to ignore. We were undefeated half-way through the year and looking formidable with the World Cup approaching in September. In mid-June we were training in Cleveland before a friendly with China when Hope found out that her father had died. It was three years to the week since I'd lost my father, and the loss was still with me every day. Suddenly we were not just fellow goalkeepers; we were sisters in grief. I sat with Hope on her hotel bed and held her hand. I hugged her and cried with her and just tried to be there and to be compassionate, the same way that Cindy Parlow had been there for me. Hope left to be with her family and attend the services in Richland, Washington, her hometown. I played the game in Cleveland against China, and again one week later in New Jersey, where we played Brazil. It was the first time we'd played the Brazilians since the gold-medal game in Athens. We won both games, 2–0, but that didn't matter as much as making sure Hope was OK and getting support as she coped with a loss nobody can prepare you for.

Hope returned about three weeks later and seemed OK.

"I am here for you anytime you want to talk, or even if you just want to cry," I told her. "I know how much this hurts." Hope thanked me. I think she sincerely believed I would be there for her, no matter what. We became closer than ever. In Hope's first game back, she played the full ninety minutes and we beat Norway, 1–0. I was so happy for her. I knew that being back in goal, doing well, would provide the best possible respite from her grief. The victory kept us undefeated for 2007, with an unbeaten streak of forty-six games. It was a good way to head to China to begin the fifth Women's World Cup. Our first game was against a hungry, technically skilled North Korea side, in a downpour. It wasn't our best showing. Hope let a head-high shot slip through her hands. Abby hit an angled rocket to tie it, but North Korea took the lead again on a deflected shot after a poor clearance. Fortunately, HAO one-timed a ball in the box into the upper corner in the sixty-ninth minute, allowing us to avert the unthinkable and get out with a 2–2 draw. The next two group-stage games, against Sweden (2–0) and Nigeria (1–0) went more smoothly, moving us into the quarterfinals against England.

I didn't know it at the time—I'm not sure how many people did—but Hope was already getting on Greg's list. She missed a mandatory team dinner and blew curfew leading up to the England game. Greg stuck with Hope and we won, 3–0. We were into the semifinals against Brazil. Hope had put up three straight shutouts since the shaky start. The day before the Brazil match, Hope was in the meal room at our hotel in China. An assistant coach said that Greg would like to have a word with her after dinner.

Hope didn't like the sound of that at all. She liked it even less when Greg told her he was going to start me against Brazil, citing my track record (I was 12–0 against them and had allowed only 0.41 goals per game) and adding that my quickness and shot-stopping ability matched up better against them. Greg had told me a couple of months earlier that if we played Brazil in the World Cup I might get the start, but I had no idea about his decision until I heard it—not from Greg, but from Hope. She was in the adjoining hotel room, and from the sound of it she was having the mother of all tantrums, complete with thrown furniture, holes in the wall, screaming, crying, and other loud noises I couldn't identify. When you see pieces of broken furniture in a hotel hallway, you kind of get the feeling one of the guests is not pleased.

Cat Reddick Whitehill (she got married), Aly Wagner, and Angela Hucles, all close friends of Hope's, were in the room with her, trying without success to console her, and to not let this become a divisive issue for the team. The veteran leaders on the team—even some who were surprised by the move—supported Greg and his decision, because that's what you do. You stay together. You put the team over self. Hope was having none of it. She was enraged and she wanted everyone to know it. And thus began her effort to marshal all the support she could for her belief that Greg had made a colossal screwup, and basically stoke a USWNT Civil War: Team Hope vs. Team Bri.

"It was pretty sad and pathetic when you look back on it," Cat Whitehill said. "That is where the mentality of the team went haywire. It started with that."

Amid the cacophony, I got a call saying Greg wanted to speak with me.

"I'm going with you as the starter against Brazil," he told me. "You've always had their number and I know you are going to have it again."

I'd done well when we shut out Brazil in the Meadowlands during Hope's absence, but that was the last time I'd been in a game. Lil and others had suggested to Greg that he work me in for a game, or at least a half, to help me stay game-sharp leading up to the World Cup, but for whatever reason that never happened. Still, I'd been on my game in training, and my associations were nothing but positive; I'd played the two greatest games of my life against Brazil—in the 1999 World Cup semis and the 2004 Olympic final.

It turned out there were other factors involved in Greg's decision. My big-game history, with a World Cup victory and two Olympic gold medals, certainly provided a comfort level. But the larger issue was that some veteran players were not completely sold on Hope; some of them apparently told Greg that they were more comfortable with me in goal because I communicated constantly and effectively with field players.

The reaction to the lineup change in the media ranged from surprise to outright shock. Julie Foudy, now a TV commentator, said she thought I'd be fine and do a good job, but questioned the wisdom of the goalkeeper switch, arguing that it could become a distraction and that it was a case of overthinking. Tony DiCicco, one of my greatest supporters, called me the best to ever play the position but thought it was a mistake at this point in the tournament. Others thought it was ill-advised in view of Hope's recent form—three hundred minutes without allowing a goal.

Even Phil Wheddon, our goalkeeping coach and another big booster of mine, didn't think it prudent to make a change in the semifinals of a World Cup.

Greg told reporters the criticism didn't faze him.

"That's not important to me at all," he said. "From Day 1 I've just tried to make decisions that will help us win the next game. The way the Brazilians play in terms of creating off the dribble in the penalty box and making a goalkeeper make reaction-type saves, I think Bri is the best goalkeeper in the world in those situations."

With cameras and tape recorders rolling, Hope took the high road.

"I was very taken back, but that's the nature of sports and it happens," she said. "He has his reasons."

Behind the scenes was a tad different. I certainly didn't expect Hope to be happy with Greg's decision; I wouldn't have been either. But I promise you that, no matter how ticked off I was, I would never have done what she did—which was to take a sledgehammer to the foundation of the team. You want to be angry about being benched? I get it. But to embark on a campaign to sow disunity, to put yourself over the team? That I don't get. It's an unpardonable offense in a team sport. It wasn't just selfish; it was the greatest attack there had ever been on the culture of that team—a culture that has made the USWNT one of the most dominant forces in global sport for going on four decades.

I felt for Hope and her loss. I grieved for her with my full heart. I know that Greg's decision hit her hard, but I also know that when you are a grown-up member of a team, you have to put your own agenda aside and think of the larger mission. Hope was not willing to do that.

It made the next forty-eight hours the worst experience of my entire USWNT career.

Look, reasonable people can disagree about a coach's decision in a high-stakes game. Nobody owed more to, or had a higher regard for, Tony DiCicco, than I did. Tony believed Greg should've stuck with Hope. Fair enough. It didn't change my opinion of him or make me want to kneecap him. Julie Foudy was my friend and teammate and in so many ways the firestarter behind some of our greatest teams; she didn't agree with Greg, either. OK, Jules. I disagree but you move on and stick together and keep the greater good in mind.

Hope Solo had little interest in the greater good. She pouted openly and talked about the matter incessantly to her closest friends and supporters—mostly the younger players. By the time we walked on the field, it was almost as if we were two squads—a split forged by one player. This is the part that people have completely whiffed on. Hope didn't even pretend to want to put the team above herself. She poisoned the well. She made herself the victim. *I can't believe Greg did this to me. It's so unfair.* She wanted to make sure Greg paid big-time for his decision. In the process, she all but guaranteed that the whole team would pay.

And the whole team did.

I did everything I could to fend off the negativity. My entire focus was to come through for my team and get us to the gold-medal game and give us a shot at winning our first World Cup since that hot afternoon in the Rose Bowl eight years earlier. I prepared as intensely as I ever had in my life, lifted up by the love I had for my teammates, visualizing myself standing strong and united with them, shoulder to shoulder and arm in arm as we rose above the quagmire and marched to victory.

That was my dream and I held tight to it from the moment we took the field. But the fact is that with everything that had happened we were like the 300 Spartans going up against the Persian Army. Of all the ways you can go into a World Cup semifinal, being divided is about the worst. These games are hard enough to win without turmoil. With it, you are asking for a disaster, which is exactly what we got.

In the early minutes, Leslie Osborne, a defender, didn't hear me calling for the ball and put a low header by me for an own goal. In the U.S. family and friends sections of the stands, Hope's supporters cheered. *They cheered.* People sitting right alongside them saw it, heard it. They cheered an own goal against the U.S. Marta, cementing her status as the world's greatest player, sambaed through three defenders and struck a low shot towards the post. I dove and got my hand on it. It's a ball I often save. I didn't save it this time. Nobody felt worse about it than I did.

Hope's supporters cheered. Again.

We were down two goals and then in the first minute of stoppage time at the end of the half, Shannon Boxx got her heel clipped by Cristiane and they both went sprawling. Boxxy had picked up a yellow card for a late challenge early in the half. Somehow the ref carded her again for getting tripped by Cristiane, and she was sent off. It was one of the worst calls I have ever seen. We were down two goals and playing eleven on ten, without one of our top players. It was a massive hole, no doubt, but we, as a team, had the strongest mentality in the sport. You never count the U.S. out. Ever.

Until now.

"Our team had given up," Cat Whitehill said. "I tried to rally the troops, but nobody wanted to be rallied. It was only halftime, but everybody just quit."

The energy in the room was toxic. If we'd had a stronger coach, maybe that could've been headed off, but that wasn't the case. I had forty-five minutes to play, a game to try to turn around. That's all I was thinking about.

Find a way to get this done.

But it was clear our spirit was irreparably broken as the second half began. The Brazilians did whatever they wanted. Marta danced on the ball as if she were fooling around at Carnival. Formiga, a midfielder, beat our defense down the left flank and centered to Cristiane, who was completely alone in front. I had no chance. That made it 3–0. Marta finished it off with one of the most magical one v. one moves you will ever see, backheeling a pass to herself, eluding two defenders and tucking the ball in the corner.

If it sounds bad, the reality was even worse. We were the No. 1 team in the world and it was the most lopsided World Cup defeat we've ever had. I thought we'd hit bottom when the game ended, but I was wrong. After major games, players file through an area known as the mixed zone, where reporters, clustered behind a barricade, bark out questions to try to grab quotes for their stories. Some people stop and talk, but after a defeat like this one, most of us just want to march on by. A Canadian reporter asked Hope if she had a comment. Hope was accompanied by Aaron Heifetz, the USWNT press officer, who fully expected this to happen and did all he could to make sure Hope did *not* stop, because he knew what would happen if she did. Heif told the reporter Hope hadn't played and there were other players who would be more relevant, and kept moving her through, away from the barkers.

Hope stopped, pivoted away from Heif, and said, "I want to talk." And talk she did: "It was the wrong decision, and I think anyone who knows anything about the game knows that. There's no doubt in my mind I would have made those saves. And the fact of the matter is it's not 2004 anymore. It's not 2004. It's now 2007 and you have to live in the present and you can't live by big names. You can't live in the past. It doesn't matter what somebody did in an Olympic gold-medal game three years ago. Now is what matters, and that's what I think."

While the Brazilians, who were staying at the same hotel, were partying it up, word spread quickly about Hope's interview. Lil, our captain, asked Hope to come to her room. A bunch of us—Abby, Christie Pearce, Boxxy, Kate Markgraf—were there. The message Lil delivered was essentially that Hope had put herself above the team and obliterated the core values that this team had been built on.

Hope didn't see it that way. "Well, I'm a professional athlete—of course I believe I could make a difference on the field, just like you guys do," she said. "We should all believe we can make a difference or else why are we professional athletes?"

Kate, who had played through a painful ankle injury, was furious that Hope had buried me after the classy way I'd handled the transition, mentoring and supporting her.

"Who the f*** do you think you are? I can't even be in the same room with you!" Kate said. She stormed out and slammed the door.

Hope apologized to me and said that she respected me and never intended to hurt me. That was her theme, over and over . . . she would never do anything to hurt me. The apology felt hollow. On her MySpace page, Hope sought to clarify things:

"Although I stand strong in everything I said, the true disheartening moment for me was realizing it could look as though I was taking a direct shot at my own teammate. I would never throw such a low blow. Never. . . . In my eyes there's no justification to put down a teammate. That is not what I was doing."

This didn't do much for me either, honestly. What do you mean, "It could look as though you were taking a direct shot at your own teammate?" How could it be construed as anything *but* a direct shot? You talked about how you would've made those saves and won the game and I was over the hill. Is that supposed to be lifting me up?

I had compassion for Hope and her terrible loss; I truly did. I said nothing about it at the time, preferring to keep my pain to myself, but it hurt like hell. I did everything I could to rise above the circumstances and deliver for my team but never had a fair shot at making it happen. I felt cheated. At a really low moment, I was betrayed by someone I considered a friend. Hope went on to have a great career, winning two Olympic gold medals and a World Cup—the same as me. I give her all the props as a world-class goalkeeper. The hurt from the 2007 stuck with me for a long time. Too long. I feel no ill will toward Hope whatsoever. I have forgiveness in my heart.

Before the bronze-medal game against Norway, we had a team meeting. Hope insisted again that people had misunderstood her message. The team voted to bar her from practice and all team activities, as well as the game.

"We have moved forward with twenty players who have stood by each other," Greg told reporters.

After the Brazil debacle in the semifinals of the 2007 World Cup, we crushed Norway to take third place. Our response was one of the proudest moments of my career. (Credit: John Toss/ISIphotos.com)

I had a strong feeling that we were going to crush Norway and win the bronze, and we did, 4–1. We played with our trademark focus and energy—exactly what we didn't have in the semifinals—and I considered it one of the proudest moments of my career because it spoke to our collective character, the way we responded to the whole mess.

As we flew home from China as a team (Hope was not on our plane), I felt honored to be surrounded by so many strong, principled, championship-caliber women. There wasn't a whole lot more to feel good about in that moment.

I never wore the crest again in a major international tournament.

CHAPTER FIFTEEN

BROKENNESS

Greg Ryan won forty-five games and lost just two in his two and a half years at the helm of the U.S. Women's National Team. The second of the two defeats—the debacle against Brazil in China—was enough to cost him his job. His successor was Pia Sundhage, a former star for the Swedish national team. Pia had to get our house in order in a hurry, with the 2008 Summer Olympics not even a year off.

"We are going to start with a clean slate," Pia told me when we met. I wasn't sure what that clean state consisted of, but it quickly became clear that Hope Solo was going to be part of it, and I was not. It's a time-honored custom for the starting goalkeeper on a soccer team to wear jersey No. 1. I'd worn it for more than a dozen years. I didn't expect to wear it if I wasn't starting, but I didn't expect to be given jersey No. 22, a number typically associated with third-string goalkeepers, either. I was thirty-six and fit and believed I had a lot of good saves left in me. I also had a hard time understanding how a player who had done everything possible to sabotage the team was welcomed back, while I was basically booted out the door. My opinion on either matter, alas, did not count. Pia's top two goalkeepers were Hope and Nicole Barnhart, and though I didn't think I was treated fairly, you can't argue with the results, because we shut out Brazil in the Olympic final in Beijing, 1–0, winning our third gold medal in four tries. As an alternate, I made the trip to China but never suited up for a game. I was given a ticket and sat in the stands with U.S. Soccer staff. It was great to be connected to a winning team, but it's hard to feel a part of the things when you never even put on a uniform. Three months later, I came on at halftime for Nicole Barnhart during a friendly against North Korea in Cincinnati. The match ended in a scoreless draw, and the only reason I remember it is that it was the last game I played for my country.

I would've retired then and there, but another professional league—Women's Professional Soccer—was starting up and my agent, Rob Raju, got me a contract with the Washington Freedom. Naomi and I moved to an apartment in Rockville, Maryland, and for the first time since the WUSA folded, I was a club team player. A balky hamstring and then knee surgery kept me out for much of 2009, but I was eager to get started in 2010. Abby Wambach, Cat Whitehill, Becky Sauerbrunn, and Allie Long were all on the club, and so was Homare Sawa, the Japanese midfield standout, and my goal was simply to have a strong, positive season or two and figure out the future afterward.

I got my first start in the third week of the season in Philadelphia. It rained that night— April 25, 2010. The only reason I know this is that someone told me. Our game was against the Philadelphia Independence, at West Chester University. At thirty-eight years old, I was normally the backup to Erin McLeod, but Erin had duty with the Canadian national team that weekend, so I got the start.

Thirty-five minutes into a scoreless match, Lori Lindsey of the Independence took an off-target shot to my left. I came hard off my line to pounce on it before an onrushing Independence forward could play it, the way I'd done about ten thousand times before. I got low and scooped up the ball, but just as I did, Lianne Sanderson, an English international and a 165-pound forward, plowed into me, hard, her knee crashing into my right temple. The two of us rolled over in a heap. I held on to the ball. No whistle blew.

When I got to my feet, I felt woozy. I took a couple of seconds to collect myself before I distributed the ball.

"C'mon, Keep. Play," the ref said.

I passed the ball out and play continued. I hoped the cobwebs in my head would clear in a minute or two. They did not. My vision was blurry and my balance was off, but I said nothing and the game went on. I felt as though I was leaning to my left, but I couldn't be sure. I kept thinking I'd lock back into my normal self and all would be fine. The ref blew the whistle for halftime and I started walking off toward our bench. I was still leaning left, staggering like a drunk coming out of a bar. That's when I had an idea this wasn't something I was just going to shake off.

Our trainer, Emily Fortunato, ran out to meet me.

"Bri, are you OK?" she said.

"No," I said.

She guided me, arm in arm, to the locker room, where she did an assessment and asked a few basic questions. I knew my name and knew I was in Philadelphia playing soccer. That was about it. I didn't know what day it was. She gave me three simple words to remember, and then a minute or two later asked me to repeat the words. I couldn't remember any of them. I felt slightly nauseous and had a headache. The overhead lights in the locker room looked like klieg lights to me. Every sound was like a crashing cymbal. Three times in my career, I had suffered a documented concussion and was removed from training sessions and/or matches. There were quite a few others that I just played through. None of them ever felt like this. The Independence team doctor examined me and wanted me to spend the night in the hospital for observation. I was a hot mess but wanted no part of staying over in a big-city hospital 150 miles from home. Our trainer promised to monitor me closely on the bus trip back to Maryland. The doctor backed off.

The Freedom placed me on two-week injured reserve and I spent the next few days following typical concussion protocol: resting in a dark room, limiting TV and computer time and any kind of stimulation. I was exhausted but couldn't sleep. The symptoms got only marginally better, crashing into me like waves on the shore. The team medical staff had me come in the following week for baseline testing. I bombed. I was functioning at something like twenty percent capacity, which is about how I felt, and to make things worse, Naomi and I were in the process of breaking up after six years together. When we lived in the Castro District, her hope was that I'd retire from soccer and we'd put down roots there. But then I decided to come back to the team, and she'd spent the last few years seeing me come and go and living in places she didn't want to live in. Naomi cared for me when I was injured and remained one of my dearest friends, but we weren't a couple anymore and that hurt like hell.

The team moved me to the one-month injured list, and then the season-ending injured list. That was fine with me, because goalkeeping was the last thing on my mind. My eyes are usually bright and almost back-lit, full of energy. Now they looked vacant. My training as a competitor and athlete was to power through everything, keep going forward no matter what, but I knew this was the worst injury I'd ever had. Even months later, I felt as if I were a different person, walking around in somebody else's body, unplugged from the rest of humanity. In the wilderness. It sucked.

At the end of 2010, the Freedom was purchased by an Internet entrepreneur named Dan Borislow, who renamed the club the magic-Jack and relocated it to West Palm Beach. Dan offered me the general manager job and said he'd pay me $75,000 per year. I still wasn't close to being right, still had headaches, but the money wasn't bad and I thought the change of scenery would help heal some of my wounds from the breakup and maybe give me a fresh start.

So I started a new career as a front-office executive. Or so I thought. The reality was that I *was* the front office. And the ticket office. And the marketing office. I had to assemble not just a roster of players, but basically an entire franchise. I worked my ass off but was stressed to the max, still had headaches, and could feel that my brain wasn't working right, as if part of it had been switched off or stuffed with cotton. Dan, who would pass away a few years later, was mercurial on his best day and seemed eager to cultivate chaos at every turn. He told players they should call him "Daddy," and the players' union wound up filing a grievance for a hostile work environment. After one bad defeat, Borislow reportedly sent a threatening email blast to the players, saying that if they don't follow his suggestions they "will be playing in a rec league within years, drinking beer and farting after the game at a local bar and telling people how good you used to be at age 26."

It was all too much. Every day I would go the beach and look at the ocean waves and cry. I didn't know what was going on, or when it would stop.

Before I signed on to be Dan's general manager, I made sure he knew I'd already committed to doing commentary for ESPN at the Women's World Cup and would be in Germany for about a month in late June and part of July. I flew to Germany as scheduled, then got an email from Dan saying I'd been fired. My initial anger turned into relief, because from everything I'd seen in my months with the magicJack, it was a vessel waiting to crash into boulders. The broadcasting role was a great opportunity, but I found out in a hurry that it's hard to do live television with an impaired brain. I had trouble keeping facts and statistics in my head. I'd try to retrieve them and it was as if the file disappeared. I struggled to make quick, cogent points in short sound bites. Sometimes I forgot words and names. I'd think of something to say and it would slip out of my grasp like an ice cube. When I looked at emails I sent, I noticed I'd leave out clauses or whole sentences. My grammar was awful. Nobody at ESPN ever said anything to me, but I was gradually phased out as the tournament reached its late stages. I would've phased me out, too.

I packed up from West Palm Beach and moved to northern New Jersey late in the summer of 2011. My agent knew I was still struggling with my injury and thought it would be good if we lived near each other so he could offer support. He helped me find an apartment—a ground-floor studio in Little Falls, a town named after a nearby water-fall, that was home to fourteen thousand people, including the Jonas Brothers. Kevin, Joe, and Nick were on the way up. I was going in the other direction. I did my best to remain my glass-is-half-full self, but it was getting harder. Money was tight and I didn't know what I would do next, or even what I *could* do next, given my brain injury. My address had changed, but everything else stayed the same, or got worse. I collected unemployment for four months, and when that ended, I made a few bucks here and there training kids, but even that got to be too much because my head pounded most of the day and all of the night.

By 2011, the Washington Freedom (and the rest of the WPS) had folded, meaning that I no longer had access to the club's training or medical staff, or its facilities. With my condition worsening and my employment prospects dim, my lawyers suggested I file a workers' compensation claim in Maryland (where the Freedom were based). They explained that because I was injured on the job and was not able to work, I stood an excellent chance of having the claim approved. That sounded like good news, and I needed good news. We had a hearing in downtown Baltimore, filed the claim, complete with detailed med-ical reports, and then the fun began. The law firm representing the team's insurance company demanded that I go see its doctors, who found—shocker alert—that I was perfectly fine.

The insurance company lawyers gave a lengthy deposition, which came down to this:

She's milking it so she can get a payday.

When my claim was approved by the judge, the lawyers switched it up, arguing that if I did indeed have a brain impairment, it was from all the other hits to the head I'd taken, not from the April 25, 2010, injury.

My lawyer, Benjamin Boscolo, referred me to a physician, Dr. Kevin Crutchfield, who specialized in treating traumatic brain injuries and had remarkable success in doing so. The first thing Dr. Crutchfield wanted to do was examine me and find out if I was a good candidate for treatment. The other side claimed that this was not medically necessary and a waste of money. They fought it for months, arguing that I needed no such evaluation or treatment, that I again was after a financial score. It took months, but the judge finally approved my consultation with Dr. Crutchfield.

"Why are they fighting everything?" I asked Ben. "All I want to do is get better and move on with my life."

"That's what they do," Ben said. "It's a cynical strategy, but it can be effective, unfortunately. They deny, deny, deny and hope you eventually will give up."

"I'm not giving up," I said.

Ben was wonderful, and fought hard for me at every turn, but we both knew this was going to be a long haul. The worst part was that even after the judge ordered the insurance company to pay me $1,347 per month, their lawyers fought it. Some months a check would come, but many others, without notice, it did not.

I'd go to the mailbox on the day the check was supposed to arrive and see nothing. I'd call Ben. He'd call the lawyer for the insurance company. The lawyer on the other side would say he did not know when the check would be coming and, moreover, that they were still contesting the legitimacy of the claim. It all went around and around. My head was hurting. My anxiety was off the charts. I'd wake up with pounding pain behind my left ear that would spend the day traveling all over the back of my head. It was agony I had never endured before. I am no baby. I have a high threshold for pain. I wished desperately that I could meet with someone from this insurance company and tell them, "What can I do to convince you I am not making this up?" I had no money and couldn't work and I was living in a studio apartment and it felt as if the walls were closing in. I was forty-one years old and had been self-sufficient since I left Dayton, Minnesota, for UMass, and when the checks didn't come when they were supposed to, it was crushing. I called my case manager at Ben's law firm, Heather Gardner.

"There's no check. How am I going to pay my rent? How am I going to live?"

"We're doing everything we can," Heather said. "You are legally entitled to this money, and you will get this money."

I trusted Ben and Heather completely, but that didn't help my financial plight. My landlord, thank God, was very understanding and let me make partial payments on my $1,200 rent. But I was getting desperate. If I couldn't count on the workers' comp checks, how was I going to make ends meet? I needed money and needed it right away. There was no way I was going to reach out to my USWNT teammates and ask for a handout. I am sure they would've helped, but I was stubborn and too proud to ask for help. My intensity and mental fortitude were my hallmarks as a goalkeeper. I was not going to go begging.

I had a 2003 Jeep Cherokee. I found out about a place that would give me cash if I handed over the title to them. That put about four thousand dollars into my bank account. It got me through a couple of months. I needed to be more aggressive and had a brainstorm: my one-hundred cap Rolex. It was a lovely watch, and I treasured it, but I was not in a place where I could hold on to things because they meant a lot to me. At the end of the day, it was just a watch. I went online and found a place where I could pawn it and get some cash for it. I drove into New York City and went to the Diamond District on West 47th Street. It was a surreal experience for me, a Black woman from small-town Minnesota, on a street in Midtown Manhattan that teemed with orthodox Jewish men with black hats and black suits and beards. One shop after another had locked front doors and millions of dollars' worth of diamonds inside.

"Top Prices Paid for Jewelry!" one sign said. That was what I wanted: a top price for my Rolex. I walked into the shop I'd researched. Two hulking security men were stationed outside it. I hit the button next to the door and was buzzed in. The owner put on his jeweler's loupe and examined my Rolex for thirty seconds or so. He offered me one thousand dollars in cash, on the spot, to pawn it. All I had to do was make monthly payments of $128 by the fifteenth of every month, and I would get my Rolex back once I had repaid the principal and interest. I signed the agreement and walked out with ten one-hundred-dollar bills. It was almost as exhilarating as the day I found that hundred-dollar bill on the floor of the Nacirema Club.

I got caught up on my rent and utilities, but I owed my chiropractor money and had medication to buy, and no health insurance to help cover it. A few months later, I didn't have the money to make my $128 payment. I received a notice in the mail that I was behind in my account and, by the terms of the agreement, needed to get it current immediately. If I missed a second payment, I would lose the watch.

The fifteenth of the next month was approaching. I had fifty-five dollars to my name and an empty refrigerator, and no access to Government Cheese. Partial payments were not going to work in the Diamond District. A few days after the fifteenth, I received a letter in the mail from the jeweler. I opened it while I was standing on my bed—something I did a good amount of the time. I liked the feeling of being off the ground. It almost made me feel like a keeper again, jumping to make a save. I stood on the bed when I spoke to Ben and Heather, and for almost every conversation I thought would be important. The letter informed me that my one-hundred cap Rolex watch now belonged to somebody else.

I stepped off the bed and threw the letter in the garbage.

CHAPTER SIXTEEN

BOTTOMING OUT

Next door to my apartment was a package room. It was full of neatly stacked brown boxes and pouches and I wondered which of my neighbors would be receiving them, and how much better their lives were than mine. I thought about how great it would be to get a package that solved all my problems, even though I knew that was straight out of fantasy land. All I got was harassing notices, and an occasional check from an insurance company that was hell-bent on making sure I never got better. I represented my country 173 times and won a World Cup and two Olympic gold medals, and now I had to fight an American company to get the care that I need?

It seemed wrong on every level.

Ben and Heather kept assuring me it would work out, and finally there was some progress. The judge ruled that I could get a second opinion from Dr. Crutchfield. I went to see him in his office in Sinai Hospital in Baltimore in January 2013. He was a former soccer player himself and had followed my career. He remembered how I looked when I played.

Wow, she is broken, he thought when he looked at me on the examination table. He gently began to feel around the back of my head, and behind my left ear, and then touched a nerve, literally, the pain so searing that I almost kicked him. He jumped away.

"I guess that's the spot," he said.

Dr. Crutchfield's diagnosis, for the purposes of the ongoing workers' compensation claim, was that I was "temporarily totally disabled." The cause was a traumatic brain injury that resulted in severe pressure being put on my left occipital nerve, which runs from between the first and second cervical vertebrae to the top of the scalp, about five inches in all.

Finally, I knew what the problem was. Better still, I had a potential remedy; Dr. Crutchfield's specialty, along with his colleague Dr. Ivica Ducic, was occipital release surgery, a procedure that entails making an incision in the back of the neck and releasing the occipital nerve from the surrounding tissue and muscle that are pressing on it. After I responded well to a series of steroid injections in my occipital nerve, Dr. Crutchfield said I would be an excellent candidate for the procedure and believed I would feel immediate relief. I wanted to hug him.

"Let's book it," I said.

The surgery, common now, was considered experimental at the time. The next step was to schedule another hearing before the judge to get approval for the surgery, which would cost about fifteen thousand dollars. The insurance company lawyers, naturally, stuck with their deny-deny-deny playbook, arguing that it wasn't standard practice and not medically necessary. They requested that I be examined, again, by their doctors. It was within their rights to do this, and of course this was going to drag things out for weeks, or possibly even months. Their doctors' opinion was unchanged from the first time. They said there was nothing wrong . . . that the problems were all in my head.

You are right, the problems are all in my head. My jackhammer head-aches, my mental deficit, my memory loss, my cognitive struggles—it's one hundred percent in my head. Maybe you'd like to be me for a day and see how you like it?

So, even though there was hope on the horizon, my day-to-day existence was only getting worse. It was coming up on three years since I suffered the injury. I was lost and broke. My Rolex was gone. My car belonged to someone else. I didn't know weekdays from weekends, because the workweek means nothing when you can't work. My memory was so bad that when I went to the grocery store or a shopping center I had to write down where I parked. I kept fighting to stay positive and hope that the next day would be better, but it never was. The headaches would be manageable when I woke up but then get progressively worse throughout the day, pounding and throbbing, and then stabbing by the end of the day, when it felt as if somebody was taking a butcher's knife to the back of my head. Every day I'd binge-watch *Breaking Bad* and *The Office* on Netflix, and wait for ten P.M. That was when I would take my Vicodin pill. I was careful with it; I was well aware the rabbit hole that a painkiller addiction could lead me down and never had more than one. It took the edge off the headaches and brought on a little euphoria. So did my preferred cocktail, vodka and cranberry juice. I knew about the dangers of mixing the two—that it can have a compounding affect and cause liver damage. I didn't care. I felt like I was in jail and a little buzz got me out of it for a while.

I was in my apartment one night, watching the end of a *Breaking Bad* episode. I'd already had my Vicodin and my drink. An infomercial came on. I've always hated those things—the way hyped-up hucksters promise you a lifetime of happiness or an incredible sex life or the best lint roller you've ever used, if you will just call the number on your screen RIGHT NOW. Usually I turn them off immediately, but this time I didn't. The infomercial was for a company called Borro in

New York City, a firm that billed itself as the leader in confidential non-bank loans, using borrowers' luxury assets as collateral. It showed classy-looking people coming in to talk to friendly loan officers and walking out with a smile and a big check. Borro looked to me to be basically a high-class pawn shop, but I was intrigued. I wrote down the number from the TV screen.

• • •

I had a goal every day and it never changed. I wanted to get outside. Some days when the headaches were bad and depression had a vice-grip on me, I wouldn't make it, but most of the time I did, even if it was a five-minute stroll around the apartment complex. If I turned right out of my building, there was a walkway that would take me to a grassy area and then to a footbridge over the river. On the other side of the river were a few woodsy trails that were serene and almost always empty. But that was a fifteen-minute walk and I wasn't often up to that. If I went straight out of my place, up the driveway, I could cross the street and stop in Little Falls Discount Liquors. I was a good customer, even if my shopping list included nothing but cheap vodka. On a sunny and brisk winter day in February 2013, I took a different route.

• • •

I walked to the left, past a parking lot and an adjacent building, following the sidewalk until I arrived at a security booth that I'd never seen manned. Beside the booth was a staircase that takes you down to the river. I descended twenty-one steps and got to a circular plaza overlooking a waterfall. This was Little Falls, though it looked plenty big to me, running probably two hundred feet across. A carpet mill had been located at this spot for more than a century; a plaque commemorates its history. I walked to the railing, slowly; it was the only gear I had. I watched the relentless power of the churning white water. Most loud noises bothered me but the constant roar of the falls was almost soothing. The misty coolness coming up from the water tingled against my face. It was the closest I've ever been to a waterfall. I peered straight down into the turbulence and in that moment it occurred to me that I could get rid of my pain forever in a couple of seconds.

It could all be gone that fast.

All I had to do was jump over the railing.

The speed was appealing, for sure, but for a non-swimmer, the churning water was a daunting sight. I took a step back.

Maybe I needed to rethink this.

A half minute passed and I was just standing there. I had a vision of myself in a dumpster with a gun. I didn't even own a gun. There are dumpsters aplenty in north Jersey. I had no idea where this vision came from. It wasn't going away.

That's stupid, I decided. If I am going to kill myself, I need to do it logically, swiftly. Here I was at river's edge. I didn't have to buy anything or go anywhere. What could be more convenient?

I studied the frosty flow of the river, dazed and conflicted.

Should I jump? Or should I walk away?

Two voices begin a debate so heated it was as if I could hear them out loud. They were almost as clear as the voice I heard in the 1999 World Cup shootout—"This is the one."

Voice One: You've never quit anything in your life. You're going to get the surgery, and your pain will be over. Your life is so close to turning around. Hang in there a little longer. You have so much to live for.

Voice Two: Nothing ever changes. The surgery won't happen for months, if then. Your pain is worse than ever. Your life is going nowhere. You have no money and no job prospects. Once you were a world-class athlete and now you can barely make it to your mailbox. You have nothing to live for.

Back and forth the voices went, at fever pitch, a tug-of-war on a rope that is about to snap. A tabloid headline trailed through my brain:

Former Olympic Champion Plunges to Her Death. No Foul Play Suspected.

I looked over the railing again. I thought of my mother, signing "Hallelujah" in the kitchen in Dayton, Minnesota, and imagined what it would do to her when she heard that her baby took her own life. I turned around and walked back up the twenty-one steps.

• • •

The months dragged on in the studio. The mail didn't often bring good news, so I wouldn't get it every day. If my phone rang and it was anyone other than Dr. Crutchfield, Ben, or Heather—or my dear friends, Naomi and Kerri—I usually would not pick up. My world kept shrinking. The one thing I felt I could control was what I put in my body. My brain was a train wreck, but I wanted to make sure I ate good food. I did a lot of juicing—the healthy kind. I'd go to the supermarket and get a variety of fruits and vegetables—kale, pears, apples, pineapple, Swiss chard, cucumber, and anything else that looked green and good. For sixty straight days in the winter and spring of 2013, I had one meal a day, and I drank it. I felt cleansed.

For most of my adult life I saw every day as a fresh possibility, another opportunity to get better. I spent years devouring self-improvement books. When I wanted to learn more about spirituality, I read Deepak Chopra. When I wanted to learn more about finances, I read Suze Orman. I became an ardent follower of Tony Robbins, finding his life strategies and positive energy uplifting. A lot of people regard self-improvement entrepreneurs as nothing more than charlatans who get rich off gullible and self-delusional people, like me. I've never seen it that way. Learning and growing are some of the best parts about being alive. I loved learning about goalkeeping from Jim Rudy. When I started working with Dr. Hacker, our team psychologist, I was excited that I could train my mind the same way I trained my body, coming to view pressure not as a burden but a necessary passage that ultimately is what creates diamonds. Even during the frustrating final years of my playing career, I was fired up about pursuing what was next. When it looked as if broadcasting might be an option, I made it a point to learn about it. As I became involved in public speaking, I studied the masters of the craft so I could get better at it. And as the extent of my brain injury became apparent to me, I read audiobooks to try to get a grasp of brain science and why a hard knock to the head could have such long-lasting repercussions.

I've always believed that if you seek/ask/pray to (pick your own verb) God or the Universe or a Higher Power (pick your own noun)—and you do it with a pure heart—your prayer ultimately will be answered. It won't be in your time. It will be in Her time. But it will happen. It doesn't mean that you won't have setbacks or hard times and that your whole life will be like a day at an amusement park. It just means that if you put positive energy out there it will somehow, someway come back to you. It happened for me after my career crash-landed when I self-sabotaged the 2000 Olympics. Once I owned that and earnestly began to pray for a way forward within two years I was at the pinnacle of my game. Before I met Naomi, I had a series of relationships that weren't especially fulfilling or healthy, as much because of what I was bringing to it as anything my partner was. When I consciously, prayerfully sought out something richer, taking a hard look at myself and what I needed to work on, everything changed.

Naomi and I had six wonderful years together, and to this day she is an angel in my life.

By the winter of 2013, though, my storehouse of positive energy was lower than my checking account balance. I couldn't summon any because I didn't remember how to. More than two and a half years of pain and insurance-company roadblocks had beaten the life out of me. Depression hit me like a runaway truck on the Jersey Turnpike. My lawyer's office called and said I had to come in for another hearing because the company submitted another objection to my getting surgery from Dr. Crutchfield.

They are breaking me, I thought. They are going to get what they want. They are going to get me to give up. I went across the street to Little Falls Discount Liquors and purchased my vodka. I could only afford a pint. Later that night, as I sipped my drink, I decided it was time to reach out to Borro.

I had an Olympic gold medal they might be interested in.

• • •

Before I could meet with the people at Borro, I had a trip to make. My gold medals were at my mom's house, in a cedar chest in her bedroom. One of my sisters helped me out with the plane fare. My mom had been suffering from Alzheimer's for a couple of years, and her disease was getting into the late stages. I wasn't sure if she would recognize me and know my name, but she did.

"Boob," she exclaimed. It was what she called me my whole life—a shortened form of Boo, because I liked to watch Yogi Bear and Boo cartoons as a kid.

"Meresie!" I exclaimed back.

She asked me about the USWNT—her brain was still stuck in that era—and inquired about my teammates, especially Mia and Lil.

"When's your next game? Who are you playing?" she asked.

I explained that I wasn't on the team anymore and that I had retired. I said nothing about my brain injury.

A minute or two later, she looked at me and said, "When's your next game? Who are you playing? Did I already ask you that?"

My mom asked me the same things a half-dozen times over a one-hour visit. Each time, she asked me if she'd asked that before. As sad as it was to see the disease overtaking her, her same sweetness still shined through. Her brain may not have been working, but her heart was as huge as ever. She noticed I wasn't wearing socks.

"Are your feet cold? I can give you some socks. I have a blanket we can put over them."

"No, no, thanks. My feet are fine." Her feet must've been cold, because she kept asking me about mine.

Near the end of our visit, I asked her if she minded if I took the gold medals with me.

She remembered she had them. I told her I needed them for some appearances I was making.

"You take them if you need them," my mom said. "You won them, after all."

I gave her a long, goodbye hug and flew home that night. Thirty-six hours later it was Borro Day, March 13, 2013, a Wednesday. I had already postponed it once because I didn't have enough money for gas. I woke up feeling dread. I wanted no part of doing this but knew I had no choice. I showered and dressed, drank my smoothie, and got in my Jeep. It was a dreary, rainy day. On the passenger seat, inside a small wooden box, was my 1996 gold medal. (I was taking it one medal at a time and this was the more valuable one.) I got on Interstate 80 heading east, toward the George Washington Bridge, for the twenty-five-mile trip to New York City. I passed exits for Paterson and Hackensack and other places I knew nothing about. Everything looked gray and grim. At almost every exit, I thought about pulling off and turning around and going back to my jail. But I kept going. I talked out loud, to myself.

"This is going to be a good thing. It will give me room to breathe," I said. I felt as though I wasn't even Briana Scurry, or in my own body. I didn't know who I was. I paid a thirteen-dollar toll that I couldn't afford, crossed the bridge, and headed down the West Side Highway in Manhattan. I passed the famous aircraft carrier, the *Intrepid.*

I'd never felt less intrepid in my life.

I got off the highway at Forty-Second Street and drove across town. Borro was in a building near Bryant Park in the heart of Midtown. I parked in a garage. The battle within continued to rage. I thought about pulling right back out of the garage and driving home.

"This is going to be a good thing," I told myself again.

I entered the building and pressed the elevator button for the twenty-first floor. I walked up to the door. It was my last chance to turn around.

I walked in.

The receptionist greeted me warmly.

"Hi, I'm Briana Scurry. I have a one o'clock appointment."

"Hi, Ms. Scurry. Yes, somebody will be right with you. Please have a seat."

The office was nicely appointed and comfortable. Two loan advisors came out—a young woman and a British guy. Both were cordial and well-mannered. We sat down in a conference room. They offered me a bottle of water. I took the gold medal out of my backpack and put it on the table. I told them the 1996 Games were the centennial of the modern Olympics and the first time that women's soccer had been a medal sport. I was trying hard to hold it together. I could tell they were intrigued by it.

"We've never had an Olympic gold medal before," the British fellow said, opening the box. He picked it up.

"Wow, it's heavy," he said.

I told them I wanted to use the loan money to start a business. I was too ashamed to tell them the truth. They explained the process to me—that they had to authenticate the medal and then appraise it, and that it would take forty-five minutes to an hour.

"That's fine," I said.

They returned ahead of schedule and told me that everything checked out and went over the details. In exchange for my collateral—the gold medal—they would give me a check for $5,000. I would pay them $199 monthly for as long as the loan was outstanding. When I wanted to get the medal back, I would have to repay the principal plus fees.

My head was spinning. I asked a couple of questions about the repayment procedure. I signed all the paperwork. They told me that $5,000 would be wired to me in a few days. My Olympic gold medal was still in the wooden box on the table in front of me. It was the medal I started dreaming about when I was eight years old, watching the U.S. Olympic hockey team beat the Soviets in Lake Placid over thirty years before. It didn't belong to me anymore, at least for now. We shook hands and said goodbye. I walked out the door of Borro, the leader in confidential, non-bank loans. I had to look at the parking stub to remember where the garage was. Back in the car, the passenger seat was empty. There was no more holding it together. I held on to the steering wheel and sat in my car and cried.

• • •

I'd hoped—perhaps naïvely—that having financial breathing room would be a panacea. It was anything but. It was a relief to know I could cover the basics for a while, but the realization that my life was so broken that I pawned my proudest possession took a heavy emotional toll. I thought about that gold medal all the time. I did what I needed to do, but I still was sick over it. The stress made my headaches worse and my depression deeper. Depression is a strange disease. It has its own ebb and flow, but it's not predictable, like the tides. Some days I would wake up and feel a glimmer of hope, and my old upbeat worldview. Other times the gloom hung so heavily over me I was sure it would never lift. I could never pinpoint what caused the depression to lighten, or what made it hit me like a tsunami. The worst wave of it I'd ever experience came late one morning, a few weeks after I'd gotten the money from Borro. I had gotten up late. I felt untethered from everything on earth, as if I were just a random mass of cells. I went outside and turned left. The sun shined, and the air was crisp and sweet with the smells of blooming and spring. The aching in the back of my head had abated for some reason.

It's a good day to die, I thought.

I never expected to be back in such a dark, despairing place, but here I was, walking back down the twenty-one steps to the plaza, past the marker for the old carpet mill. I was at the railing now again. The river was swollen from a few recent days of rain, the water falling hard into foamy rushing rapids. I put my palms on the railing. Jumping was something I had always been good at. I leaned forward and put my weight on my hands and tensed my upper body, and then, just like the last time, the lovely, light brown face of Robbie Scurry came before my eyes, and I could hear her say, "Boob, aren't your feet cold?"

My feet are fine, thanks, Meresie, I thought. I wished in that moment I could thank her for all her love for all those years. I started to cry, tears spilling over the railing. I turned around and headed towards the steps. I never contemplated suicide again.

CHAPTER SEVENTEEN

RISING

Eighteen months in Little Falls was enough. I needed to get away from the waterfall, in case I reconsidered. I had gone back to Borro and pawned the 2004 gold medal and had enough money to move into a bigger, brighter apartment in Elizabethtown, New Jersey. It wasn't luxury living, but it was an upgrade. One day I got a call from Naomi. She and her girlfriend, Fran, had started a lifestyle apparel company called TomboyX. They had organized a social with potential investors just outside DC in Maryland. Naomi asked if I would come to the gathering and model a few of the shirts. I felt crappy and the last thing I wanted to do was model anything, but I wanted to help her, so I made the trip and put on a couple of the shirts in the TomboyX line. In between times, I would lie down on a sofa to rest my head. One of the would-be Tomboy investors at the event was Chryssa Zizos, the CEO and founder of Live Wire Strategic Communications, a top-rated public relations company in the Washington, DC, metro area. Chryssa had seen some of the TomboyX styles and loved them and thought the company had carved out an intriguing niche. She was curious why one of the models—an African American woman—kept lying down on the couch when she wasn't modeling shirts.

It's kind of an inappropriate time to take a nap, Chryssa thought. But whatever. The next night, Chryssa and her partner, Karen, had dinner with Naomi and Fran. Naomi has a wide circle of friends and lives to connect people. If LinkedIn were a human being, it would be Naomi Gonzalez. She knew that Chryssa was a successful PR executive and decided to seize the opportunity, telling Chryssa about my soccer career and how I'd suffered a serious brain injury and was having all kinds of trouble getting the responsible insurance company to pay for my care.

"Remember the model at the party who was sprawled out on the couch?" Naomi said.

Chryssa nodded.

"That's who I am talking about. She is the nicest person and she is going through hell trying to get this company to do the right thing," Naomi said. "Do you think you might be able to talk to her for a few minutes and maybe help her get some publicity?"

Chryssa was swamped with a large media-training contract and wasn't in a place where she could take on pro bono project. But she had compassion for what I'd gone through and had a daughter, Sydney, who was playing travel soccer. Maybe it would be fun for her to meet a World Cup and Olympic champion. Chryssa told Naomi to have me give her a call.

Naomi texted me and told me about her conversation with Chryssa.

"She has her own PR company and knows how this works," Naomi said. "She could be the one to help you. You have to call her, OK?"

"That's great, thank you," I said. "It's nice she wants to help."

I figured I'd call this Chryssa person at some point, but I wasn't up to it right now. Being at the party with all these high-energy, dynamic women had made me feel even worse. I returned to Jersey feeling more unplugged from the world than ever. I didn't want to call anyone, and I especially didn't want to tell a successful businesswoman who I didn't know about what a mess my life was. Naomi called me a day later and asked if I'd reached out to Chryssa.

"No," I said.

"Why not?"

"I don't know."

"What are you doing? She wants to help."

"OK," I said.

"Don't tell me OK if you don't mean it," Naomi said. She was just getting warmed up. She started yelling at me. She'd never spoken to me this way—ever. "I'm not fooling, Bri. This is what you've been waiting for . . . what you have been hoping for. If you let this opportunity go by, I don't know. I don't know what I'll do. Do you want to get better or not? I am going to call you back in two days, and if you haven't called Chryssa, I am done. I love you, but I mean it. I will never speak to you again."

Naomi knew exactly which button to push, and she pushed a hot one. I called Chryssa, planning on giving her a ten-minute overview of the previous three years and seeing if she had any ideas. I wound up spending two hours on the phone, spilling it all, sanitizing nothing.

Chryssa was fully on board, pro bono be damned, and told a friend why.

"I've been doing this for a long time, and I don't think I've ever experienced anyone who was so open and vulnerable in sharing her story," Chryssa said. "Her honesty was remarkable, and her story was heartbreaking. There was no way I wasn't going to do everything I could to help."

Chryssa, I soon found out, was a kindred spirit in so many ways. She had an athletic background, having been a scholarship field-hockey player at Eastern Kentucky University. She had overcome major obstacles in her life, none greater than her dyslexia, a condition that wasn't discovered until second grade. She didn't learn how to read until fifth grade, by which time she'd been typecast as a "slow learner" who couldn't keep up. She was also kicked out of her college sorority because she was gay and wasn't all that private about it. Chryssa refused to let the homophobia define her; she became sports editor of her college newspaper and wound up becoming one of the first people in the country to get a master's degree in crisis communications.

I loved her spirit and her tenacity, and was moved that she saw something in me and my story.

"If you never say no to me, I will help you," she said. "If you agree to trust me, I will make this right for you."

I barely knew Chryssa Zizos at this point, but I trusted my instincts and had no doubt that she had my best interests in mind. Lots of agents and PR people strut around and tell you how great they are and how they are going to change your life. Chryssa never did any of that. She just went to work. She and her team got major pieces placed in the *Washington Post* and *USA Today*, and booked segments on various TV outlets. Other spots were in the works. When my lawyer let the insurance company know that I had retained a PR firm, and that major publicity was on the way, it only changed everything. Within a week or two the denial stopped and I was welcome to see Dr. Crutchfield. My monthly checks were never late again. I guess it was just one of life's crazy coincidences that the insurance company realized the seriousness of my injury the minute there was going to be major media coverage of my plight.

• • •

I moved to the Adams Morgan neighborhood of Washington, DC, in the fall of 2013. I had a network of friends in the area from my time with the Freedom, and it also made sense to be closer to my doctors. My surgery with Dr. Ducic was scheduled for October 18. In the days and weeks leading up to it I would go for snail-paced, three-mile walks through Rock Creek Park. It had winding trails, chirping birds, and a canopy of trees, and it felt like my own personal Walden Pond, an idyllic retreat that would transport me into a Zen-like state. I'd listen to Deepak Chopra's "How to Know God" on audiotape, and it was as if three and a half years of gloom were being lifted with each woodsy step.

I woke up early the day of the surgery. It was a cool autumn morning. After so much anticipation, I was completely ready for whatever was going to happen. Naomi, who flew in from Seattle to be with me, drove me to MedStar Georgetown University Hospital. I checked in at the outpatient surgery desk, got assigned to a room, and changed into a green hospital gown. It was surreal to think that this was finally going to happen, and that if the doctors were correct, I soon might have my life back. I tried not to project, but my heart was pumping hope, nonstop. I was in the masterful hands of Dr. Ducic. My only job at the moment was to bring my traumatized occipital nerve to the operating table.

Dr. Ducic briefly stopped by my room to go over his plan for the surgery. I listened intently, more excited than nervous. Naomi held my hand and rubbed my shoulder. Chryssa was there to keep me company, as well. Before the anesthesiologist came in, I looked up toward the ceiling.

"Please, please let this work," I said.

The anesthesia kicked in quickly, and I was out. Dr. Ducic began by making a two-inch incision at the base of my scalp, behind my left ear. He tweezed out little, bloody clumps of fibrous tissue that were impinging on my occipital nerve. While he was there, he also cleaned out my other occipital nerve, which showed signs of significant trauma as well. The whole procedure took less than an hour. I was back in the

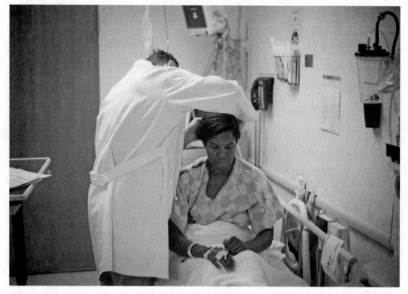

Dr. Ivica Ducic examines me before the surgery that finally freed me from pain after three and a half years. I am so immensely grateful to Dr. Ducic and his colleague, Dr. Kevin Crutchfield.

outpatient recovery area when I woke up. Naomi and Chryssa were at my beside.

I opened my eyes slowly. Five seconds passed. Ten seconds passed. I knew I was still drugged up, but I was acutely aware of one thing:

I didn't have a headache. I looked at Naomi and began to cry.

"I don't feel any pain," I said.

Naomi and Chryssa were both thinking the same thing:

Could that really be true, or is it that the anesthesia hadn't worn off yet?

The next day I woke up pain-free for the first time since April 25, 2010. I felt clear and light and was bursting with energy, as if I wanted to try to make up for all my lost time in a single day. My apartment was close to the Smithsonian National Zoo. It's famous for its giant pandas, among other species.

"Let's go to the zoo," I told Naomi.

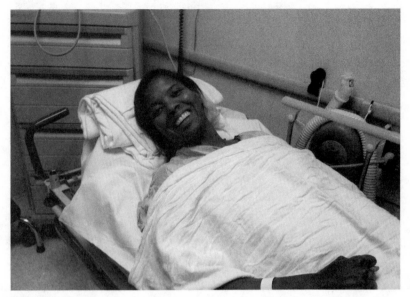

Post surgery report: No headache. No pain. New life. Who wouldn't be smiling?

"I don't think that's the best idea a day after surgery. Why don't you rest for today and we can tomorrow?"

"No, I want to go today. I feel great and I want to go to the zoo."

Naomi wouldn't take no for an answer about the Chryssa call, and now I wasn't taking no for an answer about the zoo. I wanted to see the pandas. I wanted to see elephants and rhinos and find a few panthers, too. I could show them my tattoo. So we went to the zoo and it was one of the best days of my life. I was like a little girl, her eyes the size of dinner plates, seeing big animals for the first time. I felt like an eagle who had been freed from her cage and was remembering how it felt to soar. I smiled at monkeys swinging in vines, so playful and nimble, looking as if they were smiling right back. I was mesmerized by the stripes of the tigers and the girth of the hippos. Living every day with chronic pain, all you want is for it to go away. You say prayers and beg and ask the Universe for it to leave your body but it never does. Now, finally, it had, and there were two three-inch scars in the

I was supposed to rest the day after
my surgery in October 2013, but I
was having none of it. It was a great
day for a stroll in The National Zoo in
Washington, D.C.

back of my head as souvenirs to prove it. I craned my neck up to look
at the giraffes and for the first time in so long I didn't lose my balance
when I did that. Hope was gushing out of my heart like water from
a garden hose. I was in a perpetual state of wonder as I strolled from
exhibit to exhibit. It was the first day of my new life and I loved it.

CHAPTER EIGHTEEN

THE GIFT

As miraculous as the surgical outcome was, Dr. Crutchfield reminded me I still had work to do. The pain from the head trauma masked some underlying issues, the foremost of which was my lack of balance. But I also had fine motor skills that had been compromised and cognitive deficits I had to correct. My new best friend became Laura Morris, a physical therapist at the rehabilitation center at Sinai Hospital in downtown Baltimore. For the next six months I made the one-hour trip from my apartment in the Adams Morgan neighborhood of Washington, three times a week. It was hard, grinding work and that was fine with me. It was going to help me get better. I got after it like a kid trying to make the team.

Laura helped me to understand that the repercussions of a brain injury vary depending on where the trauma was sustained. Some brain injuries impact your capacity for exertion. Others impair your balance, memory, and/or cognitive abilities. I needed to build up my ability to exert, but our larger focus was on regaining dexterity, balance, and fine motor skills, along with cognition. Laura pushed me hard, but in the kindest possible way. We'd usually start by getting my heart rate up on an elliptical trainer or exercise bike. Then I had to jump on one foot and stick the landing. I walked toe-to-heel, toe-to-heel, in as straight a line as I could. I jumped rope and did planks and side planks. The cognitive and fine motor test was one of the most challenging. Laura had me stand in a completely dark room, with a two-foot by three-foot electronic board in front of me. The board was black, with rows of small circles, one of which would light up red every five seconds or so, with a letter or a number. If the lighted red square showed "Q," I had to say "Upper case Q," then touch the square before it went out. So in the span of a few seconds, I had to see the lighted letter or number, say what it was, then touch it. It probably doesn't sound too rigorous, but when your brain has been injured you have to take baby steps, clearing the processing pathways little by little. I would do this exercise for a minute, in rapid-fire fashion, and then I'd get to rest.

Laura was incredibly gifted and thorough. Before each session, I had to answer fifty questions about my daily life in the time since the previous therapy session. *How are you sleeping? How is your attention span? What is it like when you walk down an aisle in the supermarket? Do the bright overhead lights bother you? Do you lose your balance if you bend down to pick something up and stand up quickly?*

Once a month or so, Laura would give me an Impact (Immediate Post-Concussion Assessment and Cognitive Testing) test to evaluate my memory, attention span, and visual and verbal problem solving. The results showed steady progress. After years of being stuck, I was moving in a positive direction. I was getting my brain and life back. It felt wonderful.

After just four months of working with Laura, I was doing so well I was able to accept an invitation to be a part of the 136th annual White House Easter Egg Roll, hosted by President Barack

Obama and First Lady Michelle Obama. I invited Laura to join me. The theme was "Hop Into Healthy, Swing Into Shape," an adjunct to the First Lady's "Let's Move" youth fitness initiative. It was a gorgeous spring day and Laura and I had a blast, along with about thirty thousand kids on the South Lawn. The luminaries included Fergie, who provided the music (minus the Black Eyed Peas), the Easter Bunny, and local sports celebrities, including Ryan Kerrigan and Pierre Garçon of the Washington Football Team. Angela Hucles, a former USWNT teammate who I hadn't seen in years, was also there. There were sport activity stations set up where kids could play soccer, tennis, basketball, and more. I worked the soccer part of the operation. Laura and I each got a photo with the First Lady. I went home happy and exhausted.

This was a day I couldn't have even imagined six months ago, I thought, as I drifted off into an afternoon nap.

• • •

The therapy worked wonders in all areas, and on my optimism, too. Throughout my ordeal, the best part of every day was my nap, because the pain would shut off for a little while. Not only were the naps history now, I was actively seeking to build a new life and find my way forward. Nobody helped that process more than Chryssa. Seeing the growing awareness about concussions and traumatic brain injuries, she began to pitch me as an advocate in those areas. She booked me for speaking appearances at hospitals, brain-health associations, and neurological conferences. I testified at a congressional subcommittee hearing on making sports safer. Chryssa knew I had a powerful story to share. She thought it would make for an inspiring book, and a prosperous future as a motivational speaker. She believed in me more than I believed in myself. I was at the Live Wire office one day and she was buzzing about all the things that were percolating for me . . . TV spots, articles, and upcoming speaking gigs. I was finding out firsthand about Chryssa's modus operandi as a businesswoman, equal parts creative dynamo and pit bull, both qualities being fully channeled for my benefit. She wasn't on a retainer. She wasn't getting a commission. Her payoff seemed to be watching me get stronger and healthier every day.

In the early winter of 2014, three months after my surgery, Chryssa and I went to a Spanish restaurant called Estadio in the Logan Circle neighborhood of DC. It was decorated with Spanish tile and Spanish marble, terra-cotta brushed walls, and we ate tapas and drank sangria at a little table adjacent to the kitchen. It felt as though I was on Las Ramblas in Barcelona, not 14th Street NW in Washington. We laughed and nibbled at Catalan delicacies and had too much sangria, and it had been so long since I had a simple night out that it was a revelation how delightful it could be. We said goodbye on the street. I went back to my apartment and Chryssa, who had two children and recently split up with her partner Karen after almost twenty years, headed to her new place in Alexandria.

What a gift this woman is, I thought. *Six months ago I didn't even know she existed.*

Something was happening between Chryssa and me, and it was beautiful. We low-keyed it and took it slowly, because she and Karen were still figuring out how best to work things out with each other, and the kids. We didn't see each other often in person, but when I got a text or call from Chryssa I almost felt giddy. Deep inside me there was a spark that felt ready to turn into a bonfire. As I went to bed the night we ate the tapas on 14th Street, I thought about how the darkest days I'd ever known had made this evening possible. Without my injury and pain, I never would've spoken to Chryssa Zizos. I fell asleep happy.

• • •

One day Chryssa and I were sitting on the sofa in her apartment when she brought up my gold medals.

"Where do you keep them? Are they in your apartment? A safe-deposit box? I've never seen them."

My stomach tightened. I had never told anyone about pawning them and didn't want to start now.

"My mother has them," I said.

"Why does your mother have them?" she asked.

"Well, with all my moving, it made sense to just keep them there for the time being. This way I would always know where they are. Plus having them there helps my mother remember me."

I averted Chryssa's eyes as I spoke. I am a terrible liar. She has a finely tuned BS meter.

"I think it would be great to have them for your speaking engagements. People would love to be able to see them and hold them. Why don't we go to Minnesota, visit your mom, and get them?" Chryssa said.

Now my stomach was fully in knots, and my heart was thumping so loud I thought Chryssa might be able to hear it. I didn't say anything for a few seconds. The silence felt like an hour.

"I have to tell you something," I said.

"What's that?"

"My mom doesn't have my medals. I pawned them." I thought I was going to drown in shame.

Chryssa didn't say a word. She looked sad.

"What does that mean?" she said. "I've never pawned anything. When I think of a pawn shop, I think of a ramshackle storefront next to a gas station. Can you get them back?"

I told her about Borro and my arrangement with them . . . that they fronted me cash and I had to make monthly payments until I'd repaid the principal and interest. Chryssa asked me how much I owed.

"Almost nineteen thousand dollars," I said.

We were talking on a Saturday. Borro was closed.

"Let's call them Monday morning and make an appointment," she said. "We'll find out what they need and drive up to New York and get your medals back."

"OK," I said. "But there's one problem."

"What's that?"

"I don't have the money."

"I will loan you the money to pay them off and get your medals back," she said. "Then we'll go to a local banker I know and you can take out a personal loan. It should be no problem. And it will be good to rebuild your credit by making timely loan payments."

I told you she was a pit bull.

Throughout this conversation, I didn't feel an iota of judgment from Chryssa. It would've been easy for her to look down on me for having to resort to such drastic measures. She never did. What she was doing for me was so kind. The way she was doing it was even kinder.

I was falling more in love with her by the day.

We drove to New York later that week. Chryssa was astounded that Borro was in a spiffy, high-rise Midtown office building. When we were buzzed into the office, she took in the mahogany paneling, tasteful appointments, and color-coordinated furniture.

"What the hell kind of pawn shop is this?" she said with a laugh.

"I know, right?"

I filled out some forms and handed them a cashier's check for $18,700. The customer-service person who was helping asked us to wait and came back about five minutes later with my two gold medals, in the wooden box. I said thank you and we were on our way. It was that painless to make myself whole again. We celebrated by stopping at a food truck and eating a Philly cheesesteak, then drove to Chryssa's mother's condo in Bethlehem, Pennsylvania. Chryssa's family is from Greece, birthplace of the Olympics, and from a Greek village in Smyrna, Turkey. Her mother, Poppy, is a total Olympic-phile.

She made us a wonderful dinner and then got to spend time with my medals, running her fingers over them, putting them on, admiring the rendering of Nike (the Greek goddess of victory, not the shoe company) that was on the 2004 medal.

"These are so beautiful," Poppy said.

• • •

In June 2015 we traveled to Vancouver, Canada, together for the final game of the Women's World Cup, along with Naomi and Fran. For the first time Chryssa and I walked everywhere hand in hand, arm in arm, sparks flying as we went, as lovestruck as two kids having their first romance. The trip was one of the best times of my life. I could've reached out to U.S. Soccer for tickets, I guess, but I wanted to experience a World Cup as a spectator and a fan. So we paid our own way, sat in the stands, and cheered like all the other maniacal

I attended my first World Cup final as a fan in 2015 in Vancouver, and loved every minute of it.

USWNT supporters. On the walk to the stadium, we somehow got in the middle of the American Outlaws. I had an American flag draped around my shoulders.

"Hey! That's Briana Scurry!" an Outlaw hollered. Soon I was surrounded, signing autographs and having fun with U.S. Soccer's most loyal and boisterous fan club. Our seats were right behind the goal that Carli Lloyd scored all three of her goals in. By the time she scored the third one, from a half-step inside midfield, I was so pumped up I was ready to run on the field myself. The flow of the match couldn't have been more different from the world championship we won in the Rose Bowl in 1999, but the pinnacle is the pinnacle regardless of how it happens.

Moments after the game ended, as Chryssa and I stood and cheered with tens of thousands of other U.S. soccer fans, I saw Abby Wambach sprint over to the stands. I had a good idea what was going to happen. When Abby reached the seats, her then-wife Sarah Huffman, wearing a No. 20 Wambach shirt, leaned over the railing and they shared a kiss and a hug—a moment that was captured by FOX cameras only nine days after the Supreme Court upheld the Constitutional right to same-sex marriage. It was seen by some twenty-one million viewers in the U.S. alone.

After Brandi's PK won the shootout for us in 1999, I made the same run to the stands as Abby to share the triumph with my girlfriend, Brandi. The only difference in my case was that the ABC camera turned away a few seconds before Lori and I embraced.

What a difference sixteen years makes.

When the awards presentation was over, American revelers were all over the streets of Vancouver, singing, chanting U.S.A, U.S.A., and drinking adult beverages. We decided to stop in a bar we passed along the way. Chryssa noticed a heavy security presence, and then caught a glimpse of a party of people in the back that included then-vice president Joe Biden and his wife, Jill. The security personnel turned out to be Secret Service officers. While I was in the bathroom, Chryssa approached one of the officers and mentioned that I was in the bar and asked if I might be able to meet the vice president and his wife. The officer knew who I was and said she would check. A minute or two later she came and said the vice president would love to meet me and have us join them at their table. I knew nothing about any of this.

When I was finished in the bathroom, Chryssa said, "How would you like to meet the vice president of the United States?"

"What are you talking about?"

Chryssa filled me in and I said sure, and the next thing I knew we were sitting with the Bidens and having a drink, talking about soccer then and now. The vice president had just lost his son Beau to brain cancer. You could see the sorrow in his eyes, but he was incredibly gracious and welcoming just the same. It was a delightful, serendipitous experience at the end of a joyful day.

At a postgame celebration in Vancouver after the U.S. World Cup victory in 2015, I was honored to meet then-Vice President Joe Biden and his wife, Dr. Jill Biden.

. . .

My final years with the USWNT weren't happy for me, but being back in that world wasn't bittersweet at all. It was simply sweet. I was part of the human race again. I was connected. And it was all made possible by a woman who all but led me out of the woods by the hand, motivated by nothing more than kindness and compassion. I've always believed the true measure of someone's character is revealed by how she treats someone she stands nothing to gain from . . . the hotel housekeeper, the person behind the Starbucks counter, the greeter at Walmart. Chryssa had nothing to gain from being nice to me. My life was in tatters. She didn't know the World Cup from the Stanley Cup. Long before I fell in love with her, that told me all I needed to know about her heart.

By the holiday season of 2015, I was gradually slipping into the rhythm of daily life with Chryssa and the kids, Sydney and Andrew, when they were with her. Chryssa and Karen have done a wonderful

With my stepkids, Sydney and Andrew, in New York City.

job raising them and were careful to make the kids' well-being their top priority after they split up. I loved the kids from the start. They are smart and funny and have kind souls and good hearts. At Christmas, Chryssa gave me a card.

"This is your gift," she said.

It was an invitation to move into her townhouse in northern Virginia early in 2016. It was the best Christmas gift ever.

Our relationship just got better and better. I wanted to be with Chryssa every minute. She traveled with me to Baltimore for the United Soccer Coaches Convention in January 2016. I was invited to be on a panel that was focused on head injuries. I was walking down a hallway at the convention site when I felt a tap on my shoulder. It was Anthony DiCicco, Tony's son.

I am honored to be part of a permanent exhibit at the National Museum of African American History and Culture in the Smithsonian in Washington, D.C. Not sure who that Jordan guy is.

"A curator at the Smithsonian is trying to get in touch with you," he said.

"With me?" I said. "Why?"

I was flabbergasted. Was this a joke? I had no idea what it could be about, and even less of an idea why I was hearing about it from Anthony. He didn't have many details but provided the name and contact information of the curator who had reached out to him. Chryssa looked into it and found out it was true . . . that the Smithsonian curators wanted to feature me as part of a permanent "Game Changers" exhibit in the National Museum of African American History and Culture. I donated the jersey and gloves I wore in the 1999 World Cup final against China. There is also a photo of the save I made in the decisive shootout elsewhere in the museum, and a *Sports Illustrated* cover of our Rose Bowl victory in the Title IX exhibit. The Smithsonian describes game changers as "the people, events, and institutions that

The only thing better than being inducted into the Smithsonian was sharing the day with my three angels: Chryssa Zizos, Naomi Gonzalez, and Kerri Reifel.

have forced the sports world and larger society to alter its practices, belief systems, or racial politics. The impact of these game changers demonstrates the power of sports to transform the world." The exhibit went up later in 2016, and when I went to the opening, it blew me away to see myself in the same museum as Rosa Parks and Harriet Tubman and Muhammad Ali, among many others. It never occurred to me that my career as a USWNT goalkeeper had any impact beyond helping us win some important soccer games. It remains one of the greatest and most humbling honors of my life.

• • •

Chryssa and I got engaged during a trip to Key West in June 2017 and began planning our life together. Shortly after the holidays at the end of the year, we started to explore places to live. Mostly we were looking at houses, but one Saturday we thought it would be fun to check out a new high-end condominium complex in Old Town Alexandria. The bigger units were priced at two million dollars and more. That was more than we wanted to spend, but we wanted to look anyway, for fun. We walked into the sales office and the moment we did, a nicely dressed woman in her forties—clearly the salesperson—looked me up and down. Her wariness was all over her face. If there were subtitles for her thoughts, they would've said, "What is *she* doing here? She's not someone who can afford to live in this building." It wasn't quite *Don't Let The Sun Go Down on You in Alexandria*, but the prejudice that drove it was similar. I'd experienced this many times before and chose to ignore it. Chryssa was more offended than I was.

When we sat down and talked to her, the woman looked only at Chryssa, of course. She made her sales pitch, but it was brief. We didn't want to hear it and we didn't want to live there, and were not about to dwell on it, in any case. There was too much good in our lives to worry about a racist saleslady.

A couple of weeks later, I was inducted into the National Soccer Hall of Fame at a ceremony in Orlando. I wore the power red blazer they gave me (it was the first red blazer I'd worn since 1996 Opening Ceremonies in Atlanta) and was surrounded by so many people I love: Chryssa, my soon-to-be-stepkids Sydney and Andrew, Naomi and Fran, Chryssa's mom and sister, Nicole Zizos Gulledge, and her family. A number of my former USWNT teammates were there, too. I spoke for twenty-five minutes and offered a roster full of much-deserved thank yous, led by my parents and my three angels—Chryssa, Naomi, and Kerri. I spoke about how you find out an awful lot about yourself when you are on the bottom, and about how grit and heart and resilience can power you through anything. It was another profoundly humbling honor.

• • •

On the night of my induction into the U.S. Soccer Hall of Fame in 2018, it was a deep honor, and entirely fitting, to put on this red blazer. Red is my favorite color.

Chryssa and I were married on the beach in St. Lucia on June 2, 2018. We both wore white. Sydney and Andrew were there, of course, and soon thereafter they gave me a new nickname: Bonus Mom. I love it. It was the best day of my life. My life with Chryssa is so joyful, my love for her so intense, that I feel as if I'm living a fairy tale. Meeting her when I did is another one of those instances where my timing was perfect, like being born the year before the passage of Title IX. To think that I owe the greatest gift in my life to the worst time in my life is too much for me to even comprehend. All I know is that it was no accident, because nothing is an accident.

When you are as deep in the abyss as I was, and you believe there's no hope and no point, the light goes out of your soul. You are locked in a closet, flailing about in the blackness. Not only couldn't I see a way out; I was increasingly sure there *was* no way out. And then, with my gold medals pawned and the waterfall beckoning, the door

I married Chryssa Zizos on June 2, 2018. It was the happiest day of my life.

cracked open an inch and a sliver of light came in when Ben Boscolo, my lawyer, got the approval for me to see Dr. Crutchfield, who told me he could help. A little more light came in when Naomi Gonzalez met Chryssa Zizos, told her my story and then threatened to cut me off if I didn't call her. There was enough light for me to see in the closet after I spoke to Chryssa and then she went to work, drumming up media interest in my journey, and getting the recalcitrant insurance company to back off. And when I woke up pain-free after Dr. Ducic finished the occipital release surgery in Georgetown University Hospital on October 18, 2013, I wasn't in a closet at all, but bathed in fresh, gleaming light—light that poured into me like sunrise over an ocean, that made me feel free and open to find joy and comfort I didn't know was possible. To all of those who loved me and fought for me and held on to hope, thank you for lifting me up, so I could make my greatest save of all.

With my wife and my love, Chryssa, in the mountains of Asheville, North Carolina.

Sydney, Chryssa, and Andrew: My new family, my new life, my safe harbor.
I am so blessed.

A Keeper's Best Friend: My Sunny
Bucket chilling on the beach on the
Outer Banks of North Carolina.

PIGTAILS OF HOPE

Ten weeks after George Floyd was murdered outside of Cup Foods at the corner of East 38th Street and Chicago Avenue in Minneapolis in May 2020, I was in Minnesota for a speaking engagement. I'd watched the horrific footage of the end of his life and seen and read about the murals and memorials that had sprung up at what became known as George Floyd Square. It was a few miles from where I was born, from where my parents moved to escape their grim, dead-end life in Jim Crow Texas. I had to go see it.

It was a beautiful summer day, the sun warm and comforting on my face. I thought I was prepared for the intensity of the experience, but I wasn't. It's hard for me to put into words how it felt for me to see the spot on the pavement where the cop kneeled on George Floyd's neck, and the chilling lineup of cardboard headstones for all the other unarmed people of color whose lives ended at the hands (or knees) of law enforcement officers. It was as if my own final breaths were being choked out of me. I had this visceral sense of my blooding turning cold, and then ceasing to flow altogether. I cried not just for George Floyd and the other victims of police brutality, but also for the depth of the contempt that lay beneath it, and for where we are as a country four hundred years after the inception of the barbaric, inhumane institution known as slavery.

Standing in the middle of the square, I looked at the red, black, and green stripes of a pan-African flag, which flapped over a monument. I thought of my African ancestor, Henry Gordon, my great-great-great-great-grandfather, the twenty-two-year-old man who was transported to New Orleans on that slave ship *The Union* in 1848, and I thought of my nephew Jerome Gordon-Jackson, too. Jerome was one of my favorite people in our whole family. He was stricken with a serious bout of leukemia when he was ten years old. Doctors didn't think he would recover but he got through it amazingly well, with the most positive outlook I've ever seen in a cancer patient. He recovered fully, going on to college and beginning a promising career as a special-education teacher in greater Minneapolis. On May 17, 2013, Jerome went out with friends in downtown Minneapolis. It was a Friday night. They were at a nightclub and left around two A.M. At three A.M., Jerome texted his sister, my niece Tenecia, and said he was in a Minneapolis police station and might need to get picked up. Tenecia, who was living with and caring for my mother at the time, was asleep and didn't see the text until seven A.M., when two detectives knocked on the door of my mother's house in Dayton.

The detectives told Tenecia that Jerome had committed suicide by jumping off the Hennepin Avenue Bridge at 5:11 A.M. They said nothing more. That was it; he jumped into the Mississippi River. Only later, through reports in the *Minneapolis Star Tribune* and *St. Paul Pioneer Press*, did we find out that Jerome had been pulled over and charged with DWI in the suburb of Brooklyn Park. His car was impounded and he was taken to the station. That was where he texted Tenecia. We were told nothing about any of that initially. Eventually a police report was released stating the supposed sequence of events. The report said that Jerome was "very cooperative" with officers and that his blood-alcohol level was .17, well over the legal limit. The report raised many more questions than it answered. If he was so drunk, why didn't they hold him, or take him to the hospital? The distance from where he was pulled over to the Hennepin Avenue Bridge is twelve miles. How did he get to the bridge? Where did he go after leaving the station house? Why did cops take so long to release the report? Longtime African American residents in the poorer neighborhoods of Minneapolis, like Tenecia, say there is a history of police beating Black people up and throwing them off the bridge my nephew supposed jumped off.

Tenecia and several others in the family have tried to get answers for years, without success. All they know for sure is that Jerome's body was found eight days later in the Mississippi. He was twenty-eight years old.

It's certainly possible that Jerome was ashamed or embarrassed about his DWI charge, and possibly worried that it might cost him his job. But it's hard to fathom that this young man, who had as sweet a disposition as anyone you could ever find, would take his own life because he was arrested for drunk driving, as poor a decision as that was. This was a person who was so beloved in his school district that the superintendent posted a heartfelt letter to students after his death, thanking him for his passion for helping.

"Jerome, the students you supported and loved will miss you because you were an adult who really cared about them. They will miss you and that beautiful smile you shared with them each day," he wrote.

I don't know what happened when Jerome left the station house that night, or if the police did anything wrong. I do know that something went horribly wrong on May 25, 2020, when George Floyd's life ended on the black asphalt of East 38th Street, his neck under the knee of police officer Derek Chauvin for more than eight minutes. It's impossible to comprehend how much rage Chauvin must have had to do such a thing to another human being. It's also impossible to know how he might've handled the situation if it had been a white man who purchased cigarettes with a counterfeit twenty-dollar bill. Only Derek Chauvin knows that. He has the next twenty-two years to figure it out at the Minnesota Correctional Facility in Oak Park Heights.

The whole racial reckoning that has gone on in this country over the last several years is vitally important and long overdue. As much as I embrace the mission of the Black Lives Matter movement, I believe the social strife and divisiveness in our country is deeper and more multi-layered than simple racial enmity. It's driven by the dehumanizing and toxic stereotypes that hold sway in so many places, by dangerous preconceptions that so many of us have that shape the way we see other people, by our propensity as a country to see the world in strictly black and white terms. I was appalled when I first heard about the death of George Floyd, but my instinct wasn't to paint all cops as evil and racist; that would be ridiculous and unfair. My big brother, Ronnie, was a police officer in Texas for almost forty years. His father was a police officer before him. All cops are not one way, or another, any more than all soccer players are, or lawyers are. The world is messy and complicated. We diminish ourselves when we prejudge and try to stuff a tangled-up world into our tidy, little, premade boxes. As I told you in the beginning, being a gay Black woman has given me much insight into life in a small minority group. I've been packed into my share of boxes. Once a well-known journalist from a leading publication interviewed me for a story. Afterward, the journalist thanked me for my time and said, "You are *so* articulate."

"Thank you," I said.

What I didn't say was: *Why wouldn't I be articulate? Is there a particular reason I'm not aware of? Would you have told Mia Hamm or Julie Foudy how articulate they are?*

When I was a star sprinter and basketball player in high school, a lot of people assumed—and encouraged me—to pursue those sports in college. After all, aren't those the *Black* sports?

After the 1999 World Cup, the vast majority of the publicity, and endorsements, went to Mia and Julie and Brandi. I was a world-class goalkeeper who made a penalty-kick save that helped win the final match, but I lagged far behind. Maybe it was as simple as corporate America not being ready to have an African American lesbian be the face of whatever they were trying to sell. Maybe they were too closed-minded to realize that people of all genders, of all sexualities, and of all races can look up to a champion.

I've lived my whole life intersecting with people from all sorts of races, ethnicities, and economic backgrounds. I've learned it's much easier when you focus on the things you have in common, rather than

Your 1999 Women's World Cup champions, 20 years later at a reunion in Los Angeles.

the things you don't. My parents taught me to be kind and respectful to everyone, and to not judge hastily or harshly. Look for positives and possibilities, they said, and your life will be richer. Their lessons came flooding back to me on that sunny August morning in George Floyd Square.

As I prepared to leave, I walked toward the monument in the center of the intersection and looked back at Cup Foods on the corner, a brick building with a red awning. Hot & Cold Deli, it said on the awning. On the side of the building was a mural of George Floyd's face and name, with a bright blue background and orange letters. Maybe ten feet from the mural, a little African American girl in a pink dress and matching shoes was skipping along the sidewalk. She was with a man and a woman; they looked like they were her parents. She couldn't have been more than five or six years old. She had pigtails with pink ribbons and was holding her parents' hands at first and then she broke free and ran ahead, pigtails flying behind her. She looked so carefree and happy, the picture of childhood innocence, the way we all start out, and I was taken by the simplicity and the beauty of it, forgetting for the moment about the unspeakable end of George Floyd's life, feeling uplifted instead by the promise of hers.

ACKNOWLEDGMENTS

I've read a lot of books in my life and listened to many more. I've never *written* one until now, though—a process, I've discovered, that is not unlike preparing for a World Cup or Olympics: It takes huge contributions from a great number of people to achieve the desired result.

There would've been no book at all without the efforts of Susan Canavan, my literary agent at the Waxman Agency, who not only believed in my story, but also found a perfect home for it at Abrams Books, where I was privileged to work with Jamison Stoltz, a gifted editor whose vision, patience, and deft editorial hand made the narrative so much better. Sarah Robbins, Jamison's assistant, helped in ways I can't even count. Abrams' marketing director, Jennifer Wiener, and publicists, Gabby Fisher and Jennifer Brunn and Mamie VanLangen, forged a plan to spread the word about the book and help readers understand this was more than just another athlete memoir. Managing editor Mike Richards and Sarah Masterson Hally, the production manager, did the heavy lifting behind the scenes to make sure the whole process stayed on course. Thanks, too, to Michael Jacobs, Abrams' CEO, and Michael Sand, the adult publisher, for being passionate soccer fans and believing in the possibilities of this project.

It would take another book to thank the coaches and teammates who believed in me and supported me along my journey. Coach Dave Tank of Anoka High School taught me about what belief and hard work can achieve, and what a championship team culture looks like. Pete Swenson (who I can still hear screaming, "Don't Let Up"), my one and only club coach with the Brooklyn Park Kickers, made it his mission to get me to the right college program, and connected me with Jim Rudy, the coach of UMass and a goalkeeping savant who took a raw talent and molded her into an All-American. Jim told his longtime friend, the legendary Anson Dorrance, he needed to invite me into U.S. Women's National Team camp. Anson listened, and he and his successor, the late, great Tony DiCicco, saw something in me, and for that I am forever grateful. April Heinrichs, who took over the USWNT after Tony stepped away, was, for a short time, the bane of my existence, because she dared to tell me I wasn't fit. April was right. She was also open-minded enough to give me a chance to regain my starting spot on the USWNT and lead us to the 2004 Olympic gold medal.

A keeper is nothing without the players in front of her. In high school and with the Kickers, my stalwart teammates included Colleen Carey, Laurie Menke, and Shannon Jaakola, along with the Kickers' ace striker, Denise Swenson. At UMass we had warriors all over the field, especially Paula Wilkins and Colleen Milliken. On the Atlanta Beat Cindy Parlow Cone, Homare Sawa, and Sun Wen made us one of the top clubs in the late, lamented Women's United Soccer Association. And where would I have been without my captain, Carla Overbeck, on the USWNT? Carla anchored the best backline on earth—Joy Fawcett, Kate (Sobrero) Markgraf, Brandi Chastain, and Christie (Pearce) Rampone completed it—and there were others on those teams who could play a little soccer, too . . . people named Hamm, Lilly, Wambach, Foudy, Milbrett, and MacMillan, to name just a few. Cat (Reddick) Whitehill was another star from the North Carolina assembly line, and a person of high integrity besides. Angela Hucles was as great a friend and teammate as you could want.

You always can tell who your friends and allies are when things are not going well. Thanks to my former agent, Rob Raju, for being there during the hardest time of my life. My attorney, Benjamin Boscolo, and his case manager, Heather Gardner, were tireless advocates throughout the legal nightmare that followed my traumatic brain injury. They promised me we would prevail and they were right. All Dr. Kevin Crutchfield did was free me from years of pain and give me my life and vitality back. How are you supposed to find the words to thank someone for doing that?

Patrick Renegar, my manager at Live Wire Sports & Entertainment, lit the spark that led to this book, and it was his research and resourcefulness that set things in motion and connected me with Wayne Coffey, my coauthor. Wayno, as I call him, has become not only part of our family, but someone I love and trust very much. No one could have told my story better and for that, my friend, I thank you from the bottom of my heart.

Nicole Zizos Gulledge sells playgrounds by day and does genealogical research the rest of the time, and I am so grateful to her for tracing my ancestry all the way back to African Motherland. This book begins with a foreword from Robin Roberts, who has been a role model and inspiration, on the screen and off, for decades; thank you for being part of my journey, Robin.

Throughout my life I've had a philosophy about friendship: I'd rather have a handful of true, loyal, loving friends than a stadium full of casual ones. Nobody has been more blessed in this department than me. Kerri Reifel, former standout goalkeeper for the University of Arkansas, has been an angel in my life for close to thirty years, a person I trust implicitly, a kind and steadfast soul who would always tell me the truth, even if it hurt. Naomi Gonzalez, a former massage therapist and girlfriend, is another angel who has blessed my life. Naomi has a healer's heart whose compassion and presence did more to get me through the grief I felt after my father passed than anyone. Her love and kindness never stopped even after we were no longer a couple. Naomi and Kerri were both there for me when I needed them most, and I will never forget it. When you find angels like these, you hold on to them for life.

My oldest brother, Ronnie, did the Galveston Police Department proud over nearly four decades of service, and has done our family proud his whole life. Ronnie spent hours helping to fill in pieces of Scurry/Gordon family history I wasn't aware of. You didn't sign up to be family historian, Ronnie, but you've got the job now. My sister, Daphne, the one sibling I grew up with, was as devoted and protective as a big sister can be, and that was just one of her profound gifts to me. My precious niece, Tenecia, is not just the younger sister I never had, but gave my mom so much love and care in the final years of her life. Bless you, T.

On June 2, 2018, I married Chryssa Zizos, my greatest angel of all, on a Caribbean beach. Chryssa was already my agent and the person who had done more to build my career as an inspirational speaker than anyone. Now she was my wife and I was a "bonus mom" to the two best stepchildren I could ever ask for—Sydney and Andrew. It was perfect. It was the best day of my life. The only regret I have is that my parents, Ernest and Robbie Scurry, weren't there to be a part of it. Being a parent now, I've come to appreciate how much time, effort, and devotion it takes to be a good one—the sort of parent who fills her kids with positivity and empowerment. My parents did that for me every day of my life, a gift that truly never stops giving.

After moving all over the country for basically my entire life, I am rooted at last in northern Virginia. We live in a beautiful home that overflows with love and kindness and my ever-loyal dog, Sunny

Bucket, who is deaf and has only one eye but never runs out of affection. I feel as though I am living a dream and it all starts with you, Chryssa. You are my greatest love. You are my moon, my rock, my everything, my wife. I love you to the depths of my soul.

Briana Scurry

Alexandria, Virginia

INDEX